DATE DUE

OC 27 '98			
SE 29 '99			
NO 19 '99			
OY 12 '00			
JE 8 '01			
JE 11 '01			
AO 2 '01			

DEMCO 38-296

BORN FI' DEAD

BORN FI'
DEAD

A Journey Through the
Jamaican Posse Underworld

LAURIE GUNST

HENRY HOLT AND COMPANY
NEW YORK

Henry Holt and Company, Inc.
Publishers since 1866
115 West 18th Street
New York, New York 10011

Henry Holt® is a registered trademark
of Henry Holt and Company, Inc.

Published in Canada by Fitzhenry & Whiteside Ltd.,
195 Allstate Parkway, Markham, Ontario L3R 4T8.

Library of Congress Cataloging-in-Publication Data
Gunst, Laurie.
Born fi' dead: a journey through the Jamaican posse
underworld / Laurie Gunst.—1st ed.
p.   cm.
1. Gangs—Jamaica—Kingston.   2. Gangs—United States.
3. Drug traffic—Jamaica—Kingston.   4. Drug traffic—United States.
5. Jamaican Americans—Social conditions.   6. United States—
Social conditions.   I. Title.
HV6439.J252K664   1995   94-34554
364.1'06'097292—dc20   CIP

ISBN 0-8050-3205-3
ISBN 0-8050-4698-4 (An Owl Book: pbk.)

Henry Holt books are available for special promotions
and premiums. For details contact: Director, Special Markets.

First published in hardcover in 1995 by
Henry Holt and Company, Inc.

First Owl Book Edition—1996

Designed by Brian Mulligan

Printed in the United States of America
All first editions are printed on acid-free paper.∞

10 9 8 7 6 5 4 3 2

For Brambles, Trevor, and Shenda
And the sufferers of Kingston—
Past, present, and to come.

CONTENTS

ACKNOWLEDGMENTS

As this book defined my life through ten years of research and writing, it created its own small world of supporters and friends. Their encouragement and criticism lifted me out of the isolation every writer knows. To Jervis Anderson, who believed in this work at a crucial moment, I owe a special thanks.

Philippe Bourgois and Terry Williams, colleagues in the field of street ethnography, understood the peculiar joys and sorrows of working in the underworld of drugs and gangs. They read the manuscript through countless drafts and shone their own considerable light on what was sometimes a dark path.

T. J. English and Samme Chittum are friends and veteran journalists with tough minds and compassionate hearts. They listened and lent their own superior wit.

Flo O'Connor, coordinator of the Jamaica Council for Human Rights, spoke with me at length about the history of political violence in her country. I am indebted to her for her insights and courage.

I would like to thank the Harry Frank Guggenheim Foundation for providing support during the final stages of writing. The manuscript benefited from a master's seminar at the Foundation in March 1993 at which the following scholars were present: Basil Wilson, Gustavo Gorriti, Anita Waters, Ansley Hamid, Philippe Bourgois, Philip Kasinitz, and Robert Trivers. I am especially grateful for the kindness shown to me by Karen Colvard and Joel Wallman, project directors at the foundation.

INTRODUCTION

W hen I began working on this book a decade ago, I con-
ceived of it as both a work of history and a traveler's
tale, the story of Jamaica's political gangs and the record of my
journey into their labyrinth. This story began in the ghettos of
Kingston, a chessboard of war zones with human pieces; for as
long as the majority of Jamaicans can remember, politicians have
armed and paid Kingston's most notorious gunmen to enforce
their rule in the capital city's thronged slums. The worst of the
violence came between 1975 and 1980, so it seemed to me as I
set out on this journey that the heyday of the gangs was in the
past. And I thought that the saga of the "posses," as the gangs
have come to be called, ended where it had begun, in Jamaica.

When I moved to Kingston in 1984, the downtown ghettos
were quiet and the sufferers—the honorific title that Jamaicans
give to the poorest of their poor, the ones with the courage
and resourcefulness to endure—were still recovering from the
undeclared civil war of the 1980 election. The death toll from
that campaign has never been officially tallied. But Michael Manley, Jamaica's prime minister at the time, dedicated his 1982 book
Struggle in the Periphery "to the memory of seven hundred and
fifty people who died so needlessly, many in the first flower of

youth." This was his epitaph for a generation that was sacrificed to the fires of Jamaica's political strife.

I began moving with the sufferers at a time that superficially resembled a period of healing and peace. It seemed like a good time to begin writing the untold story of the tribal gunmen who had fought for Manley and Edward Seaga, his archrival. The secret symbiosis between the politicians and their mercenaries has always been a dangerous subject in Jamaica, but it seemed a little less so after Seaga had defeated Manley and his new, right-wing regime began restoring the island to America's favor. But the lull was ominous and deceptive. Even as I sat in rumshops and tenement yards, watching young men light glass pipes of crack instead of the ganja they would have smoked in a mellower time, I was already hearing the first rumors of an outlaw exodus to the American promised land. The "rankings" who had controlled Kingston for Manley and Seaga through the 1970s were leaving their ghetto hell for the cities of the United States, transforming their island gang alliances into mainland drug posses. This is a story without an end.

As I write this introduction, placing an arbitrary punctuation mark in an ongoing saga, I have just spoken with a reporter from the *Miami Herald,* Lisette Alvarez, who called this morning to interview me about yet another posse massacre. This time four people were shot dead at a Dade County dance hall. One of the victims was a girl who was celebrating her seventeenth birthday. Eighteen people were wounded when gunmen opened fire with the Glock 9 mm handguns that have become the trademark weapon of the gangs. Alvarez told me the Miami police were still uncertain about the motive for the shootings, but they thought the fight was sparked when two men from rival posses argued over who had fathered a woman's child.

The U.S. Bureau of Alcohol, Tobacco and Firearms has been

tracking the posses since their mainland debut in the early 1980s, and it now reports that the gangs have killed forty-five hundred people in the United States since then. The gunmen began migrating to America just after the 1980 election in Jamaica; by that time Kingston's top-ranking mercenaries had already begun trafficking in homegrown marijuana and transshipped cocaine. They soon branched out from Jamaica into the American market, and the money they made from the drug trade snapped the leash that had once bound them to their politician-patrons. The party leaders, menaced by an outlaw underworld they could no longer control, turned the Jamaican police loose in the ghettos to execute their former paladins. This reign of terror sent posse men by the hundreds on the run to the United States. They brought with them a killer enthusiasm honed by years of warfare with one another and the police, and when they came onto America's mean streets, they were afraid of no one. Their timing was superb: the Jamaican posses quickly proved themselves indispensable to the Colombians, Cubans, and Panamanians who controlled the supply of cocaine and needed street-level dealers to sell the cheap new product called crack.

But long before the posses began migrating to America, they were learning bad-guy style from Hollywood. These island desperados are the bastard offspring of Jamaica's violent political "shitstem" (as the Rastafarians long ago dubbed it) and the gunslinger ethos of American movies. They are a Caribbean cultural hybrid: tropical bad guys acting out fantasies from the spaghetti westerns, kung fu kill flicks, *Rambo* sequels, and *Godfather* spinoffs that play nightly in Kingston's funky movie palaces and flicker constantly behind young men's eyes. The posse men see themselves as Clint Eastwood in *Dirty Harry*, Al Pacino in *Scarface*, or—if they are old enough to remember the 1960s— the rampaging misfits from Sam Peckinpah's *Wild Bunch*. I was captivated by this crazy synthesis between Hollywood and Jamaica's Johnny-Too-Bad renegades; it was my way into the culture of this outlaw world.

I moved to Kingston to teach history at the University of the West Indies, but my real purpose was to write the secret history of the gunmen and their links with Jamaica's elected leaders. I had been going to the island for almost ten years, long enough to know something of downtown Kingston from reggae musicians and Rastafarian elders, the lyric poets of rebellion. But it was a far cry from backstage encounters with Bob Marley or Jimmy Cliff to the ghettos that spawned their music, a distance measured by the boundaries of color and caste. Years before I came to UWI, a visiting Australian lecturer was stabbed to death at the Palace movie theater downtown by a famous criminal named Donovan Chin Quee, a half-Chinese outlaw who worked on and off for Edward Seaga's Jamaica Labour Party (JLP). No one on campus had forgotten this slaying, and my colleagues warned me to stay out of the places where the sufferers lived.

"Not one of us has any reason whatsoever for venturing into certain parts of this city," said the timid East Indian professor from whom I rented a house. "And if we do, we get what we deserve." Us and them—the line of demarcation, never to be crossed, that separated the downtown poor from the fearful but fortunate uptowners.

But I had a reason for crossing this line. The Jamaican sufferers come from the same tradition as the griots of West Africa; they are the storyteller-historians who preserve the legends of a people, and they alone are the keepers of the posses' saga. I couldn't chronicle the exploits of gang leaders who were also Robin Hood heroes in the ghettos unless I went to stand with the sufferers on common ground. Downtown Kingston was the "groundation" for everything I had wanted to understand about Jamaica since my first trip to the island in 1976.

That initiation coincided with the years when a fiery and eloquent politician named Michael Manley began leading his People's National Party (PNP) and Jamaica into a postcolonial reckoning with the past. The island had gained its independence from Great Britain scarcely a decade before, in 1962, and it was struggling to come to grips with a legacy of slavery and colonialism that persisted with a vengeance. The decade of the 1970s was a fever-dream of raised consciousness and high hopes, the first time in Jamaican history when the downtown, downside reality of "sufferation" gave the lie to the island's polite British parliamentary facade. As reggae music and Rastafarian redemption put Jamaica on the world's cultural map, its deep and painful schism between rich and poor, light-skinned and dark, was forced out into the open as never before. In an anguished reappraisal of the past, islanders began confronting the truths of a history that Peter Tosh lamented as "Four Hundred Years," four centuries of Babylonian captivity for the black race in Jamaica and the Americas.

At the same time, Manley took up the larger struggle of small, underdeveloped third world states against the overwhelming dominance of the old and new colonial powers. Even as Manley's PNP raised this banner, Edward Seaga began turning the rival Jamaica Labour Party into a reactionary force, thundering against Manley's warming friendship with Fidel Castro and his brave but foolhardy support for myriad third world insurgencies.

The United States embraced Seaga with predictable fervor. The American eagle hovered fiercely over Jamaica's doomed experiment in democratic socialism and eventually routed it with the same methods the State Department and the Central Intelligence Agency had used elsewhere. The American press painted a harsh portrait of the island, the International Monetary Fund (IMF) devalued Jamaica's currency and destabilized an economy already battered by the oil price shocks of the 1970s, and travel agents discouraged their clients from going to Jamaica, thereby crippling the industry on which the island depended for its survival. And a tide of high-powered weapons flowed like bloody currency from the United States into the hands of political gunmen. Jamaicans were traumatized by the rising violence, but only a few dared to suggest that the killing was done at the behest of elected leaders.

Jamaica became yet another theater of the worldwide cold war. The island's contortions were a claustrophobic replay of those in Chile, in Nicaragua, in a dozen other outposts of strife where the superpowers played out their East-West death dance. This drama not only went on in the corridors of the State Department, the World Bank, and the IMF; it played constantly in the rubbly streets of Kingston, where Manley and Seaga armed their rival posses to maintain control of political constituencies in a tangle of slums and shantytowns. It was this misery that claimed my heart and mind.

I was then working on my doctorate in history at Harvard, shuttling back and forth between the tumult of Jamaica and the cool, battleship-gray stacks of Widener Library. My dissertation was on the origins of the African slave trade to the Spanish Caribbean, and there was for me a certain resonance between this bitter history and Jamaica's contemporary reckoning. Every trip I took to the island showed me a present heavy with the burden of the past.

Jamaica became my teachment, as it has for thousands of other watchers and listeners around the world. It is an island with a densely compacted history that contains every movement of consequence in the western hemisphere: native societies devastated by European conquest; the extermination of aboriginal peoples and their replacement by African slaves; the long sleep of colonialism and the slow, painful awakening into the struggle for nationhood. "This is a small island," Jamaicans like to say of their mountainous country, "but it's big like hell in the middle." Its history is similarly grand.

The island's insistent voices yanked me, again and again, out of the safety and removal I was learning to mistrust in academia and into that place my too-comfortable colleagues blithely referred to as "the real world." As I listened transfixed to the rambling, apocalyptic lectures fired at me by Rastafarian visionaries or the headmen of small villages deep in the Jamaican bush, I came to see that these men were giving me history lessons every bit as crucial as the ones I was hearing in Harvard Yard. Buried for years in archives of dead voices, I began learning the dangers and delights of listening to the living. In many ways the risky work that I found later, venturing mapless into the unknown terrain of the posses, was just the logical extension of looking for truths in the places where my first Jamaican instructors taught me to look.

I remember being summoned for the first time into the myriad contradictions of Jamaica's colonial past by an old man named Mann Rowe in the tiny village of Accompong. It was the Feast of the Epiphany on January 6, 1976, and Accompong was holding its annual celebration in honor of its founder, a rebel slave named Cudjoe. Cudjoe's people fought two guerrilla wars with the British in the eighteenth century and won their freedom a hundred years before Queen Victoria gave it to the rest of England's slaves. The colonizers called these rebels Maroons, a corruption of the Spanish word *cimarrón,* meaning wild or untamed. Their descendants are still living in five autonomous Maroon townships scattered across Jamaica's mountainous interior, and Accompong is their proudest community. Mann Rowe was then the keeper of its traditions and its history.

He and I sparred together for the better part of the day in his small house, knocking back glasses of the overproof white rum Mann loved and reasoning about the tangled history of England and Jamaica. There were framed pictures of Queen Elizabeth and Winston Churchill on Mann's walls, and late in the day I asked him why he honored these modern British incarnations of the power his people had long ago fought to a standstill. Without a word, he rose and fetched his copy of the treaty that Cudjoe had made with the British in 1739. He turned its pages to the place where Cudjoe had signed his name with an X.

"Young miss," Mann said, pointing to the photographs, "we and those people up there are of one spirit. Once it was for us to fight the English for our freedom. And then time come for that mon, Sir Winston Churchill, to stand firm for all the world 'gainst the Hitler bizness. Same spirit. Is only time separate us."

Mann smiled. "History is a mystery sometimes, eh?" he said.

By the end of the 1970s, after many trips to Jamaica and my first tentative forays into Kingston, it was the mystery of Jamaica's worsening tribal war that caught and held me. It seemed that every time I opened a *Gleaner,* the island's daily paper, there was a story about a killing in downtown Kingston that was said to be the work of one "political activist" or another, some Johnny-Too-Bad who was rumored to be working for the PNP or the JLP.

Who was the shadowy PNP enforcer named Winston "Burry Boy" Blake, and why was he so powerful that Michael Manley himself chose to join Blake's funeral procession in 1975, after the gunman had been shot dead by a JLP supporter in West Kingston? Snipers from the JLP fired on that cortege as it snaked its way past Tivoli Gardens, Seaga's own West Kingston fiefdom.

Who were the political mercenaries who set fire to a PNP tenement-yard on Orange Street one hot May night in 1976 and then shot the firefighters who tried to extinguish the blaze? Eleven people died and five hundred were left homeless. This viciousness was made even more surreal by the *Gleaner's* gutless response to it: no one dared to name Manley or Seaga as the men behind such outrages. Rumors flew and whispers floated from Kingston's uptown verandas. Downtown, the sufferers burned and bled.

The gunmen infused their cruelty with a certain cinematic style, a cool detachment from the agony they inflicted. Most of these paladins had come of age in the 1950s and 1960s, when Hollywood churned out countless westerns, and Jamaicans began a long love affair with the legendary bandits of the silver screen. No one who has seen Perry Henzell's 1973 masterpiece *The Harder They Come* can forget the scene where its country-boy hero Ivan O. Martin comes to Kingston hungry for fame as a singer and goes to his first movie in town. He and a new, city-slick friend are at the Palace watching a rotgut spaghetti western called *Django,* starring Franco Nero, and the audience of young people is mesmerized by the violence. As the light from the screen flickers across their ardent faces, they watch Nero crouch behind a log in the mud of some nameless frontier town, facing down a posse of white-hooded vigilantes who stalk toward him with their guns cocked, laughing. Ivan holds his breath, certain that the hero is doomed, until another kid in the audience mocks Ivan's naïveté.

"Hero cyan' dead till the las' reel!" the kid whispers. And he's right. Nero leaps up from behind the log with a Gatling gun and mows down the whole posse. The Kingston audience howls with delight. They know the rules of this game.

At the end of his own last reel, when Ivan is a hunted outlaw himself, he makes his final stand on a deserted beach near Kingston. Cornered by a squadron of soldiers, he flashes back to that scene from *Django* and staggers out from cover, shouting for a fair chance to shoot it out with the Jamaica Defense Force.

"Jus' send out one mon!" he yells. "One mon who can draw!" He clutches his revolvers, but the soldiers cut him down in a barrage of machine-gun fire. Like hundreds of Jamaican gangsters before and after, he lives and dies with gunslinger bravado acquired from the movies.

I discovered the power of that myth as I came to know the gunmen and sufferers of Kingston. We shared an affinity with the Wild West, and this carried us across many a cultural bridge. There were night-long sessions of talk that were accompanied by ancient, scratchy jukeboxes blaring tunes by western balladeers like Marty Robbins and Tex Ritter; there were veteran outlaws who were brought to tears by "Ghost Riders in the Sky." There was the tense afternoon in a shantytown near Kingston where I had gone to meet a ranking nicknamed "Billy the Kid" who was very reluctant to talk to me until someone mentioned that I'd only recently come to Jamaica from Wyoming.

"Whoy," Billy breathed in a reverent whisper. "I know 'bout that place! Nuff-nuff bad-mon come from out there! Hole-in-the-Wall, Butch Cassidy an' the Sundance Kid. . . ."

Of course, I had been wrong to assume that the posse saga ended in Kingston. By the time I left the island in 1986, the gangs were well established in the United States. Their Jamaican beginnings were in some ways only a prologue to what they became here, an apprenticeship in the ways of badness. But they had been taught essential lessons in Jamaica—by the politicians who used them, by the police who gunned them down when their brief period of usefulness was over, and by a poverty from which death is often the only release.

If you are a Jamaican youth who expects to die before you reach twenty, but find that somehow your nine lives keep spinning out one after another in a miraculous reprieve, it isn't that hard to summon up the nerve to carve out a niche as a street warrior in the American drug trade. If you are a Kingston sufferer, living inside the hell that's been created for you by the greed and folly of the United States and the corrupt establishment of your own country, it is logical that you will do anything to get out. The sufferers' rage can be contained for a while in the shantytowns of Kingston, but sooner or later they will bring it here, for this is their frontier.

And then one can follow them, as I did, into their American hegira. Put them on streets where there is nothing but the drug trade and then throw in the guns, the ones meant for combat: assault rifles, rapid-fire weapons like the Uzis and Glocks which let off an orgasmic spurt of bullets, enough to drop at least a few people. Remember that some of these youths have never held a gun before, but others are experienced killers. It doesn't really matter; if you are in the line of fire, it's your turn to die. And if you live, you can bear witness to the power of the posses.

PART ONE

Born Fi' Dead

From Babylon
to Brooklyn

The five men from the Renkers posse carried baseball bats, flashlights, and a set of chains into the basement of the derelict building on Pacific Street in Brooklyn. It was just before Christmas 1986, and the basement was cold, dark, and empty except for a boiler. The men were bundled in hooded sweatshirts and the Triple-Fat goose down trench coats that were then de rigueur for crack dealers who had to spend long nights on freezing streets. They would go home later, after tonight's mission was accomplished, to change into silk and linen for the dance at Love People One, the Renkers' favorite disco on Empire Boulevard.

The youth they had come to discipline cowered in the corner by the boiler, already pleading for his life. At seventeen Norman Allwood was the Renkers' youngest soldier, an African-American "Yankee boy" among Jamaicans. He had been nothing but a liability to Delroy "Uzi" Edwards, the Renkers don, chronically shorting Edwards on money and stealing crack from the Renkers stash. A few weeks before this night Allwood had failed to deliver four hundred dollars he owed and Uzi shot him in the leg, a favorite punishment, as a warning. Allwood hid from him after that, getting down out of sight on the floor of the apartment he shared with his sister Janet when Delroy cruised the street in his black Mercedes-Benz. But now the kid's luck had run out. Dane Trail, one of Delroy's cousins, held a gun on Norman Allwood while he begged for mercy. Trail had a reputation as an enthusiastic disciplinarian, a soldier loyal to his don. But he, too, would die soon in an unsuccessful Renkers bid to take over a rival posse's crack spot in Brooklyn.

Conroy Green, a soft-spoken, bespectacled gang member, was down in the basement with his fellow posse troops. The memory of Allwood's terror that night would come back to haunt him, along with remorse for his own cowardice. "The kid kept crying, 'Dane, help me! You know better than to think I would steal.' And Dane was just lookin' at him, blank, like, 'You're not talkin' to me.' So I figured if he knows this kid this well and he's just goin' to let them do that to him, what do I look like, talkin' up for him? So I kept my mouth shut.

"I had to tie him up. Well, I felt . . . I knew it was wrong. I felt wrong. Really an' truly, I thought they was just goin' to give him a little beating, a spanking. This was the first time I saw Delroy and them discipline somebody. I didn't know they were goin' to end up killing the guy. They didn't know. He just died on them while they were trying to get information from him."

Delroy Edwards stood off to one side, watching. He was in his late twenties then, a handsome man whose eyes had already acquired the faraway, affectless gaze of someone used to killing. Short and stocky, with a body bulked up from lifting weights, Delroy had earned his nickname from the gun he favored and his reputation from his days as a mercenary in Kingston. On the crumbling, bullet-pocked concrete walls of Southside, the war-torn ghetto where the Renkers posse was born, Uzi's name was scrawled in green, the color of the Jamaica Labour Party. It was the JLP that had given him his first job as a Southside ranking. The party hired him for a princely ten dollars a week during the 1980 election campaign to shoot the PNP out of Southside, part of the neighborhood that was Michael Manley's own constituency.

When I met Delroy a few years later in the maximum security visiting room at Rikers Island, he told me how he had picked his posse's name. "It means stinky," he said with a puckish grin. "It's like the smell when you piss against a wall."

But Delroy was still just a "fryer" then, a young chicken in Kingston's posse parlance, even after he'd killed a few people in Southside. He was a minor soldier in the political wars, and once the election was over he was nothing but a petty criminal with the police breathing hard down his neck. So he came up to Brooklyn and regrouped the Renkers with a ragtag assortment of old friends from the Southside streets and American homeboys like Norman Allwood. He rode the crest of the crack wave, acquiring a dozen booming drug spots, a fleet of new cars, and an arsenal of fine guns. The Renkers cleared as much as fifty thousand dollars on a good day, with special two-vials-for-the-price-of-one deals on busy Saturday nights and holidays. But their violence was so extreme that the police eventually took them down; Delroy and his minions killed six people and wounded seventeen.

Now it was Norman Allwood's turn to feel Delroy's wrath.

"They say it takes more heart to beat somebody than to stab or shoot them," said Conroy Green, musing about why Delroy chose to discipline Allwood the way he did. "I guess it's easier to pull the trigger of a gun."

So they lit into the youth and beat him unconscious. When he came to and began to whimper and writhe, Kenneth Manning got vexed. Manning was in his fifties, the oldest man in the posse and a relative of Delroy's uncle from Kingston. He walked over to the boiler for some scalding water and poured it over Allwood. "Manning was kind of, you know . . . laughing," Conroy Green recalled. "The kid's skin started to strip and he started moving again. Kenneth said, 'Oh, you not dead yet?' He was laughing at him. After that we left him hanging, chained to a beam. He died sometime during the night."

The men drew straws to see who would dispose of the body; Jamaicans are intensely superstitious about being around the dead. Delroy ordered them to dump the corpse in a section of East New York that belonged to a rival posse called the Forties. This gang hailed from a PNP neighborhood in eastern Kingston named Rockfort, and the Forties was then waging a war over drug turf in Brooklyn with the Renkers. Island politics added an extra, vicious kick to their Brooklyn vendetta. "Delroy wanted to make it look like a Forties killing," Conroy said. "So he wanted us to shoot the body, since he said that otherwise the cops and Jamaicans would know the Renkers did it. We had the reputation for beating people."

A sanitation worker found Allwood's remains in a Dumpster three months later. The corpse was frozen solid and difficult to identify after the mutilation done by the Renkers. But Janet Allwood knew it was her younger brother; she had been waiting through the winter for his body to be found.

It was not until the spring of 1987 that police from Brooklyn North Homicide were finally able to arrest Edwards on a gun charge that stuck. They had been dogging him since 1982, when he was charged with slaying the only witness to his father's murder. He was acquitted, but the police and most of the Jamaican community thought Uzi himself had killed his father, eager to take over the ganja business that Lloyd Edwards had going in his little grocery store in Crown Heights.

In the summer of 1989 Delroy was tried on multiple charges of murder, assault, and conspiracy to distribute cocaine. It was a federal trial, the first successful prosecution of a Jamaican posse leader under the Racketeering-Influenced and Corrupt Organization (RICO) statute. It took a team of more than twenty federal agents and New York police to finally get Edwards off the street, and when the jury found him guilty on all forty-two counts of the indictment, the prosecution team held an impromptu celebration. A few months later he was sentenced to 501 years without parole and given a fine of over $1 million. None of this had any impact whatsoever on the street in Crown Heights, except to open up Delroy's former turf there to a host of competing dealers.

Conroy Green and a dozen other Renkers men went to prison for much shorter sentences; all of them had cooperated with the prosecutors. Green had been their star witness, so they placed him in the federal witness-protection program, and when he comes out he will be given a new name. He has been a model prisoner, and when I went to visit him shortly after the trial, the guards left us alone for the afternoon. We sat in an orange-carpeted room with vending machines and no bars on the windows, with the sound of birdsong fluting in. It was sweet but mournful background music to our voices.

Conroy looked studious that day, with his rimless glasses, and he chose his words with care. He called me "Sis," a Jamaican term of endearment; I was one of the few people who accepted his collect calls from prison in the empty months after the trial. Conroy still had a few robbery charges pending, so he refrained from talking about those cases, but he was open and articulate about the things he'd done with Delroy Edwards and what it had been like to grow up in the rough Dunkirk neighborhood in Kingston and then come to America as a teenager.

Dunkirk is a PNP zone in downtown Kingston, and it was already a hotbed of gang warfare by the time Conroy was growing up. His parents were hardworking people who tried to steer clear of the violence. His father drove a bus between Kingston and the countryside, and when some of his passengers gave him pound weights of ganja from their cultivations he would give these to the Dunkirk gangs to sell; Conroy thought this was what gave him and his family "cool runnin's"—good standing—in the neighborhood. But the tribal warfare intensified so terribly in the late seventies that his parents left Jamaica for good and moved to Albany, New York. Shortly after the bloody 1980 election, Conroy came up to join them, and in the summer of 1986 he went to Brooklyn to visit a cousin. There he met Delroy Edwards, who was just beginning his brief run with glory.

"I just saw this young guy with all these people around him," Conroy recalled. "And I thought maybe I could get into this, too. I told myself, It can't be all that bad. Uzi talked that first night I met him about the drug game, how he survived, being in shoot-outs, and keeping from getting arrested. And he talked a lot about Southside, how the politicians didn't even give them guns at first. The first gun the Renkers had down there was a one-pop they made out of bicycle handlebars, the curvy kind. You cut them where they curve so it's shaped like a gun, then you load a spring on it with a nail and put a bullet in.

"Delroy said they fought off the Tel Aviv posse, which was PNP, with that one-pop until they started getting guns from the JLP—two little thirty-eights. He said everybody wanted them and this caused a lot of cutthroat. Who had those guns ruled."

Conroy started working for Delroy soon after that summer

night, drawn to the don by the promise of money and respect. Both men had been on intimate terms with violence since their youthful days in Kingston, and both knew that being affiliated with a violent political posse from Kingston could only enhance their standing among Jamaicans on the streets of New York. Conroy understood the 1980 election as a watershed for the posses, the time when young men like Delroy Edwards made a name for themselves. "Being a youth down there during that time, the killing was like a natural thing."

Conroy and I talked mostly that day about violence, in one shape or another: the reality of killing as opposed to the cinematic versions of it that he and his crew had grown up with; the evanescent way that Kingston's familiar mercilessness meshed with the Hollywood imagery his friends cut their teeth on as youths. He thought that even though the movies didn't necessarily engender the violence, they framed it; they gave it style.

"To an outsider, it might look like, 'Damn, these guys are mean!' But being from Jamaica, you see it growing up, you see it all your life. Even before I killed somebody, I felt like I killed before. I think maybe Hollywood had a part in the rude-boy thing, with the movies they put out, like certain westerns. Jamaicans act out a lot of that stuff, want to be tough like outlaws. Even Delroy. Every time he would shoot somebody, we would say, 'Hey! You just got another notch in your gun.'

"When I shot at people, I felt like I did it before. It wasn't like I was trembling and asking, What is this I'm doing? It was like I was into it all along. And I think that's just from social settings, from growing up around all that violence, the way Jamaica was with politics. The way it was when I was just a youth comin' up."

It is just after Labor Day 1992. I am sitting in a small room at the downtown Manhattan headquarters of the Federal Bureau of Investigation with an agent, Bob Chacon. He is setting up a VCR so that we can watch a videotape seized by the FBI in December 1990 when police and federal agents raided the Brooklyn headquarters of a posse called the Gully.

"You're not going to believe this thing," Chacon says. "It's really amazing."

The videotape was part of the Gully's archival stash, home movies of high times like posse dances and the annual West Indian Labor Day Parade down Brooklyn's Eastern Parkway. But the video Chacon wants me to see was made in Kingston during one of the last "treats" that the Gully put on for the sufferers at home. These treats were held every Easter, a season of great celebration in Jamaica. In the days of slavery, Easter—like Christmas—was a time when masters might give their slaves a new article of clothing or a tiny ration of meat. Now the Gully posse's don, Eric "Chinaman" Vassell, was continuing this tradition with funds derived from cocaine and heroin instead of sugar and rum.

Eric Vassell started out as a petty thief in McGregor Gully, a tight-knit ghetto settlement in eastern Kingston that is fiercely loyal to the People's National Party. He migrated to Brooklyn in 1981 and began selling first ganja and then powder cocaine. Soon he was the only Jamaican posse leader to branch out into heroin, and this turned out to be a brilliant entrepreneurial move. After the New York police initiated Operation Pressure Point to drive heroin dealers out of Manhattan's Lower East Side, Vassell reaped a whirlwind of profits from the brisk smack business on his side of the East River, and he shared his luck with the people back home.

Vassell had a string of colorful aliases, including "Chinaman," because of his half-Chinese ancestry, and "Brooklyn Barry," for his standing in the borough. He liked to give his heroin catchy names too, like "Obsession" and "No Way Out." His posse troops started calling him "The IRS" because of his habit of taxing them for funds to buy VCRs, Walkmans, tapedecks, shoes, clothing, food, and guns for the Easter treats in McGregor Gully. They were the only bright spot in many a Gully sufferer's bleak year, the time when a schoolchild would get new shoes or a posse member's baby-mother (the mother of his child) received some clothing and money for her child. The guns that Vassell sent down were another matter—he called them "vote-getters"—and they ensured that the violence tearing the Gully apart would only escalate. But that was just another of the contradictions inherent in the posse system, and it was momentarily obscured by the joyous partying that went on around the treats.

The scene Bob Chacon cues up on the VCR is a beauty pageant for preteen girls, filmed by Crat Vassell, Eric's brother and public relations man. Crat had panned his camera out over the packed, klieg-lit night crowd on the Gully's soccer field and then closed in on the stage where the girls paraded in their best dresses. Some wore frilly, ruffled pastel concoctions that reminded me of white First Communion dresses, and other contestants were decked out in slinky polyester. But each one was wearing a satin sash across her budding breasts, inscribed with the name of whichever posse soldier had sponsored her. There was Miss Sean, Miss Jukie, Miss Ever-Reds.

Chacon is visibly rattled by the girls' prepubescent sexual vibe, and I too recognize that unsettling mixture of innocence and vampishness that lets you know how mercilessly short their childhoods are going to be. Meanwhile, Whitney Houston's voice throbs over the sound system, proclaiming that no one can take away her dignity. The next tune is a soul version of Bob Dylan's "Knocking on Heaven's Door," his ballad for a gunfighter. Chacon and I shake our heads at the aptness of the song. He points to the girl with the sash that says "Miss Jukie" and tells me that Jukie himself wasn't long for this world by that time; just after the treat he was blown away by a rival dealer as he stood at a pay phone in Brooklyn.

Just before the winning beauty queen is announced, a little girl steps up to the microphone with a prepared speech of gratitude for Eric Vassell, even though he is far away in Brooklyn too.

"We can remember the first day we had this treat like it was yesterday," she trills. "This is the fifth year since Barry and the Schenectady Crew"—she has a hard time with the unfamiliar word, the Brooklyn street where the Gully posse was based, and the mistress of ceremonies has to pronounce it for her—"from the United States of America have shown their love and care for us citizens of McGregor settlement. We are grateful for this kind of togetherness, and we pray that this will never cease. The Schenectady Crew, words cannot say how much we love and care for you. Barry, you are extremely loving and caring, and that's what makes you one in a million."

Chacon has his own idea about what makes Vassell one in a million. Like the other federal agents and New York police officers who staged the 1990 raid on the Gully's headquarters, he is still smarting over the fact that Vassell slipped through the dragnet and got away. Chacon knows that Vassell is back in Jamaica, almost certainly in McGregor Gully, protected by the PNP and the sufferers who worship him. And Chacon knows what happened to some of the forty-two other Gully men who were not so lucky and were picked up in the raid. One of them was a young man named Anthony Williams, who got the nickname "Modeler" because he loved stylish clothes. Chacon was the one who cut Modeler down from the bar in his cell where he had hanged himself.

"He was a sensitive, religious kid," Chacon says. "And he felt betrayed by the whole situation. He had no money, he was living day-to-day, friendless. Vassell deserted him, and he knew it. So he pleaded guilty in the case, promised to cooperate. But he got into a fight in Manhattan Correctional and they put him in solitary. That was too much. He read his Bible, wrote a farewell letter that reeked of remorse to his mother and sister in Jamaica. Then he left the Bible open to a passage about mercy and forgiveness and hanged himself. He was a sweet kid, always smiling in the pictures of him we found from before the Gully days."

When the tape finishes, Chacon turns to me with a tired smile. I notice for the first time that his blue polo shirt has "Jamaica" embroidered near the collar, a souvenir from one of his working trips to the island. I ask him if he'd ever go there for pleasure.

"Not on your life," he says.

I ask him if he thinks Eric Vassell might be arrested in Kingston and extradited to stand trial in New York. He says this is pretty doubtful. "When you see how dons like Chinaman are loved by the people in Kingston, you understand why they're untouchable. No one down there is going to cooperate with us to get them extradited. They're safe. Totally safe."

Groundation

Darkness had already fallen on the September evening in 1984 when I flew across the island into Kingston. After so many years of short visits, I was coming back to my adoptive country to live.

Nervous with anticipation, I pressed my forehead against the humming plastic porthole and remembered a prophetic conversation I'd had seven years before with John Womack, the professor who would become one of my dissertation advisers. It was the beginning of the fall term and the history department was having its annual reception for new and continuing graduate students. I had spent that summer in Jamaica, living with an enchanting, hard-drinking Irishman who taught elementary school in Montego Bay, and had returned to Cambridge full of a confusion I was coming to know all too well.

Jamaica was in a shambles that summer, beset by economic crises and escalating political violence, and many of the teachers I knew in Montego Bay were quitting their jobs to leave Jamaica for good. A headmaster there had begged me to stay and teach, and the plight of so many schoolchildren made me wonder why I was coming back to thrash through an advanced degree.

I walked into the History Department party alienated by the

unquestioned privilege and power that emanated from the building's neoclassical Great Space, the atrium where we gathered, and I caught a glimpse of Womack standing on the fringes of the crowd. He was something of a legend to many of his students; the university's only Marxist historian, he had written a magisterial biography of the Mexican revolutionary Emiliano Zapata, and his lectures, to which he came wearing jeans and cowboy boots, often centered on bitter subjects like the role of torture in Latin American regimes. One of my friends thought he resembled Jack Nicholson; he definitely had the same brooding force. I barely knew him then except by reputation, but because he had lived in Mexico I thought he might understand the disjunction that comes from straddling the abyss between the first world and the third.

"So how is Jamaica doing under Manley?" Womack asked, and I described the island's travail along with my own. When I was finished, he just shook his head. "If you want me to," he said, "I can paint the scenario for the next ten years of your life."

His unexpected candor was a breach of the usual decorum that prevailed between faculty members and their anxious, worshipful students. So I held my breath and waited for my fortune to be told. "You'll keep going back to Jamaica again and again," Womack said softly. "And the place will never be anything else to you than what it is now, a loved mystery. But you won't ever be really comfortable here again, either, and eventually you'll become a kind of exile in both places."

This was more than I'd bargained for, a Zen whack from the master. "How do you know this?" I asked.

Womack gave me his best Jack Nicholson smile. "Mexico," he answered.

I never forgot that conversation. It was a prelude to the doctoral wranglings that came later, when I would leave my carrel in the library, exhausted by the melancholy that comes from too much reading, and stop by Womack's office for encouragement. But now I had chosen to leave that world, with all of its seductive familiarity, for the uncertainty he had warned me about years before. And I remembered his words as a kind of valediction.

Peering into the blackness of Jamaica's night sky, I conjured up the landscape below from memory. Beneath us was the Grand Ridge of the Blue Mountains, seven thousand feet of ferny rain forest blanketed by clouds. The country men had dug terraced cultivations into those mountainsides, steeper than a Mayan pyramid. I thought of them trudging home in the darkness with cutlasses tucked under their arms, wearing jaunty wool caps sent home by relatives in England or America and walking in rubber Wellingtons with soles caked with red clay. I pictured the crops they coaxed from those cultivations, the same ones that had sustained Jamaica for the past three hundred years: cassava and yam, Irish and sweet potatoes, dasheen, leafy green callaloo, breadfruit, and papaya. I'd learned but kept forgetting which of these were indigenous to the island and which had been brought in, first from West Africa and then from India and the Pacific. The slave ships brought the first ackee, the bright orange pod that holds its tender yellow fruit in a tight, poisonous embrace until the pod opens and releases the deadly hypoglycin, making the ackee safe to eat. The breadfruit came in with Captain Bligh on the *Bounty,* from Tahiti; all of these foodstuffs came and went across the oceans in the same imperial commerce that brought the slaves.

Shiva Naipaul's novel *A Hot Country* lay open on my lap. His vision of the West Indies was like his brother's—it swerved between pity and contempt. I had put the book down after we crossed Cuba and I read, "The history of this patch of earth was written in blood. Pain was the only thing that had flourished on its red soil. Only in pain had they been self-sufficient."

I had fallen to remembering my first trip to Jamaica, just in time to catch the fever of the 1976 elections. By then the two parties had been kicking power back and forth between them like a soccer ball for so long that only older people recalled elections without violence. Michael Manley was prime minister, but he was already in deep trouble with his own fractious party and with the United States, and the island was flying with rumors of American plots to destabilize Manley's government. Philip Agee, a rogue CIA operative who turned into a whistle-blowing apostate, had come to Jamaica in the fall of 1976 and identified several agents on the island. The American ambassador, Sumner Gerard, denied Agee's allegations, but that did nothing to quell the fears about destabilization. Manley retaliated with a program of socialist discipline that he called "Heavy Manners," and the slogan was scrawled on every wall. It was eloquent patois that rallied Jamaicans to stand firm against the gun terror Edward Seaga was unleashing with the JLP.

Hoping to stem the rising tide of gang violence that engulfed Kingston, Manley declared a state of emergency in the summer of 1976, "detaining" (locking up) 593 people. Some of them were the leaders of the city's most dreaded gangs, and others were politicians from both parties who were suspected of being warlords. Manley waited to set a date for the coming election until November, when he went to Montego Bay and delivered one of the most charismatic performances of his career. He stood before a crowd of 120,000 ecstatic supporters in Sam Sharpe Square, all of them mindful of the slave for whom the square was named: the man they lovingly called Daddy Sharpe had led an 1831 uprising of such magnitude that it hastened the day, three years after, when England freed its slaves. Manley, too, was mindful of Sam Sharpe's legacy as he whipped the crowd into a frenzy that blazing afternoon, finally naming December 15 as election day.

I watched him from the seashell-pink roof of a bank in the square as he brandished the scepter everyone called the "Rod of Correction." The rod was said to have been given to Manley by Ethiopia's Haile Selassie when young Manley visited East Africa in 1970, and by the time of his first victory in the 1972 election it had become the PNP's most powerful symbol of authority and righteousness. The crowd went wild when Manley raised it high. His followers were calling him Joshua by then, the prophet who would lead them into the Promised Land.

"Lick them, Joshua!" the crowd roared as if with one voice. "Lick them with the Rod of Correction!"

I was new to the feverish world of Jamaica's leader worship and I had never seen anything like this before. But the young man who was standing beside me on the roof had witnessed many such performances. He explained that, to the people of this sleepy tourist town, whose apartheid beaches had only recently been desegregated by the PNP government, Manley was very like a god. At that moment their leader was proclaiming that socialism held no terrors for Jamaica, because what socialism really meant was love.

Manley swept to victory in December, despite the violence at polling stations and some dubious counting of votes. But the rift between the PNP and the JLP only widened after the election, with Seaga leading an intransigent opposition and his momentarily defeated gunmen sitting in their ghetto limbo, licking their wounds and spoiling for revenge. Meanwhile, the island's elite saw Manley's victory as a signal of worse to come, and many of them left Jamaica for good; they had already sent their capital to banks abroad. Manley wasn't exercising any rhetorical restraint either; soon after the election he warned the JLP "high-ups" that if they didn't like the way he was running Jamaica, there were plenty of flights to Miami.

My sister and her husband were living that winter with their three daughters in the village of Anchovy near Montego Bay in a house they'd rented from a businessman named Lester Bell. Bell was a diehard Labourite—a "Labour-wrong," as Manley's people were then calling Seaga's supporters. His hilltop mansion was built by workers who earned a dollar a day, toiling up the steep grade with hundred-pound bags of cement on their heads, and Bell treated them like beasts of burden. He claimed to love Jamaica, as long as he felt it was his. But now he railed against "this damned freeness mentality" that the PNP was spreading among the sufferers. His workers were demanding the new minimum wage of forty dollars a week; some of them were sprouting dreadlocks and wearing T-shirts with revolutionary slogans and images of Marcus Garvey over their hearts. There had been a spate of frightening crimes in and around Montego Bay, seemingly aimed at the rich. Lady Sarah Churchill was raped at gunpoint in her cottage at Round Hill, one of the most exclusive resorts in Jamaica, and the attack took on the contours of a political act. Lester Bell and his wife began smuggling their money out to Canada and making plans to leave.

The Bells often came out from Montego Bay to check up on us, puttering and fretting on the breeze-swept veranda where Mrs. Bell kept her treasured orchids. She bustled through the house on unnaturally tiny size-four feet, barking orders at the maid and the gardener, who only hummed softly to themselves as they washed and scrubbed and watered. When we went to town one evening to have drinks with the Bells, their watchdogs growled at the bush sounds in the gardens and Lester went for the shotgun he kept propped by the door, aiming it into the darkness and cursing with fear. Already sick with a bad heart, he died in Canada a few years later. His farewell to Jamaica was to strip the Anchovy house of every wire and fixture, turning it into a derelict shell so that none of the locals would "capture" it after he was gone. Capturing unoccupied land and dwellings has always been the sufferers' way of taking back what they think should be theirs to begin with.

Years later, my sister and I returned to that house. It was a ruin, captured by dampness and rot. The gardens had reverted to jungle and the beautiful mahogany windows and doors were warped beyond repair. Lizards and mongoose scuttled through the terraced grounds, and the only thing left of grandeur was the sweeping view of Montego Bay from the veranda. We remembered the nights, after the Bells had gone to Canada, when we threw open the doors of their forbidden palace to our Anchovy friends, drinking overproof with the crew from Campbell's rum-shop down the hill and getting them to teach us how to play dominoes and dance. My sister and I listened for the echoes of our laughter in the ghostly silence that had settled over the house.

Almost a decade had gone by since then, but the Jamaica I remembered from the seventies had changed so much that the days of Michael Manley's "Heavy Manners" might have been from another century. Seaga was now prime minister and Manley, once so vigorous and vocal, was ill with cancer and had gone into a kind of internal exile—a prophet without honor in his own land. In one of his more belligerent moments, Seaga had recently vowed that he and the JLP had the power to "lock Jamaica down tighter than a sardine tin." It seemed as if he had kept his promise: all of the political energy of the Manley years had vanished without a trace.

Coming into Norman Manley Airport, we circled over the

sprawling plain of lights that Kingston becomes at night. I thought about the man for whom the airport is named, father to the former prime minister and the leader who midwifed his country into independence. In 1969, thirty years after Norman Manley founded the PNP and began the long struggle for nationhood, he lay dying at his home in the Blue Mountain foothills. His wife Edna, an artist and activist who had stood beside him in every political fight, bent down to catch his whispers. He was hallucinating, murmuring that he had a train to catch, but Edna begged him to forget about that train and stay a little longer with the people who loved him.

"No," Norman answered. "Life here costs too much." Those were his last words.

The passport officer who rustled through my documents was tired and hot, sweating under the slow-twirling fans. There were so many Jamaican arrivals and departures stamped in my passport that he had to smile. When he finally found the work permit from the university, I imagined what he must have been thinking: Jamaicans leave their homeland by the thousands to seek work, but this foreign woman has found a job on the island. Between 1980 and 1990, 213,805 Jamaicans came to the United States, 9 percent of its 2.4 million people. Other countries sent greater numbers, but Jamaica had the highest percentage of population. This massive migration inflicts wounds that bear a strong resemblance to slavery's forced partings: children often grow up without ever knowing their mothers, and the pain of separation has become a fixture in the island's soul-scape. No one questions the necessity of this endless sundering; without the money that workers abroad send home, their families would perish.

"So what you goin' to teach us?" the immigration officer asked, playfully but with an edge to his voice. I was relieved to be able to say that it was American history, not that of his own people. He stamped me my allotted time and I passed through into the echoing customs hall, where another sweating officer rifled through my duffel bags in search of contraband and guns.

My friend Nelson from the history department was waiting outside to take me to the new home I hadn't yet seen, a small faculty flat on campus. But we decided to have a drink first in Port Royal, the old pirate town on the tip of the same sandy peninsula as the airport. We both loved Port Royal for the echoes of its past; although the place is nothing but a sleepy fishing village now, in the seventeenth century it was the Sodom and Gomorrah of the English Caribbean. Every slave ship bound for the English colonies unloaded some of its surviving passengers at Port Royal, while sea dogs like Francis Drake and Henry Morgan whored in the waterfront brothels. There were so many criminal enterprises that the women had a jail of their own.

On a bright June day in 1692, an earthquake and tidal wave buried most of the town beneath the sea, killing two thousand people and heaving galleons into the streets. A friend had taken me to the graveyard of the little Anglican church in Port Royal, rebuilt after the quake, where one of its miraculous survivors is buried. He was a French Huguenot named Solomon Galdy, a slave trader who was thrown into the sea by the earthquake's first shock and then rescued by a passing ship. We stood before his grave and wondered why he had been spared.

The evening cool brought Port Royal's small population out into the streets, where women set up kerosene lanterns and little glass cases full of fried fish and the cassava wafers called bammy. Nelson and I bought beers and carried our greasy paper bags of fish to the waterfront, sitting on a beached boat and looking across Kingston Harbor to the city's lights; they flickered like stars in the air currents that wafted over the water. When I went to use the toilet at Gloria's rumshop, I noticed that my favorite dirty mural—a tiny man disappearing between the mountainous buttocks of a grandly fat woman—had been erased from the wall behind the bar. The barmaid told me that some image-conscious people from the prime minister's office in Kingston had asked that it be painted out; Seaga wanted to develop Port Royal for tourism, and the mural was a little too raw.

Sated and mellow, Nelson and I went on to town in the late-night hours when the city wears itself out into languor. Pedestrians loomed up in the milky clouds of exhaust that make night driving in Jamaica a test of concentration, and goats and cows, trailing their ropes, grazed along the roadside. We sped by the smokestacks of the cement company and the Pillsbury flour mill, and I thought of the gunman named Copper, a Robin Hood from the 1970s, who used to rob the mill and distribute flour to the poor.

The Windward Road turned from an industrial strip into a Kingston thoroughfare at the corner of Mountain View Avenue, where a cluster of rumshops had their wooden doors open to the sidewalk and night-long domino games were in full swing. Through the open car window came the familiar click and slap of plastic-ivory pieces being slid and slammed onto the board tables, and the shouts, curses, and laughter of the players. Fragrant smoke from jerk-chicken stands floated in as well, and I got Nelson to stop and let me buy some for tomorrow's lunch; the vendors come out only after dark. "Night food," I joked to him as I got back in the car, and we both laughed at my intentional misuse of the phrase; what it really means, in the perfect grammar of patois, is sex.

The sounds from the rumshop jukeboxes were the only thing that had changed; they weren't playing reggae anymore, and the songs were all rapid-fire dance hall tunes with a lot of gun sounds on the tracks. We heard the real thing after we turned onto

Mountain View Avenue and skirted the shantytowns that lie at
the base of Wareika Hill. Sparse streetlights disappeared up into
the dense darkness of bush-covered slopes that are the last, best
refuge of Kingston's outlaws. Wareika is part of Long Mountain,
which stretches like a hump of wilderness across the city's eastern
flank. The western ridge falls away into shanties that are crowned
absurdly by a wealthy neighborhood called Beverley Hills—
robbed with predictable regularity by Wareika's gunmen—and
the eastern side of the mountain slopes down onto the Mona
plain, where the university is.

Nelson and I listened to the gunshots together; they were single
shots. "Stalking," he said. "Someone's looking for someone."

Looking up at the fortress of that hill, I mentioned Copper,
and Nelson told a story from his days at the university in the
early seventies, when student radicals saw Kingston's outlaws as
revolutionaries. Sometimes the gunmen themselves would mate-
rialize like phantoms at student union dances. But Nelson remembered another appearance, a night when Copper showed up
at a medical student's flat with a bullet in his shoulder. Both
men were awed by the legend's presence and his bravery; Nelson's friend had no anesthetic, but Copper ordered him to cut
the bullet out anyway.

"Just do it," he said. And they did.

The city noises evaporated once Nelson and I reached the
campus at Mona, and the rumshop soundtrack was replaced by
croaking tree frogs and night winds. On a whim, I asked Nelson
to drive by another favorite place of mine before we went home,
the ruins of the church that once belonged to a visionary preacher
named Alexander Bedward.

It stood in a grove of ackee trees just off a sandy lane in
August Town, the working-class settlement close to campus, and
I had often seen the white-robed Bedwardite women walking

up the Mona Road to that church on Sunday mornings, when their hymn singing would ring through August Town. I wanted to see the Church by moonlight and to remember the revivalist "shepherd" who had prophesied the fall of Jamaica's white aristocracy. He was one in a long succession of apocalyptic souls driven mad by his country's sorrows, a Jamaican version of a Sioux Ghost Dancer. He was their contemporary, in fact.

Bedward started having visions in 1891, long before the authorities locked him up in Bellevue, Kingston's mental asylum. In a dream he saw that "the Black Wall shall crush the White Wall," and his Baptist followers took his prophecy to heart. So did the police, who jailed him. But Bedward celebrated his release in 1920 by vowing to fly: he would take to the skies on the last day of that year, from the branches of one of the ackee trees in his August Town churchyard. He was going home to Africa, and if his flock kept the faith, they would follow him home as well.

By that time Bedward's fame had spread to the rest of the English-speaking Caribbean and through the Central American countries where Jamaican laborers had migrated. Many believers came from as far as Panama to watch him fly. When his wings failed to sprout, the police locked him up again, this time as a madman in Kingston's Bellevue asylum. He died there ten years later, but his congregation endured.

Nelson and I stopped at the moonlit churchyard. He said it was fitting for us to be remembering Bedward, since that autumn marked the 150th anniversary of emancipation in Jamaica and the founding of August Town itself by newly freed men and women. The island's post-emancipation history was Nelson's own specialty, and he loved to talk about that period. But he was also a witty and scathing observer of the contemporary scene. He'd earned his doctorate at Oxford, and he came home with a repertory of stories about what it had been like to be a brown-skinned Jamaican in the mother country. He told them with his best dry humor, but they were always about pain. One day when he was working at the British Museum, he queued for a bus and accidentally brushed against a white Londoner in the line; the man promptly swung around and called the café-au-lait Nelson a "black bastard."

"My friend," Nelson replied, not missing a beat, "my mother in Jamaica would weep hot tears to hear you call her lovely brown son black."

I was slow catching on to the torturous complexity of Jamaica's racial consciousness, although race was high on the country's agenda that fall because of the observances surrounding the 150th anniversary of freedom. These ceremonies made a lot of people uncomfortable, mainly the light-skinned few whose ancestors were the master class. I realized that class itself, not color, is one of the safe categories in which Jamaicans frame discussion about the gap between the skin shades. Because the overwhelming majority is black, point-blank discourse about race is often too threatening to the fragile order of Jamaica's establishment and its prevailing fiction of a plural society. So the bitter fact that color itself is what most often consigns many people to poverty is obscured by polite, British-inspired talk about the evils of the class system. And the illusory ease with which lovers choose partners of a different shade simply masks a deeper racism: these couplings are possible not because race is not an issue, but for exactly the opposite reason: the darker partner knows that the child born of a union with a lighter-skinned lover or spouse will have a better chance in life. Jamaicans have not relinquished their preference for "bright" skin, "good" hair, and white-featured faces.

A few weeks after I arrived, there was a car accident in the countryside in which two young people from a wealthy family were killed. I overheard an elderly black woman at a Kingston bus stop lamenting the deaths with a friend. "What a sad ting, eh?" she said. "An' the two o' dem so nice an' white!"

The daily *Gleaner* was meanwhile full of stories about the emancipation celebrations. Remembering the decade before, when Afrocentricity allowed Jamaicans to begin being proud about having overcome slavery, I was astonished that all of this was once again a source of shame and confusion. "Why glorify pain and a heritage of slavery?" asked a white *Gleaner* columnist. "In Australia, they don't celebrate the arrival of criminals and jailbirds shipped by the thousands from the British Isles to colonize. Why does Jamaica celebrate slavery?" White Jamaicans kept confusing commemoration with celebration; they would prefer to forget. As a black journalist answered, "The aim is not to look back in shame and anger but to reminisce with pride and a sense of having overcome considerable odds."

In a downtown museum not too far from where the slave market once was, the Institute of Jamaica had mounted an exhibit on slavery and emancipation. There were leg irons, collars and manacles, whips and chains. There was a famous eighteenth-century diagram of how to pack a slave ship, showing the prone bodies laid hip-to-hip below deck. There were tracts by English antislavery agitators written at the beginning of the nineteenth century, when the trade was already three centuries old. And, for comic relief, there was a satirical cartoon in the manner of Rowlandson and Hogarth about a young, eager Englishman named "Johnny-New-Come" who was undone by the West Indies. The delicately tinted panels told the story of Johnny's rise and fall: how he began as a conscientious planter, riding through the sugarcane fields on a handsome horse, but soon began drinking rum and lazing through the long, scorching afternoons with an array of dark-skinned beauties. In the end he lay on his death-bed, reduced to a skeleton by malaria and lust.

The centuries unraveled as I walked past the display cases filled with relics of atrocity and redemption. Then I rounded a corner and almost collided with a contraption that could only have come from a fiend's dream. It was an iron punishment cage, suspended from the ceiling by its headpiece. Rusting hoops formed an exo-skeleton for the torso and the legs. Bending close, I saw the iron crotchstrap hammered sharp as a knife and the spikes on the footpads of the stirrups—an artfully crafted device, most likely forged by a blacksmith who was himself a slave. A solitary guard heard my camera click and strolled over to gaze at the cage with me. I asked him where the thing had come from, and he said that workmen had recently unearthed it while digging a new foundation on an old sugar estate.

The university itself was built in the 1940s on land that had once been a plantation, and the campus was full of ruins. Old maps of the Mona estate showed slave cabins in neat rows among the ackee trees that still grew behind my flat, and a colleague from the history department was leading a student dig under the trees. He took me to the archeological museum in Port Royal, housed in the barracks where Royal Navy sailors once conva-lesced from yellow fever. The curator let us wander through the air-conditioned storerooms where uncatalogued artifacts were kept, shelved in cardboard boxes up to the ceiling.

The one I chose to open happened to be full of *zemis*, baseball-size stone carvings made by Arawak Indians. I lifted one, a tiny, smiling face above crossed arms.

"We really don't know what these were for," the curator said. "There aren't any Arawaks left to tell us."

I described the zemi to my next class; we were doing early New World history at the time, and the students were savoring the story of Columbus's disastrous sojourn in Jamaica. The admiral was shipwrecked on the island in 1503 with a mutinous crew of disappointed, angry sailors. They raped and plundered through the Arawak settlements until the natives refused to bring them any more food, and then both crew and Indians turned against Columbus. In a stroke of genius, he accurately predicted a lunar eclipse and thus convinced the terrified Arawaks that he was a god. But he went back to Spain in disgrace anyway, having failed to find enough gold. By the end of the 1520s, when Spain had conquered Mexico and Peru and turned its back on Jamaica, the Arawak tribe had already been exterminated by forced labor, starvation, and disease. Yet a few survived, escaping from the coastal plain up into the Blue Mountains, where no Spaniards followed them. When archeologists dig in the remains of Maroon encampments, they sometimes find shards of Arawak pottery scattered amid the iron and glass brought to the settlements by the African runaways.

Just before Christmas that first semester, I climbed the 7,280 feet to the top of Blue Mountain with another history professor, Neville Hall. Our party camped halfway up the mountain and then rose three hours before dawn to reach the summit at sunrise. Climbing in the darkness, we passed close enough to the ruins of the Maroon village called Nanny Town for all of us to think about the warrior-chieftainess for whom it is named, the sister of Accompong's Cudjoe. Legend has it that when the British bombarded Nanny's settlement with cannons and guns, she took these missiles into her cunt and fired them back.

Panting uphill in the cool night air, Neville and I saw torchlight flickering through the bush on a ridge above us.

"You nuh' see Nanny's ghost up there?" he asked in a whisper that brought goose bumps up on my arms.

Although the archeologists still dream of finding Nanny's

gravesite, her Maroon descendants say it will never be found because she never died. I thought of some children I'd watched one night years before, when Alex Haley's "Roots" was on Jamaican television, playing Kunta Kinte on the beach of a fishing village near Montego Bay. They reenacted the scene where Kunta is beaten to make him forget his African name, so taken with their play that the voices of their mothers calling them home to bed rang out unheeded across the beach. When the boy who played Kunta collapsed on the sand, exhausted by the pretend beating, one child cried, "Kunta dead!"

"You fool?" a little girl whispered. "Kunta cyan' dead! Him live forever!"

So if you ask a Jamaican where Nanny is buried, they will know you've missed the point of her life.

Like most Jamaicans, I began rising before dawn to catch the morning coolness; it was the best time to read papers and write lectures. The only sounds were birdsong from the ackee grove and the distant shouts of boys from the Poco Flats shantytown near the university. They came across the dew-soaked lawns with long sticks and crocus bags, knocked the ackee down, and then sold it at Papine market. They also scavenged through the garbage dump next to my flat for food scraps and anything else that looked interesting.

I had taken some photographs of a woman named Miss Addie who sold papayas at Papine, and after giving her the good ones, I tossed the other pictures in the trash. When I went to Papine a few days later, Miss Addie held up one of the crumpled, grease-stained photographs in an angry reproach. "What you tink I let you tek me picture fah?" she rasped. "You don' know someone can fix yu' bizness like so?" A Poco Flats boy who knew her had found the picture and returned it to her; Miss Addie was sure that some obeah man could have used it to "fix her bizness"—to work the black magic that Jamaicans call "high science." After that I was careful about what I threw out. There was no privacy, even in trash.

The Poco Flats children were persistent beggars, clanging on the aluminum louvers of my ground-floor flat with a stick if I didn't answer their first, softly hissed requests. It was impossible for me to refuse them, even though Jamaicans commonly ignore beggars. I wrote about the children to an anthropologist friend who was then in Costa Rica doing research on a banana plantation; he was a Marxist, and I expected him to write back with an order not to give alms and thus stall the coming of the revolution. But he was deep in his own third-world reversals by then.

"Keep giving," he wrote. "Now that Reagan is in for a second term, we will probably all be giving to beggars for the rest of our lives."

The boys from Poco Flats left the campus at dusk. Then the students from the dorm across the yard cranked up their boom boxes full blast to study by. I got used to working with the accompaniment of heavy dance hall tunes; like the ones I'd heard with Nelson on the drive from the airport, they were all full of gun sounds and deejays who spat out their lyrics with ballistic style. The current hit was by a group called Blood Fire Posse, and the song was titled "Every Posse Get Flat."

I had to ask one of my students what a posse was.

"Well," she smiled, "it's like your crew, your friends. Or a gang. You know . . . it comes from the westerns."

"So what does 'get flat' mean?" I asked.

"It means to hit the floor when the shots start fire."

Life on campus was full of ironies, most of which grew out of the contradictions between Jamaica's reality and the lovingly preserved illusion that UWI was like Oxford and Cambridge. Teaching was based on the tutorial system, perfectly suited to an

English university where there is a surfeit of splendid libraries, well-prepared students, and an army of dons for one-on-one sessions of brilliant exchange.

But this was Jamaica. My tutorials had twenty or thirty students each, and they were all supposed to read the same books from a meager library and produce a weekly paper. They competed with other students for those books like dogs scrapping for scarce bones. The reserve books had a way of disappearing, or of coming out of the stacks with entire chapters ripped out by some desperate scholar; I was lucky if one or two came to the meetings having read anything. No one could afford to buy the five paperbacks I had assigned for the American history course. They cost between fifty and two hundred dollars each in Jamaica's IMF-emasculated currency, and that was double what my students spent for food in a week. Many were women with children, and they fed themselves last. They came to class exhausted, and I learned not to be insulted if some dozed through lectures or didn't turn up for days at a time.

The campus had its tribe of homeless people and half-mad groundskeepers. Ras Dizzy made the rounds every day, a shadow of the Rastafarian who had once been a major Kingston artist. Dizzy had been beaten by the police so many times that he was deranged with justified paranoia. He would come by my office bringing scribbled poems about the fall of Babylon and primitive paintings he did when he could scrape up enough money for supplies.

"I'm goin' to the country," he vowed after a savage encounter with some rogue cops left him badly hurt. "Dread cyan' live in dis ras-clot city again."

A crazy groundskeeper named Winston always came by my office on Friday afternoon to ask for a few dollars to buy his white rum. He wore a blue felt officer's cap and a tattered wool tunic with gold buttons, even in the blazing heat; it looked like the uniforms once worn by London bus conductors. But Winston carried it with military bearing.

"I served His Majesty in the late war," he proclaimed, brandishing his machete like an officer's baton and railing against cruel students who taunted him about his drinking. After every outburst he would straighten his tunic and shout, "Back to university!" and resume his work of hacking at the thorny bougainvillea bushes.

The mood in Kingston that fall was somber. Jamaica's foreign debt was then a massive $4 billion, the largest per capita in the world. Seaga was "rationalizing" and restructuring the economy to service this debt, further crippling a country already battered by the oil price shocks of the 1970s. Translated into the terms of a sufferer's existence, all the prime minister's fancy financial wizardry meant was hunger. The government dropped subsidies on essential foods like rice, cornmeal, and flour. Prices soared as the International Monetary Fund repeatedly devalued Jamaica's dollar. Protein was just a dim memory: ackee and salt fish, the national dish, became a delicacy when salt fish went up to ten dollars a pound, then twenty dollars, then thirty dollars. "Chicken fly so high we only see his shadow," mourned Barbara Gloudon, the popular host of a radio call-in show. "He's gone to banquets elsewhere."

Clinics and hospitals around the island were forced to close as the health-care system was rationalized, and the same bitter IMF medicine was spooned down the throats of schoolteachers, who went on strike. The Caribbean Basin Initiative (CBI), David Rockefeller's brainchild, was Seaga's post-Grenada showpiece. The CBI was hyped as an economic boost for the region, but its real purpose was to turn the islands into offshore sweatshops where American manufacturers could exploit cheap labor. The program launched a string of garment factories on Kingston's waterfront, nonunion plants where ten thousand women and girls, handpicked from Seaga's West Kingston constituency, worked for twenty cents an hour stitching Nike running shorts, Hanes pantyhose, and Liz Claiborne sportswear. Guards stripped the women at the end of every shift to make sure they weren't stealing garments, and Seaga's goons beat up any union organizers who tried to get inside the factories. But the women were grateful to have work.

The CBI was also working miracles in the countryside. Now foreign agribusiness firms could lease the best arable land and grow winter vegetables for export. These farms were high-technology plantations with state-of-the-art machinery and a barefooted workforce of laborers who migrated from one rural parish to another in search of jobs. I met a young Israeli at a party in Kingston who was an overseer at Spring Plain, an agrofarm in the parish of Clarendon, and he invited me on a tour of the place. Hebrew-speaking masters roared across the irrigated fields in fancy jeeps, yelling at the ragged laborers and complaining to me in English about the dearth of a work ethic among Jamaicans. Guards patrolled the fields and shipping areas with high-powered weapons; a few weeks after I was there, a worker was shot to death for allegedly pilfering produce. In the packing shed, cartons of perfectly sized and shaped zucchini, tomatoes, and cucumbers were waiting to be flown to America and Europe. But Spring Plain nevertheless went bankrupt a year later, and the shady Israeli entrepreneur who had leased it vanished into thin air. The farm was rumored to have been a front for his cocaine trafficking.

On the political front Jamaica was eerily moribund, a one-party state for the first time in forty years. Manley and the PNP had boycotted a snap election Seaga called in 1983, just after the invasion of Grenada had raised his popularity in the polls. Man-

ley's stated reason for the boycott was Seaga's unwillingness to
bring the voters' lists up-to-date, but the real reason was that he
knew he would lose. His refusal to contest the JLP left Jamaica
without an opposition party in government.

This one-party rule brought out the worst of Seaga's autocratic
tendencies. He took to announcing tough new policies and aus-
terity measures like royal fiats, and then he spent an inordinate
amount of time away from Jamaica with foreign dignitaries and
the international moneymen who called the shots. His friends
were Ronald Reagan and Eugenia Charles, the leader of Domin-
ica who had masterminded the Grenada invasion; several of his
ministers were close to the Duvalier regime in Haiti. None of
this would have mattered had conditions in Jamaica not been so
dire, but as things were, this closeness with wealthy and powerful
right-wing allies threw Jamaica's distress into stark relief. There
was an ugly interlude when John Rollins, an American tycoon,
tried to evict squatters from a stretch of prime oceanfront land
he owned near Montego Bay; when lawyers defended the squatters' claims, Rollins went to his friends at Citibank and tried to
convince them to freeze its loans to Jamaica until the government
did his bidding.

Jamaica was beginning to resemble Haiti, and some of Seaga's
critics compared him to the Duvaliers. Although he is white,
there were echoes of Duvalierism in Kingston's police terror and
the way Seaga manipulated his black followers, turning up in
West Kingston for dances in revivalist tabernacles and taking part
in the dark ceremonies of Pocomania, a cult whose practitioners
often double as obeah men. His spiritual mentor was a widely
feared Pocomania shepherd named Mallica "Kapo" Reynolds, an
intuitive painter and wood-carver whose work was installed in
its own room at Kingston's National Gallery. Kapo had a reputation as a science man, a high priest of the dark arts. When

Manley developed cancer in 1985, the word on the street was that Kapo had followed Seaga's orders to fix his rival's business once and for all, and that Manley was therefore doomed.

This atavistic return to superstition and occultism was paradoxically paired with a fresh passion for anything American and white; dreadlocks, dashikis, and black pride went underground, replaced by a sinister longing for status and the trappings of privilege. Beauty pageants were big again, even though Manley and his elegant, dark-skinned wife Beverley had tried in the seventies to discourage these contests because they invariably favored women with light skin and white features. Now they were back with a vengeance, and all of the winning contestants were brown or tan. Black women flocked to watch models with narrow noses and "good" hair sashaying down the runways at luxury hotels like the Wyndham and the Pegasus.

A Jamaican Miss Universe contestant named Ruth Cammock caused a scandal when she sued her Dryad deodorant sponsors after they pulled her from the pageant because she was too dark. "You should learn to face reality," they told her. "Naturally we prefer a person with lighter skin and taller hair." Althea Laing, Miss Jamaica Fashion Model of 1985, admitted that she was a rarity among beauty queens. "They're calling me the black statement," she said, "because Jamaica is into the brown thing."

A woman fittingly named Grace Virtue wrote a letter to the *Gleaner* about the Ruth Cammock affair. "One hundred and fifty years after emancipation, we quote Marcus Garvey and sing Bob's songs, but for the majority of us beauty does not exist unless it comes decked in the garb of a fair skin and straight hair. I say black was never beautiful. For a fleeting moment in the 1970s it seemed as if we were finally accepting ourselves, but this upsurge seems to have taken a nose-dive."

Author Rex Nettleford, one of the island's most gifted and

prolific critics of its racial schizophrenia, lamented the resurgence of beauty pageants and the spectacle of "combatants locked in covert and overt conflict as to the true worth of that melanin which resides obstinately in the skins of the vast majority."

Jamaican women, like their sisters everywhere, were the miners' canaries for their country's poisoned air. SuperCat, the undisputed don of dance hall, came out with a hit song called "Boops," about the way ghetto girls had to find a sugar daddy if they wanted to eat. "Boopsism" became the talk of the town, a code word for female despair.

Kingston's men lost a champion of promiscuity when a man named Charlie Mattress died in his nineties. Charlie had fathered forty-eight children with different women, and some wit proposed a fund in his honor to reward men who sired at least twenty children with ten or more women. Mike Henry, the minister of culture, didn't think the proposal was funny at all, and he struck back with a nasty speech about how poverty was just a disease brought on by excessive breeding. Another expert on the population problem said that the poor with too many children simply had nothing better to do.

But it took courage to do it in Kingston. Women labored three to a bed at Jubilee Lying-In, if they could get to the childbirth clinic through the nightly barrage of gunfire that peppered the streets around Kingston Public Hospital. The hospital was dangerously close to the border between the JLP's West Kingston stronghold and the PNP's Concrete Jungle garrison. Gunmen had recently murdered a hospital porter and torched two of the wards, then killed a policeman and his girlfriend. She was in labor at the time, and he was trying to get her to Jubilee. Winston Spaulding, the JLP's minister of national security, blamed the killings on the Concrete Jungle gang; the PNP blamed Seaga and his thugs from Tivoli Gardens.

Everyone thought the crime wave in Kingston couldn't get any worse, but it did. Dealing with it had transformed the police force from a British-inspired constabulary into a tribe of killers in uniform; by the time I moved to Kingston, they were committing a staggering one-third of the island's homicides. Americas Watch sent a mission to Jamaica to investigate police brutality and condemned the force for shooting criminal suspects—along with innocent bystanders—on sight. Morris Cargill, the *Gleaner*'s curmudgeon columnist, responded to the Americas Watch report by admitting that the police "do shoot down known murderers and armed gangsters when they catch them, sometimes in cold blood. This is not the best way of justice, but in our present circumstances my only complaint is that they don't shoot enough of them."

The deadliest member of the police force was a killer cop named Keith Gardner, who earned the nickname "Trinity" from a spaghetti western. He'd become famous in the 1970s for walking his prisoners at gunpoint from one lockup to another, like some Wild West lawman. He used to show up at downtown dances with a brace of pistols and an M16, dressed all in black like a gunfighter. Trinity learned badman-ism from the inside, growing up in Concrete Jungle and then rising through the police force to become Seaga's bodyguard for the 1980 election campaign. His closeness with the prime minister allowed him to rub shoulders with celebrities, and the walls of his office at the Halfway Tree police station were decorated with framed color photographs of him with Nelson Mandela, Jesse Jackson, and Queen Elizabeth. Trinity reckoned that he had been in a total of ninety-seven shootouts, but he modestly claimed not to be counting anymore.

"I think the moment you start counting, you are becoming degenerate," he told me once, in a voice so soft that I had to lean forward to catch his words above the hum of the air-conditioner in his office. "You must think like a criminal, but you do not necessarily learn to behave like them."

A few years later Trinity shot and killed his wife in a domestic quarrel and then became a born-again Christian. It was thought that perhaps he had calmed down somewhat, but his colleagues on the force were still as deadly as ever.

A few months after I arrived in Kingston, some rogue cops executed a university graduate, Patrick Lewis. He was riding with some friends in a stolen car on the Red Hills Road uptown when the cops ambushed the car and shot him in cold blood. Lewis was a veteran leftist with ties to both the PNP and the Workers' Party of Jamaica, the island's Communist party; according to press reports of his death, that was enough to warrant his execution in this new Jamaica.

But most of the other police homicides were random killings with no political motive. They killed a shoemaker in the parish of St. Thomas as the man sat under a tamarind tree with some friends. The first shot didn't kill him, and when he begged for his life, one of the cops laughed. "Now you dead, bwoy. Me a' go kill you," he said. The police didn't like to leave witnesses. A few weeks later they picked up a sixteen-year-old Kingston schoolboy named Garfield Chin and shot him once. After they found a Bible and a letter from his girlfriend in Chin's pockets, they teased him about the romance and then stuffed him in their squad car trunk. Chin begged for mercy. "You a' talk?" one cop asked. Then he fired a single shot into Chin's head. There were usually one or two stories like these in the *Gleaner* every day. I would clip them in the evenings after work and slide them into a fattening file marked "Police Killings." Fifty-seven people died in the first two months of 1985; twenty-nine of them were killed by cops.

Soon I had a miscellaneous file I couldn't name, so I called it "Distress Signals." Some of the stories recounted weird events in the parishes outside Kingston; some were about cannibalism. "A man said to be of unsound mind was beaten to death by citizens in Ashton district, Westmoreland, on Saturday after he was found eating what was believed to be the remains of a man chopped in two." Some were about madmen who were stoned or beaten to death by mobs, or about the mentally ill who were treated like criminals. The file also held stories about crop theft and what country people did to the thieves. I clipped the story of a twelve-year-old schoolboy named Miguel Miller who hanged himself after he failed his Common Entrance admission exam for high school. Even if he had passed, the odds still would have been against him: high schools had space for only one-fourth of the forty thousand children who took the Common Entrance every year.

I clipped a lot of stories about ganja and cocaine. As the U.S. Agency for International Development (US AID) funded ganja-eradication missions led by the Jamaica Defense Force, the *Gleaner* ran daily cautionary tales about hapless farmers whose fields had gone up in smoke. Meanwhile, Air Jamaica planes were getting impounded in Miami and New York with huge quantities of weed in their cargo bays. But ganja was an old story; the presence of cocaine was new. It was news when a shipment was seized from some pleasure boat off Jamaica, or when a fisherman found a stray kilo bobbing on the waves after the rest of the shipment was picked up at sea.

None of these random articles told the full story of Jamaica's tragic mating-dance with cocaine—how it first appeared during the 1980 election campaign, when Seaga's gunmen were the ones who used and peddled it; how most of the drug came into Kingston's Newport West wharves in shipping containers, and that it was no coincidence that these wharves were controlled by the JLP; how cocaine had turned Seaga's mercenaries into madmen and—too late—shown the politician-warlords that they had created monsters they could no longer control.

But cocaine was not the only contraband that was coming into Newport West.

The *Gleaner* ran a screaming headline on October 4, 1984: ARMS CACHE: FBI, INTERPOL CALLED IN. The story said that two fifty-five-gallon steel drums had mysteriously shown up on the wharves; it did not mention that the customs officer who had been bribed to clear them happened to be off that day. When another worker opened the barrels, he found a twenty-two-gun arsenal that included an M16, an M1 Enforcer, five assault rifles, two .44 magnums, and more than six thousand rounds of ammunition. The *Gleaner* dropped the story after that.

But for American authorities it was only the beginning. Federal agents from the Bureau of Alcohol, Tobacco and Firearms traced the guns to a string of pawnshops in Florida's Dade and Broward counties. They were part of a much larger cache—210 weapons—bought in Florida and Ohio by a posse called the Shower. Spawned in Tivoli Gardens, the Shower had been running things for Seaga since the 1980 election. But by 1984 it had moved its base of operations to Florida, and its two leaders, Vivian Blake and Lester "Jim Brown" Coke, were running ganja and cocaine from Miami to New York.

Jim Brown—who had taken this nickname from the American football star—had only just left Kingston when I arrived. He had killed so many people for the JLP in 1980 that he became the undisputed "don-gadda" of the streets, and his deadly reputation was reaffirmed in May 1984 when he went into a Kingston ghetto with twenty Shower men and killed twelve people in a single night of terror. He left the island soon after that and promptly sent those twenty-two guns down from Miami to his friends in Tivoli Gardens. A month after the shipment was intercepted, Brown was robbed outside a drug house in Miami where he'd just bought some cocaine; he thought the people inside had set him up. So he went back and killed everyone there. To make certain that all six were dead, he went through the house and finished each one off with a bullet to the head. It took another three years for the Miami police to figure out who Jim Brown was and to link him to the 1984 slayings. By then the Shower had become the deadliest posse in the United States.

I was years away from knowing any of this when I read the *Gleaner*'s gun-cache headline that October morning. But it seemed even then to be an ominous sign of further trouble. Although I was beginning to see that Jamaicans are experts at coping with duress that would spark an armed insurrection anywhere else in the world, I kept expecting the lid to blow off as I watched the violence and sufferation escalate in Kingston. "Pressure drop" was what the reggae singer Toots Hibbert had called it years before, but now it seemed as if that pressure was becoming unbearable.

The lid did blow off, in early January 1985, when Seaga announced in an evening speech to Parliament that the price of gasoline was shooting up to eleven dollars a gallon; we knew this meant steep increases in the cost of everything else. Seaga acknowledged "the pain that you all feel," but he said that the IMF's impending devaluation of the Jamaican dollar necessitated the increase and that, as a result of the favorable exchange rate for Americans, tourism would enjoy its best season ever: $400 million Jamaican in earnings. So no one was supposed to complain.

Roadblocks were going up across the island before Seaga had finished his speech. By morning Kingston's streets were full of angry crowds, clustered at intersections blocked by fallen trees, burning tires, and the husks of blackened cars. Some of the barricades were like neighborhood block parties—small, spontaneous combustions of protest—but the ones in PNP strongholds turned deadly when the JLP sent its goons into the streets to quell the demonstrations. Gunmen from Wareika showed up with their arsenals; three people were shot dead by police in Nannyville, a PNP area, and others were killed on the Windward Road. Manley disclaimed any party connection with the violence and said Jamaicans had simply "reached the limit of their capacity to endure hardships and suffer in silence."

Seaga left the island for Miami to appear on the "MacNeil/ Lehrer NewsHour" and reassure the frightened American tourists that Jamaica was still a safe destination. It was the height of the winter season, and rioting on the island was Seaga's worst nightmare come true. American television crews got into Kingston in time to send back scary footage of shouting mobs and burning barricades, making Jamaica look like a miniature South Africa. When islanders learned that their leader had skipped out to the mainland to parlay with the people who really mattered, they got even angrier.

Classes were suspended at UWI and the campus was dead quiet except for the sound of radios. No one wanted to sample the action at the Liguanea roadblock nearby; when I traipsed across the lawn to check on Neville Hall, the adventurous colleague who'd taken me up Blue Mountain a few weeks before, he flatly refused to accompany me to Liguanea.

"I had enough excitement in 1980," he said. "If you want to check out this latest manifestation of our collective unrest, you'll have to go by yourself."

But Trevor Munroe, a government professor and the leader of the Workers' Party of Jamaica, rallied some students for a march down the Mona Road. Munroe was fearless; he'd had his skull cracked many times in the 1970s when he worked as a WPJ organizer on the West Kingston docks, so an uptown roadblock was a picnic by comparison. One of his students had a boom box and was playing the latest song by Trinidad's reigning calypsonian, the Mighty Sparrow; it was called "Capitalism Gone Mad," perfect music for the barricades.

The sufferers at Liguanea were in a celebratory mood, even when Trinity careened up in a police Jeep and began threatening the crowd. He and Trevor Munroe got into a brief, intense shouting match, but the professor stood his ground and Trinity left. Fortified by the rhythms of the Mighty Sparrow, we watched as more Jeeps full of soldiers and police tried to dismantle the roadblock, turning back when the sufferers dragged more debris from a stockpile in someone's yard. A helicopter from the Jamaica Defense Force hovered so low over the crowd that I could see the pilot's face. He was laughing.

"Soldier-bwoy-dem feelin' the pressure same as we," said the gray-haired man beside me. "Dem nah' gwan shoot at we today." The radios told us that in other parts of Kingston there was plenty of shooting going on, but no one wanted to surrender this chance to fight back.

I recognized people I knew in the crowd: a few of my students, the buxom higgler women who sold fruits and vegetables every day at Liguanea, and the pushcart man who sold jelly coconuts in the shade. Since there was no produce coming into town, the higglers were celebrating their day off, flinging raucous, good-natured insults at one another instead of sitting on their scraps of cardboard in the burning sun and haggling over the price of mangos.

There was a Rasta woman named Plummy who always had the best produce, and she was at the roadblock in her Sunday best, dressed in a patchwork skirt of red, gold, and green with her resplendent locks tied into a towering head wrap. She was brandishing a big, unlit spliff, her gesture to the freedom of the moment. "Whoy, dawta!" Plummy beamed, clapping me on the back in sisterly greeting. "What a day we live to see, eh? Lookin' like the big-men-them get a lickle of their own back at last."

The gas price riots, as the press called them, lasted for three days. But by the evening of the second day, Kingston's streets were clear enough to drive. So I went down to the Pegasus Hotel in New Kingston, the city's business district, to see how the foreign journalists who always stayed there were faring. They were sitting in rattan chairs by the pool, trading stories and trying to straighten out the details of the island's political scene. Jamaica had not been on anyone's list of stories worth covering since 1980, so the riots had caught the media by surprise.

But Seaga's silky-voiced, all-female public relations team was at the Pegasus, urging the journalists to leave Kingston and write some positive stories from under a palm tree in Negril; the government had chartered several small planes to take them there. One of the women mistook me for a correspondent and began her pitch. "It is essential to our government that you play down the extent of these disturbances," she said. "If more scenes of violence and disorder make it into the American media, it will be disastrous for our tourism." She spoke with dignity and composure, but I felt ashamed for the position she was in.

The riots changed nothing, of course. When the streets were cleared and the country returned to normal, gasoline was selling for the promised eleven dollars a gallon and the cost of living went up one more notch. The sufferers were still drinking salt water to fill their bellies and Seaga was still firmly in control.

When classes resumed, some of my students wanted to talk about the protests, but others were anxious about expressing their views. The current regime had impressed them with the importance of pleasing Americans, and only a few dared to risk offending a teacher whose country held theirs hostage. So there were a lot of embarrassed apologies for the recent bad behavior. But the brightest of my students, a woman who later won a Fulbright scholarship to Johns Hopkins and became a historian herself, wasn't apologizing for anything. She was furious, and her eyes sparkled with tears.

"You know what offended me the most?" she said, her voice quaking. "Seaga just ignored us. He went and talked to the Americans, told them it was still safe here for them. What about us? Whose country is this, anyway?"

Brambles

The rains came hard that spring, forty days of biblical intensity. Bridges washed out and country trucks listing with workers and sugarcane overturned in flash floods, spilling men and women into ravines. The flooded roads lured highwaymen, who held up stranded motorists and demanded money to push their cars through the water onto dry ground. Kingston's streets turned into swift-running streams, threatening to drown schoolchildren. The country areas were hit hardest—farmers lost all of their crops, but many told tales of heroism and kindness, of friends who swam through flooded fields to rescue precious livestock. When the sun came out again and the waters receded, the mud-caked rural parishes started digging out.

The JLP seized on the floods as a prime public relations opportunity: it sent members of Parliament out to their constituencies with seeds and tools for replanting the fields. I got an invitation from a woman I knew in the Office of the Prime Minister to tour one flood-ravaged section of the parish of St. Ann, represented by Neville Gallimore, the minister of health. A friend of Haiti's Baby Doc Duvalier, he was the emissary Seaga sent to Haiti a year later when Jamaica wanted the dictator to leave Port-au-Prince peacefully. My friend Dorothy told me to be at Jamaica House early the next morning to catch a ride with Gallimore's entourage.

The scene at government headquarters was the usual chaos, with drivers trying to organize their vanfuls of media people and bodyguards. There was a slim, tobacco-brown photographer from the Jamaica Information Service, the island's press agency, who was standing apart from the throng. He was draped with camera equipment, wearing it along with a bulging photographer's vest and a natty cap that reminded me of a horse trainer. He was scanning the *Gleaner* for the day's lineup of horses at the Caymanas Park racetrack, looking up now and then at the confusion around us with a glint of mirth in his eyes.

We started talking before we knew each other's names. He told me he'd lived all his life in Central Kingston, the waterfront ghetto that was Michael Manley's constituency and a little hotbed of tribal war. We soon discovered we had a friend in common, a Kingston actor whom I was seeing then, and the photographer told me the two of them had grown up together in Central in the days when it was the city's residential and commercial heart, before the tribal violence of the 1970s devastated the neighborhood. The actor had moved up in the world; he had earned a UWI degree, which gave him a measure of status, along with plenty of painful conflicts about the downtown and uptown worlds he still tried to straddle. But this photographer had stayed where he was born, and he wore his sufferer's struggle like the badge of honor it was.

"I is a ghetto mon, born an' bred," he said proudly. And then he gave me his hand. "They call me Brambles."

It was high noon by the time we got out of Kingston and on to Spanish Town Road—later renamed Mandela Highway—a speedway that goes by the city's industrial terraces and the sprawling shantytown called Riverton City. The first shanties had

gone up around a garbage dump, and now the area was a home
to thousands; the children of Riverton City formed their own
posses to fight off the john-crow buzzards they competed with
for food. Dead animals by the dozens littered the highway, sending up wafts of putrid scent. I was riding in Dorothy's fancy car,
and her driver went so fast that one of our tires exploded from
the heat. When he stopped to change it, kneeling down on the
melting asphalt, I saw the gun tucked into the waistband of
his pants.

Past Spanish Town, we started rising into cool green hills like
the hollows of Kentucky or Tennessee, lush limestone mounds
with tiny valleys and villages tucked between them. Our first
stop was a town named Cave Valley, where Gallimore was to
speak to his constituents and then tour their sodden fields. By
the time we got there I was carsick from the diver's homicidal
speed and went to stand in the shade of a rumshop wall. Gallimore was already haranguing a small crowd, raising high the
rakes and hoes he had brought. They were gifts from America,
Gallimore said, because Mr. Seaga and the Americans were
very close.

The young men in the rumshop listened coolly to this speech.
Their parish was prime ganja country, the source of the lamb's
bread and kali weed, potent strains of ganja whose profits bought
their sexy fishnet T-shirts and acid-washed jeans.

"Cho!" one of them hissed after a long pull from his Red
Stripe bottle. "What a fuckery that mon there chant! Him come
up here fi' tell we is pure orange an' banana we mus' plant again.
An' him know is ganja we haffi' grow up here fi' survive! No,
mon. No way Seaga can hold disya' place when next election
come round. Seaga fight too hard 'gainst the ganja-men-dem."

There was proof of his bitterness on the rumshop wall—one
of the powerful pieces of local art that had come out of some

Kingston printery and become collector's items. This one was called "Jamaica Ganja Eradication." Four army helicopters are landing in a burning ganja field; one soldier is suspended in midair like a terrible angel, his M16 already aimed at the farmer who stands with his weeping wife and children to watch their livelihood go up in smoke. A black mongrel dog is barking in futile defense, and there is a strange female face framed in one of the helicopter's windows: a white woman, smiling benignly, like one of the placid, incongruous observers in medieval crucifixion scenes.

"Who's the white woman?" I asked.

"You don't know 'bout she?" the young man scoffed. "Is the Iron Maiden, that. She flyin' on all the ganja missions now. Some American 'ooman from DEA or CIA or FBI—one o' dem ting. An' she wicked to ras! Yeah, mon. Dis what Seaga mean fi' we. So you better believe is Manley we gwan' vote for nex' time. It never coulda' go so with the ganja-men inna' Manley time."

St. Ann's parish is where Bob Marley's mother Cedella raised her son after his white English father left them. Marley is buried across the hills from Cave Valley in the village of Nine Miles. Marcus Garvey, the father of pan-Africanism, was also born here in the main town of St. Ann's Bay, down the coast from where Columbus landed. The parish has always had a strong sense of itself, made stronger since the 1970s by the money ganja brought in. Herb by the ton was smuggled out on boats from Ocho Rios and small planes that landed on strips built by the ganja barons, just like the roads they paved and the houses they built and the electricity they brought into dark dwellings perched on steep hills. Everyone knows who their real patrons are; they are not the politicians who live in Kingston and only show up in places like Cave Valley when it is time to raise votes.

I kept my eye on Brambles from the rumshop, admiring the

way he darted through the crowd, kneeling to take pictures and climbing around for better vantages. He moved like a cat and smiled to himself, loving his work. When Gallimore's contingent left the square for the nearby fields, I followed behind Brambles and an old man with a harmonica who played a sweet, lilting jig for Gallimore as we walked. Dorothy had gone back to town with her gun-toting bodyguard, so I rode with Brambles's media crew to the day's last stop, a village called Gibraltar, where a crowd of farmers had been waiting patiently since early morning for the city people to arrive.

Gibraltar was in another constituency, represented by a woman with the sonorous name of Princess Lawes. She was one of the JLP's rising female stars; Seaga liked working with women because they were both ambitious and practical, better at cooperating than the male MPs, who generally behaved like roosters in a yard. But Lawes had thrown practicality to the winds that day: her white crocheted suit and black patent-leather heels were far too elegant for a country visit. The red clay had demolished her shoes and she looked very uncomfortable among her peasant constituents with their bare feet and tattered clothes. They were waiting for us in a one-room schoolhouse, sitting on rough wooden benches and eager for the seeds and tools to replant their fields.

But Gallimore had given almost everything away in Cave Valley and there was not going to be enough to go around. Somehow I was recruited to untie the plastic bags full of seeds and divide them into smaller amounts, working frantically while Lawes stood at the front of the schoolroom and delivered a speech.

"These seeds we have brought for you were given to our prime minister by the people of America," she said. "They love

us and they love Mr. Seaga. Do you know what the letters *JLP*
stand for? They stand for 'Jesus-loving people.' And that is what
we are."

But the people of Gibraltar were in no mood for soothing
talk about Jesus. They were tired and angry, and they began first
to murmur and then to shout and stomp. Brambles had ducked
out for a smoke under the guinep tree in the schoolyard, and I
went out to join him just before a small riot exploded inside.
The long-suffering farmers rushed to the front of the room and
engulfed their member of Parliament in a shoving throng, grabbing for a handful of pumpkin or cabbage seeds.

Brambles was smoking one of his Craven A's and smiling his
catlike grin. "This nothin'," he said. "I see some true riots inna'
my time. You should 'ave seen this country in 1980. Nuff-nuff
guns fire inna' my neighborhood then."

He glared at me suddenly for emphasis.

'Labourites kill a bredda right inna' my yard on Foster Lane,
shot him in the lane and chased him through my gate. Cornered
him behind the fridge on my veranda and finished him off right
then and there. Is so much killin' I see. Is me haffi' spend the
better part of that mornin' cleanin' up the blood. I thank God
my pickney [children] not there that night."

Brambles told me he had a son and daughter who lived with
him, but the boy wasn't born till after the election. "Ricky was
in Pet's belly still. An' seem like him come into this world already 'fraid from what his mother see in them time."

Princess Lawes had made her escape from Gibraltar while
Brambles and I were talking under the guinep tree. Now the
rest of the crew from JIS were piling into the van for the long
ride back to Kingston. Even though I was riding with them, I
felt a sense of urgency about asking Brambles for the favor I
wanted before we got into the van with everyone else.

"Would you take me with you on a walk downtown sometime?" I asked. "Just so I could get to know the area a little."

He laughed. "You 'ave car an' you still like walk foot? Is rough down there now, you know. Well-rough."

He looked me up and down, considering how much of a liability I would be on the streets of Central Kingston.

"The place is cosmopolitan-like, still," he mused. "It was the waterfront once, so people used to seein' sailors an' foreigners 'bout the place. Is not like West Kingston. That place is full o' nothin' but pure obeah-yard an' people fresh from country, and them suspicious to ras."

We were in the van by then, beginning to climb out of Gibraltar's narrow valley onto the better road to town.

"You know that Rosalyn Carter came down to Raetown once, when her husband was president?" Brambles said, almost to himself. Raetown is the fishing beach on Central Kingston's eastern flank; the Manley government had started an urban development project for the fishermen there, and they brought Mrs. Carter to see it. Brambles covered her tour. "The lickle sheds Manley built are derelict now," he said.

"All right," said Brambles, bringing himself back from the 1970s. "Mek me tell you what we a' go do. Is walk you want? All right, we walk. You meet me tomorrow, ten o'clock, on the corner of East Queen Street and High Holborn. There's a football field there, an' I will walk up from my yard to find you."

He was quiet for the rest of the trip back to Kingston, and when the van left me at Jamaica House, he hardly said goodbye. I wondered if he would even show up as I waited the next morning, standing next to a little scrapboard stand where an elderly higgler was selling cigarettes, matches, and oranges. She peeled me one and then hung the spiraling skin neatly on a string above her, saving it to make tea.

The street was roaring with market day traffic, and the new Japanese minibuses everyone called "quarter millions" were farting a black pall of diesel smoke through the harsh sunlight. The rumshops, barber shops, tailoring establishments, and cookstands were all doing fast business, and the street vibrated with Saturday morning energy. I looked down High Holborn and saw Brambles swinging toward me with his loose, easy gait, wearing his camera like a necklace.

"Whappum?" he said casually. "You find this place with no problem?"

"It's hard to miss a football field," I said, and we stood for a while side by side, watching the kids shout and sprint their way through the soccer match.

"So we walk," Brambles said after a while. "I show you Parade."

The square is downtown Kingston's heart, presided over by the ice-blue-and-white Ward Theatre, a Victorian wedding cake of a building, where Norman Manley launched the PNP in 1938. The hall next door, where Marcus Garvey's voice once rang out, had been torn down, and the site was a bus yard now, clamoring with activity as the rusted buses unloaded country people and their crocus bags full of produce. The buses were beautifully painted, with names like *King Alphonso* and *Conquering Lion,* but they were in terrible condition. I'd lost a dear friend, a Montego Bay musician, to one of these buses; he fell through the rotting floorboards and was ground to death in the gears.

We walked across Parade to the new covered market Seaga had built for the higglers, who were now being called "informal commercial importers" in recognition of the fact that their weekly runs to Miami and Panama furnished Jamaicans with most of what they wore. You could glimpse their power and authority in the Miami airport: woe to any overzealous airline employee who told them they couldn't put their refrigerator-size boxes of Pampers and soap powder in baggage. The higglers sat in their palace on Parade with mounds and racks of lacy panties and fluttering bras, cheap Indian cottons, and plastic shoes, calling out good prices and friendly insults to anyone who tried to bargain them down.

"This place, goin' on down King Street, used to be where everyone came to buy 'pon a Saturday," Brambles said. "But then the big-mon-dem build the plazas up in Constant Spring and Liguanea, and is only we sufferers come to Parade now."

We crossed to East Street and walked down it until we came to the sea; I wanted to see the spot where the famed Myrtle Bank Hotel had stood, a palm-fronded palace beside the United Fruit Company pier. "It opened a magic window on the world," wrote Vic Reid, a Raetown child who grew up to become a poet, novelist, and historian. The Myrtle Bank catered to the first white tourists from England and America who came on the United Fruit Company's ships, and Reid remembered the tourists as "dons (noble and Mafia) and dolls (debutantes and tarts)."

But the affluence belonged only to foreigners, something Brambles knew for himself. We stood in the hot wind off the water and he spoke of being a little boy and watching the rich people getting off the ships. "I used to hang 'round the pier by the Myrtle Bank in them times. Used to dive naked for the coins the cruise ship passengers flung over the side. I was one o' the best swimmers."

The JLP tore down the hotel and the pier in the early 1960s and built new wharves, Newport West, on the West Kingston waterfront, close to the party's own stronghold, where it could control who got work on the docks. That was when Central

Kingston began to die. "The Labourites always hated this area," Brambles said, "because they could never control it. Too cosmopolitan, too open to the sea."

We turned north, away from the water, and began walking into the residential core of the neighborhood, crossing old streets and lanes named for English sovereigns and tropical commodities: Georges, Hanover, Rum, and Gold. It was at a dance on Gold Street in 1980 that PNP gunmen opened fire on a crowd, a reprisal after someone stoned Manley in a motorcade. Three people died.

"Notice that the police station is right across the street," Brambles said as we strolled by. "But no one came to pursue the gunmen. Gold Street is no-man's-land."

Gold Street was just one of several demarcations that split the neighborhood in two: to the west was territory that belonged to a PNP gang called Tel Aviv; to the east was Foster Lane (where Brambles lived), High Holborn, and Fleet Street. That section was known as Southside, a little JLP enclave within the heart of Central. Its reigning gang was the Southies, sometimes called the Renkers, and they got their guns from the JLP. We walked by a crumbling brick cottage on Fleet Street with graffiti that said EDDIE MY LOVE, meaning Seaga.

Even with the rot and crumble, the bullet marks, and the rubble from burned-out buildings, there was something left of Central's former grace. Behind twisted zinc fences and scrap board dwellings rose the leafy branches of mango, ackee, breadfruit, and almond trees, planted decades before by the neighborhood's proud householders. Some of the concrete walls in front of the old cottages were topped now with broken glass to repel marauders, but the cottages themselves were beautiful despite their dilapidation. They still had carved wooden tracery above doors and windows and names etched into their gates. EVELIN'S COTTAGE, said one; HARLEM, said another.

"This place was sweet once," Brambles said, "before politics turned people 'gainst each other. This was where you came to stowaway 'pon a boat for America, in the days before planes."

He told me he had watched his mother walk onto a ship bound for England in the early 1950s, and he never saw her again. His aunt raised him. "She was strict. You didn't cross her 'less you wanted a beating. But thru' I grow without a mother, I feel me own pickney never goin' to go without me."

It was a promise he struggled to keep.

We had come to the wooden gate of his yard, and we paused to look up and down Foster Lane. It was no wider than a car, and the ceaseless pour of neighborhood sounds reverberated up and down its tunnel. Shouts and calls came from all sides, along with music, crowing roosters, and barking dogs; Central sounded like its own small village. But most of all it was the crying of children that became for me the signal sound of the ghetto— wailing punctuated by laughter. In the upstairs window of the rumshop across from Brambles's yard, a woman leaned out, bare-breasted, to catch stray breezes from the harbor. She was laughing into the sun and she looked down at me and smiled.

Brambles opened his gate to the self-contained world of a tenement yard, where ten people lived in a row of three twelve-square-foot rooms lined up along a concrete veranda. His room was on the Foster Lane end of the row, so it had a window that looked out over the shard-topped wall. I went to stand by it and instinctively drew away to the side, still looking out. Brambles laughed.

"You stand like a gunfighter," he said. "Tactical."

He had two pieces of furniture: a double bed and an old glass-front cabinet where he kept china, glasses, and utensils. His cameras and archive of photographs and slides were hidden under clothes in a corrugated cardboard barrel. Neatly pressed shirts hung on a line across the bed. That was where his children slept; Brambles told me he usually bedded down on the concrete veranda.

"Nuff-nuff time I don't even sleep down here," he said. "I just bleach all night." To "bleach" is to never close your eyes into darkness. "Is too much noise 'bout the place fi' sleep."

His daughter Natalie was sitting on the veranda, playing house with her box of treasures: a blond Barbie doll and some old doll clothes, Brambles's empty aftershave bottles, and a shard of mirror. She paused every now and then to gaze into it, admiring the fresh cornrows a neighbor had given her that morning. She was nine and already an almond-eyed beauty, much darker than Brambles and conscious, he said, of the difference in their skin. She resembled her mother but adored her father and often stayed up with him at night, listening to the talk between him and his friends.

The yard had its matriarch, an old woman named Auntie, who sat, sewing, in the far corner by her room; she earned a few dollars doing piecework for a tailor up the lane. Carol, the single woman who lived with her baby in the middle room, was washing dishes at the standpipe. Brambles's yard had running water, a toilet, and a shower, and that made it the kindest of all of the neighborhood tenement-yards I came to know. None of them had water, and many had no latrines either. People pissed on the ground and defecated into buckets, emptied later into the gully that flowed along South Camp Road into the harbor. At times later in that year, I would sit on the veranda while Brambles took a shower and listen to the water sluicing over him, feeling intense pleasure at the sound. Next to food, water is the ghetto's greatest luxury.

We passed the rest of that first afternoon sipping cold beer and reasoning on the veranda, until the shadows lengthened and the neighborhood came to Saturday-night life. Some of the sufferers whom Brambles called "the professors of poverty" came by his yard to check me out. One was an older man named Keith who used to be a sailor. Brambles called him an elder, even though he was barely out of his forties; I was beginning to see that living to that age qualified someone as a survivor.

"Down here," said Keith, "we 'ave all the time in the world to observe the way things go and none of the power to change them. So we is all philosophers of a sort."

He took us later that night to his favorite brothel in Raetown, the Seaview Club, where a string of Christmas tree lights garlanded the gatepost and the rooms upstairs were painted a faded, gaudy turquoise. There was no one there, and it looked as if there never would be.

A Tel Aviv youth named Bruce came with us, and he brought along a little notebook with verses he had written to no one in particular. One had a long title: "What I Have Learned in Life, Through the Acknowledgments of My Hardships, Desperate Needs and Hostile Tribulations: One Should Never Give Up to the Failures of Survival. Such as Illiteracy, Folly and Helplessness." When I asked Bruce how he lived, he murmured, "By the mercy of God. I jus' try not to get stagnant an' tryless." He was in love with words for their power, but he had nowhere to use them. So he spent long hours talking with the grizzled ex-leader of the Tel Aviv gang, a veteran street fighter named Dixie Dawkins, and he and Dixie reasoned the time away, redeeming their lives with talk. That was one of the strategies for survival downtown.

Another young man named Winston Gray showed up at Brambles's yard with his guitar. He strummed songs by Sam

Cooke and Otis Redding and sang in a soft tenor; we did "What a Wonderful World" together. Winston loved country music best, especially sentimental gunfighter ballads. He laughed when I said I had an American friend who called country music "the white man's reggae."

Then the old man everyone called Chronicles came by the yard; Brambles had told me about him and how he had gotten his nickname from his perfect memory.

"Life down here is jus' a daily burning," the old man said. "When election time come, politicians hand out lickle work—gully-cleaning project and street sweeping an' such ting. It is so ironic. The ghetto youth will starve just to dress expensive an' impressive in foreign clothes an' shoes. What we call trash-an'-ready. Many a youth stays in his yard all week, keepin' his threads only for important occasions like a funeral or a dance."

The next night was Sunday, when Raetown holds its weekly street dance that goes on until dawn beside the high brick walls of the General Penitentiary. The deejays set up booming speakers and duel with each other to see who can dig up the best oldies, the most danceable favorites from the glory days of ska, reggae, and rhythm and blues. The Raetown dance has been going on for so many years that it's become a Kingston institution, the only downtown fete that uptown people come to. Classy women from Barbican and Stony Hill bring their dates to skank for a few hours, unmindful of color and caste, next to the sufferers. Their outfits are always a study in contrasts, since the uptown girls are usually in sequins and satin and the ghetto daughters come in their most casual street wear: track shorts, tube tops, and the ubiquitous hair curlers. But the music is what matters, and it brings everyone together in a unifying force field of sound. It's the same music black and white Americans danced to in the era of civil rights—the Four Tops, Wilson Pickett, Martha

Reeves and the Vandellas, Gladys Knight and the Pips—mixed in with Burning Spear, Toots and the Maytals, and Bob Marley. "Forget your sorrows and dance."

But the police are always there too. The *Gleaner*'s gossip columnist wrote about the Raetown dance and the cops a few days later: "The only thing I found disturbing was a police Jeep passing through, minus license plates, and the driver with gun in hand firing shots in the air. No fear was shown by the large crowd, but as one reveler put it, 'A' so dem police-bwoy gwan all the while. Dem jus' come fi' frighten people.' It was a very happy gathering, but I do wish the guns were silent."

Brambles and I stayed at the dance until just before daylight, and by then it was too late for me to drive back uptown alone. We walked across South Camp Road to his yard, passing by the little bridge that spans the gully where a group of men hang out until dawn. I fell into bed with Natalie and Ricky, and Brambles took his blanket out to the veranda, bleaching till the sun rose to the sound of crowing roosters and barking dogs.

Blood for Blood,
Fire for Fire

The guns that traumatized uptowners were so commonplace in Central Kingston that Brambles's children vied with each other to identify them. They lay awake in the night and listened to the different sounds made by single-shot revolvers and rapid-fire automatics; the revolvers were antiques by then, high-powered weapons being the norm since the 1980 election campaign.

For almost fifty years the people of downtown Kingston have lived with intensifying violence—institutionalized warfare with the police, political banditry, and the quieter brutality of being bulldozed or torched out of their tenements so that one politician or another could build a housing project for his supporters. This has been going on, in one wave after another, since Jamaica went into the first birth pangs of nationhood in 1938.

There have always been two Jamaicas: the peaceful island nostalgically remembered by the few, and the one experienced by the rest as the "daily burning" that Brambles's friend Chronicles knew. He was in his early seventies, old enough to remember the late 1930s and early 1940s when Norman Manley and his first cousin, Alexander Bustamante, founded the two parties that led Jamaica into independence. Late at night, when Chronicles came home to Foster Lane from his daily round of scrounging up a little money from his friends on the docks, we would sit on Brambles's veranda and reason about history by the light of a kerosene lantern. In many ways, he said, the politicians and their gunmen took over where the slave masters and their overseers left off: the practice of intimidation was a logical outgrowth of the brutal intimacy that had always prevailed between the powerful and the powerless.

"The gang bizness did not come from nothing," Chronicles said. "And you mus' understand that this violence passed through many stages. When I was a young mon comin' up, we used to throw bricks and bottles to break up the other party's meetings. I remember when Norman Manley told us to bring brooms to PNP rallies, because everyone had one in their yard, even the poorest. So we'd carry our brooms to all the meetings and chant, 'Sweep them out!' against the JLP. The broom became the PNP's symbol."

Chronicles smiled at the innocence of those days.

"Everything start to change up when the first guns started comin' in, in the sixties. And then things only got worse. Yet the violence was always there, the PNP and the JLP playing divide and conquer with us sufferers. You may be surprised by how much politics means to us in the ghetto, but the reason is because we know that if our party loses, we will starve."

Jamaica's two parties were born in the refining fire of a labor rebellion that started in the late spring of 1938. The First World War had raised the price of sugar, bringing a brief moment of higher expectations to the island's workforce. But then the worldwide depression came, and these hopes were crushed in the postwar crash. The sugar industry was monopolized by one British company, Tate and Lyle, which poured capital for labor-saving new machinery into several big estates and began laying off workers; those lucky to still be employed were earning a shilling a day. One of the plantations was Frome, in the parish of Westmoreland near Negril, and it was there that workers first rose up, set the cane fields on fire, and went on strike for a living wage.

Conditions were just as bad on the United Fruit Company wharves in Kingston. Lord Olivier, one of the island's colonial governors, used to go down to the pier where the workers died from malnutrition, tuberculosis, and yaws. He watched them staggering under their loads of bananas, "expressionless all but for a kind of unquestioning patience of beasts of burden, the look of all yoked animals, in their eyes."

But in the spring of 1938 the beasts of burden proved they were human. When the Frome sugar workers set fire to the fields, Kingston's dock workers joined the uprising. Soon the wharves were paralyzed by a strike that spread quickly to the ranks of all of the city's workers: firemen, garbage collectors, tram conductors, and the night-soil men who hauled excrement away from the city's yards before dawn. Kingston erupted into mass demonstrations and torchlit rallies.

The city's small middle class—teachers, barristers, civil servants, and businessmen—had been watching for many years as social conditions got worse, and they were edging toward action. Their leading voice was Norman Manley, the soft-spoken, Oxford-educated barrister who went out to the cane fields at Frome and promised the strikers he would help them get their living wage. But while Manley and his supporters sympathized with the downtrodden black laborers Jamaicans call "Quashee"—the African name that stands for the very black and poor—educated reformers were not yet ready to cross the line of caste and color and join Quashee's ranks. So far the strikes were a black people's struggle, and the colored elite knew it. So they watched, and they waited.

But the working men and women were not waiting for them. For fifteen years they had been listening to Marcus Garvey and his Jamaican disciples preach the doctrine of black self-determination, and now they found a temporary leader from the ranks of Garvey's United Negro Improvement Association, the Harlem-based UNIA. His name was St William Grant, and he was a militant who wanted nothing less for his country than full independence from England. For a brief moment it looked as if the working-class rebellion might just transform itself into an anticolonial movement. But Grant had a rival for Quashee's loyalty, a fiery, near-white demagogue named Alexander Bustamante. "Busta," as everyone called him, soon eclipsed Grant in the sight of the masses, and his rise to power changed Jamaica forever.

Bustamante had only recently returned to his native Jamaica from a long pilgrimage through the Caribbean; he had cut cane in Cuba and worked on the Panama Canal. His origins were shrouded in mystery, and he liked it that way. His real name was Clarke, but he chose Bustamante for its Latin flair, and he promoted his own legend as a self-designated defender of the poor. He was a ghetto moneylender at the time the 1938 uprising began, so he already cracked a whip over the sufferers' heads.

With his light skin, wavy hair, and strong-featured face punctuated by enormous bushy eyebrows, Bustamante was a riveting presence. He was a ladies' man—a distinct, reputation-raising advantage in the lusty world of Jamaican politics—and a ferocious speaker who held crowds spellbound with a combination of angry rhetoric and bad grammar. "Bread!" he would roar. "The people want bread!" And then he would spell it out: "B-R-E-D!"

Bustamante's color gave him a definite advantage in a colony where blackness was no virtue. To this day Jamaicans sometimes refer to themselves as Afro-Saxons, admitting that they are still bedeviled by their reverence for English skin and English ways. Even though Bustamante loved to fulminate against the local elite, he always proclaimed his adoration for the British monarchy—a Jamaican paradox that has prevailed ever since slaves rose up against their masters and turned for salvation to the Crown.

Within weeks of the onset of the Kingston general strike, Bustamante had ousted St William Grant from the leadership of the labor movement and had taken charge of the city's docks.

"My people!" he shouted at rallies, "you don't have to think. I will think for you!"

"The Chief!" they roared back. "We will follow Bustamante till we die!"

When I asked Chronicles about those times, he was still bitter over the Chief's demagogic triumph. "I always believed that Grant owed Busta money," he said, "and that was why he lost out. But I will tell you this: Busta was one of the greatest tragedies in Jamaican history. If Grant had been the man to lead us, maybe this country would have had a real black-oriented government. Instead what we got was white-mon rule. And we black people never learned to think for ourselves."

Bustamante's main strategy in the beginning was to keep Jamaica in a state of unrest. He played on race and the threat of violence, the trump card in the sufferers' deck. "There will be bloodshed," he warned. "I expect everyone in this country to follow. . . . The niggers in this country shall rise. This will be war. We want revolution in this country and before whites destroy us, we will destroy them. The Negro blood has been shedding for the past 102 years and the time has come when we shall shed theirs."

The British locked him up. With Kingston in turmoil, the Colonial Office in London was looking for someone a little less incendiary to intervene with the strikers, someone who belonged to the elite but to whom Quashee might still listen. "Such a man will be reviled and hated by one class," wrote William Makin, a progressive newspaper editor. "He will quite possibly be betrayed by the other."

Norman Manley was that man. He and Alexander Bustamante happened to be first cousins, but their affinity ended there. Manley was a Rhodes scholar whose Oxford studies were cut short by World War I. He joined the British army and was decorated for heroism, and it was in the trenches that he got his first taste of racism, as a brown Jamaican among white Englishmen. He married Edna Swithenbank, the English-born daughter of a Methodist missionary and his Jamaican wife, and brought her home to Jamaica after the war. He began practicing law, and by 1938 he was both a King's Counsel and a keeper of the island's social conscience, the founder of a group called Jamaica Welfare, which politely lobbied the Colonial Office for reform.

Manley launched the People's National Party in the fall of 1938, six months into the labor rebellion, with a moderate platform of Fabian socialism and a call for gradual decolonization. The Colonial Office had no particular objections to Manley, especially after his peacemaking efforts during the strikes, but it wanted Jamaica to have a two-party Westminster system in place before the island would be ready for its first election under full adult suffrage in 1944. Independence would not come for another eighteen years.

It was clear that once the British let him out of jail, Alexander Bustamante would found a second party to harass Manley's PNP. He started the Jamaica Labour Party as soon as he came out of prison, in 1942, and from then on became acutely conscious of his new political profile. The Chief quieted down considerably and began acting in a more statesmanlike fashion, trumpeting his loyalty to king and country. In 1944, with the war coming to an end and Britain ready at last to unload her fractious Caribbean colonies, Bustamante and the JLP contested the first elections and trounced Manley. The PNP won only four seats in the House of Assembly and Manley lost in his own constituency. He and Bustamante alternated as premiers until independence came, but Bustamante was the one in power when it did. It was the Chief who waltzed with Princess Margaret on the night of August 6, 1962, when the Union Jack was lowered for the last time in the National Stadium and Jamaica's black, gold, and green flag was hoisted above the euphoric crowd.

But the formation of Jamaica's two parties was not the only power struggle that dominated the years leading up to independence. The other, more violent fight went on between the two labor unions founded by Bustamante and Manley and aligned with their parties. The JLP had its own union, the Bustamante Industrial Trade Union (BITU), while the PNP had its Trade Union Congress (TUC). These unions battled to represent sectors of the newly mobilized workforce; thus politics and unionism locked in a deadly fusion that turned Jamaica's working people into two armed camps. The BITU and the TUC went into cane fields, bauxite plants, and shipping facilities to fight for supremacy, and violence became the norm in unionism and politics alike.

"Before the bosses would even sit down at the bargaining table," Chronicles said, "the unions had to bring in thugs to demonstrate their power. And this was where a lot of the first gang violence began. The BITU controlled the docks—it does to this day—and the TUC fought back elsewhere, in sugar, bauxite, the building trades, the city workers. Those were hard fights, and the strong-arm men carried the day."

Chronicles had known one of the founders of the PNP, Wills O. Isaacs, who had also organized its union. Isaacs never shrank from a fight, and when someone asked him in 1944 whether he regretted Jamaica's descent into partisan violence, Isaacs shot back, "What are a few broken skulls in the growth of a nation?" Central Kingston was then part of Isaacs' constituency, and he became the first PNP politician to play gang hardball with the JLP. He founded his own garrison of street fighters, Group 69, and led it into the fray when Bustamante's men broke up PNP rallies with stones and beer bottles.

"Busta played rough right from the start," Chronicles said. "And he really saw himself as some kind of king. I remember going down to a meeting one night at the Myrtle Bank to hear him speak, with Norman Manley on the podium behind him. And Busta looked out over the crowd and said, 'You see my cousin. It is the two of us, him or me. And if it is not me, it is him who will rule you. We are a royal family.'

"The two of them locked Jamaica down tight. The JLP took Winston Churchill's V-for-victory signal, the two fingers raised, as their sign. Later on, in the black power time, the PNP started using the clenched fist. You know what we say those two signs really mean?"

He held up his two fingers and then closed them into a fist.

"We two hold them tight. It's the same leader with two different faces. One was white and the other was brown, but it didn't make much difference."

As the two parties evolved in the years leading up to independence, their constituencies divided along lines of race and class. The PNP became the party of educated, brown-skinned professionals, and its outlook was cosmopolitan and internationalist. After Manley became premier in 1955, he devoted much of his energy to forming a West Indian federation of British colonies, knowing that unity would be their best hope for economic development after independence. But Bustamante opposed the federation, as did many Jamaicans, full of a large-island sense of superiority that made them reluctant to band together with little islands like Antigua, Saint Lucia, or Saint Kitts. The federation's defeat in a 1961 referendum was a crushing blow for Manley; Bustamante became prime minister six months later, ushering Jamaica into the independence whose groundwork Norman Manley had laid.

Meanwhile, the JLP was turning into a kind of schizophrenic entity, the party of the black have-nots and the reactionary haves, an odd alliance that still persists. Bustamante set the tone, with his claim to speak (and think) for the poor while assuaging the class fears of the rich. Irish writer Patrick Leigh Fermor, while visiting Kingston in 1950, met both Bustamante and Manley and described the JLP leader as a "pistol-packing, hard-living humorous ex-rabble-raising demagogue, whose every word and gesture have an engaging histrionic phoneyness."

As Jamaica inched toward nationhood, world events began to impinge on its internal affairs. The Cuban revolution sent shock waves through the Caribbean, beckoning other islands to confront their own entrenched elites. The civil rights movement in the United States sent the message of racial equality around the world and struck with gale force on an island whose black majority harkened not only to the nonviolent words of Martin Luther King, Jr., but also to the angrier voices of leaders like Stokely Carmichael, H. "Rap" Brown, Huey Newton, and Eldridge Cleaver. The ruling JLP banned black power literature, but it couldn't jam the airwaves that poured American soul music and rhythm and blues onto Kingston's ghetto street corners, along with the news of the changes that were coming in the United States.

And like the street corners in American ghettos, the ones in Kingston were mirroring the country's social dislocation and already spawning little gangs of their own. Most of their members wielded only ratchet knives, but a few had started to carry guns. Although these gangs had not yet been drawn into the political web, they were already angry rebels spoiling for a fight, Johnny-Too-Bads who worshiped the gunfighters in Hollywood westerns. They were the perfect street warriors, waiting in the wings for the politicians to recognize their usefulness.

The island economy of the 1960s was an added source of both hope and disillusion. Bauxite and tourism were booming, but their new success didn't make a dent in the lives of most Jamaicans. The bauxite plants belonged to big multinationals like Kaiser, Revere, and Reynolds Metals, and even though they paid the highest wages on the island, this in itself created a labor aristocracy that only made subsistence farmers and the peons on sugar estates all the more aware of their poverty.

Tourism was even more socially corrosive. It brought seasonal, low-paying jobs to a few people who lived in the small towns on the north coast, and this work came with a wicked, atavistic fantasy: the Jamaica Tourist Board wanted white visitors to see the island as the Old South of *Gone With the Wind*. "You can rent a lovely life in Jamaica," cooed one tourist board advertisement. "Rent-a-villas, rent-a-cooks, rent-a-maids, rent-a-nannies, rent-a-gardeners. It starts with a country house or hilltop hideaway that comes equipped with gentle people named Ivy or Maud or Malcolm who will cook, tend, mend, diaper, and launder for you. Who will 'Mister Peter, please' you all day long, pamper you with homemade coconut pie, admire you when you look 'soft' (handsome), giggle at your jokes and weep when you leave."

Ivy, Maud, and Malcolm were living in dirt-floor shacks where children with rickets sat dull-eyed in the yards. They walked miles to work in hotel kitchens and scraped uneaten food into the garbage, then they walked home along scalding roads while the tourists sped by in shiny cars. So if Ivy, Maud, and Malcolm wept, it wasn't because you were leaving.

None of the prosperity from bauxite and tourism trickled down into Kingston. The city was swelling every day with migrants from the rural parishes who were running from the countryside to a city where they envisioned plenty of work, decent housing, running water, and transportation. What they found were the "dungles," garbage dumps and empty land that had turned into shantytowns blooming on the waterfront of western Kingston.

"Me did think town woulda' be pretty-pretty," said Joycie, a sweet-tempered, withered prostitute who was one of Brambles's oldest friends. She had come to Kingston in 1960, a young country girl with stars in her eyes. "But I got off the train there in the west by Coronation Market an' the depot, an' all I could see was pitchy-patchy shanty an' zinc fence, magga dog an' hungry-belly pickney. Not a true house in sight. Lord, I wanted to go right back home. But I was proud in them days, an' I thought I could mek something outta' meself in Kingston. You know, once you go a' town, is like you go a' foreign. You cyan' come back unless your pockets full."

The shantytowns had spawned their own culture of African redemption by then—Rastafarianism—and the locksmen were living in the West Kingston dungle. The lion-maned, barefoot prophets took their philosophy from Marcus Garvey's pan-Africanism and their inspiration from Ethiopia's Haile Selassie; when Rastafarianism was born in the late 1930s, Ethiopia was the only African nation unfettered by colonialism, and Rastafarians believed that Selassie was the living incarnation of Negus, the black man's true God. "Rasta is God without any apology," Brambles loved to say, quoting one of the brethren's prayers. They challenged every one of Jamaica's cherished social norms: "churchical" Christianity, hair-straightened Afro-Saxon primness, and the "politricks" that flourished in its intractably corrupt, Babylonian "shitstem."

So there was war between the Rastas and society in those early days; when the locksmen ventured out of the dungle they were hounded through the streets and beaten by the police, who took special pleasure in shearing off their dreads. Most of the brethren were apolitical in the extreme and wanted nothing to do with Babylon. But black American militants saw this Jamaican brotherhood as a potential revolutionary vanguard. In 1960 this ephemeral alliance sparked a brief uprising, one of the stranger episodes in the island's long history of revolts.

It began when Claudius Henry, another Jamaican-born visionary in the tradition of Alexander Bedward, returned to his homeland from the United States. Henry brought with him a small cadre of black American radicals from a group called the First Africa Corps, based in the Bronx. Soon this vanguard was joined by militant Rastafarians who harkened to Henry's preachments that he was the "Repairer of the Breach" between Africa and the Caribbean. The Rastas believed that he would shepherd them back to Africa. But meanwhile, Henry was stockpiling guns, bought with the proceeds from several bank robberies committed in New York City by a rogue police officer who belonged to the First Africa Corps.

In June 1960 the West India Regiment raided Henry's guerrilla camp in the hills above Kingston. Five of his men shot their way out of the ambush and through several police roadblocks, killing two soldiers and wounding three others. Among the guns and revolutionary literature discovered in the raid was a letter from Claudius Henry to Fidel Castro:

"Dear Dr. Castro," Henry wrote, "We wish to draw your attention to the conditions which confront us today as poor underprivileged people which were brought here from Africa by the British slave traders over 400 years ago. We now desire to return home in peace, to live under our own vine and fig tree, otherwise a government like yours that gives justice to the poor. All our efforts to have a peaceful repatriation have proven a total failure. Hence we must fight a war for what it ours by right. Therefore we want to assure you, Sir, and your government that Jamaica and the rest of the British West Indies will be turned over to you after this war which we are preparing to start for Africa's freedom is completed, and we her scattered children are restored. We are getting ready for an invasion on the Jamaican Government, therefore we need your help. We have the necessary men for the job. The Black people of Jamaica are with you and your government one hundred percent and desire to see that Jamaica gets into your hands before we leave for Africa."

It took another week after the raid for the police to hunt down the militants who had escaped. Their leader, Henry's son Reynold, was hanged for treason a year later. Norman Manley, Queen's Counsel, was one of the barristers who prosecuted the case, and his arguments against the Rastafarians who followed Claudius Henry did not endear him to the brethren. But Henry himself became a passionate partisan of the PNP; he served eight years in prison and came out in 1969, still a believer in the inevitability of African repatriation. In the 1972 election he threw his weight behind the young Michael Manley, believing that this son of a famous father had seen the light and would soon send Jamaica's black captives home to Africa to be free.

Despite its magical-realist undertones, Claudius Henry's aborted rebellion was a very real distress signal, a warning to Jamaica of how deep the fissures of race and class were. David D'Costa, a white Jamaican journalist who began working for the *Gleaner* and the BBC in the 1960s, saw the Henry affair as a harbinger of what was to come. "Our established society has always been very fragile," he said. "The problems are insoluble, and you will never really be able to meet your own aspirations. The more decent a society you postulate, the more impossible reaching your own goals becomes, given the expectations that you yourself engender.

"What I saw happening in the sixties was this established society beginning to break its own bonds. It couldn't meet its own aspirations and therefore it became hypocritical in its own eyes. The judges, the lawyers, the teachers all talked a standard which they knew could not be met. In their heart of hearts they knew the situation was racing beyond them."

Like many other uptown Kingstonians after the Henry rebellion, D'Costa started carrying a gun. Coming home late and slightly drunk one night to his home on Stony Hill, he almost shot someone he thought was a prowler lurking in the bushes. But it was only the gardener boy, too shy to come forward and ask D'Costa for his pay.

"The next day, I took the gun to the Constant Spring police station and turned it in. I said, 'Here, you keep it. I never want to see it again.' The detective on duty asked me what had happened and when I told him, he laughed. 'But you would have had every right to kill the boy,' he said, 'and we would have looked after you.'

"And that was really my first glimmering of what class, what color meant in Jamaica. I could have killed an innocent child and been 'looked after' for it by the police. I never carried a gun after that."

But while D'Costa was turning away from weapons, the rest of his countrymen began using them with deadly frequency. Gun violence was already a fact of life in the ghettos, where the two political parties had embarked on their struggle for supremacy.

The sufferers were soon to be introduced to a young politician who would take this internecine violence to a new level. He was the son of a Syrian-Lebanese family from Kingston, but he was born in Boston and educated at Harvard; in 1954 he came home to Jamaica to carve out a place for himself. His name was Edward Seaga.

Seaga had a bachelor's degree in sociology. He had a keen interest in Afro-Jamaican revivalist cults and their music; he quickly made friends with shepherds at the revivalist tabernacles and wrote a pamphlet about their religion, and he also opened a little recording studio in West Kingston where he started producing mento, ska, and some early reggae music. Seaga's ties to the Pocomania church led by Kapo Reynolds let Seaga tap into one of the deepest veins in Jamaica's religious life—despite Seaga's white skin, his alliance with Kapo sent a crucial message through West Kingston: this foreign-born white fellow had serious credentials as a roots man, and he was nobody's fool.

Legend has it that Seaga wanted at first to join the PNP and that Norman Manley turned him away because he disliked the young man. But Alexander Bustamante recognized Seaga's political skills and received him into the JLP, appointing him to the Legislative Council in 1959. Seaga won the West Kingston seat in Parliament three years later; he has never lost it since. The JLP then named him Minister of Welfare and Development, a position he soon began abusing so savagely that the sufferers called him the "Minister of Warfare and Devilment."

Seaga saw that the surest route to power lay in building housing for his supporters, and in 1966 he embarked on a particularly brutal siege of slum clearance in the West Kingston shantytown called Back O' Wall. The neighborhood was packed with PNP supporters and Rastafarian squatters living in tiny shacks built out of flattened gasoline cans, hammered cheese tins, and salvaged lumber. It had not been easy to build, but the people of Back O' Wall had managed to make a community of their own.

Seaga routed them with bulldozers and squadrons of police; the destruction of Back O' Wall was something that no one who witnessed it ever forgot. Some of the Rastas tried to fight back, and a few lay down in front of the advancing machinery. But they were no match for the police with their rifles and tear gas. When the shanties were leveled and the bulldozers had scraped them into piles, work began on a housing project called Tivoli Gardens, where Seaga rewarded his supporters with homes. They became his people for life.

The PNP did not stand idly by while Seaga became the patron saint of West Kingston. A young politician named Dudley Thompson ran against Seaga and lost, but in the process began to carve out a power base of his own in western Kingston. He was a short man with pudgy features, and he wore a knitted tam to signify his solidarity with the sufferers. People called him "Cuddly Dudley" behind his back, but he took himself very seriously; a British-trained barrister like his friend Norman Manley, Thompson went to Kenya with the legal team that defended Jomo Kenyatta against charges of sedition, and after that he started calling himself "the Burning Spear," like the African freedom fighter.

Thompson and Seaga fought a proxy war in the streets of West Kingston, mustering small armies from the ranks of the neighborhood's top gunmen. These gangs were the ancestors of every political posse that came later. Seaga's main squadron was the Phoenix, whose leaders were Zackie the High Priest and Frank "Bad Word" Gillespie. One of the Phoenix members was a charismatic youth named Claudie Massop, who was already apprenticing himself to these masters and rising through the ranks; he would become the undisputed don of Tivoli Gardens in the 1970s.

The Phoenix had allies in other parts of the city where the JLP was trying to capture support. In Central Kingston the Phoenix was aligned with a gang called the Max, based in the little corner called Southside. The Max threw its force behind the JLP, and Southside gradually became a Labourite stronghold within PNP-dominated Central Kingston; this divide-and-conquer strategy soon became the parties' standard operating procedure throughout the city.

Faced with the certain prospect of escalating gang warfare, the PNP started creating its own mercenary squadrons. In Central Kingston a gang called Tel Aviv began fighting off the Max from Southside; its leader, Dixie Dawkins, told me they had picked the Israeli name after the movie *Exodus* came out, "because Tel Aviv was known to be impregnable."

Over in western Kingston, Dudley Thompson began assembling a fighting force of his own—two gangs called the Vikings and the Spanglers. The Vikings had taken their name from the movie starring Kirk Douglas, and one of their leaders, Glen Pusey, started calling himself "Dillinger," after his favorite American outlaw; thus began the time-honored tradition of gunmen modeling themselves on Hollywood desperados. The outlaws vied with each other for the distinction of killing top rankings from opposing gangs: Dillinger claimed the honor of being the man who shot Zackie the High Priest, the JLP gunfighter from Tivoli. When the dust had cleared and Zackie was buried, the grieving Tivolites named a street after their fallen hero.

The Spanglers, the other PNP posse, were based on Regent Street in West Kingston, and their leader was a robber named Big Uzi—the gun was already becoming famous in Jamaica following its use in Israel. Soon the Spanglers and the Phoenix were gunning for each other; in retaliation for the murder of their leader, Zackie the High Priest, Phoenix gunmen invaded a dance in Southside and killed a Spangler named Rashi, who was said to be Dudley Thompson's protégé. When the case came to trial, Thompson pressed unsuccessfully for Rashi's killers to get the death penalty.

The JLP Phoenix and the PNP Vikings got their chance to fight a full-scale street war in the spring of 1966, at the same time that Seaga was bulldozing the squatters out of Back O' Wall. A series of bitter industrial disputes broke out that April across the island, from the cane fields at Frome (where the 1938 labor uprising began) to the Kingston waterfront and the tourist hotels around Montego Bay. The strikes were sparked by a power struggle between the unions, but the violence soon spread to the West Kingston streets as displaced sufferers from Back O' Wall saw their chance to vent some of their rage. The Phoenix and the Vikings rampaged against the police up and down the waterfront, along the Spanish Town Road, and through the narrow streets of western Kingston. The gangs had pistols, dynamite, and homemade bombs, but the security forces had rifles and tear gas. The army sent in troops by helicopter and by sea; the gangs were outgunned, but they kept on fighting. By the end of that summer, twenty people were dead and five hundred had been arrested. Fifty guns were seized, along with eight hundred rounds of ammunition and enough Molotov cocktails to burn down West Kingston.

By fall Kingston's violence had taken on a frightening and permanent new pattern: now the gangs were attacking dances, movie theaters, and rumshops downtown, and some of the gunmen were going uptown to rob the homes of the rich. The ruling JLP declared a state of emergency that stayed in effect until the 1967 general election, in which it won a majority of parliamentary seats. By then the gunmen who worked for the politicians had become the new lords of the streets, politely hailed as "community leaders," who could wage war and make peace. Some started calling themselves "the Untouchables"—in homage to Eliot Ness—because they were beyond the law's reach.

Dixie Dawkins, the Tel Aviv leader from Central, was one of Brambles's friends. He was graying and pretty much retired from active duty by the time I got to know him, but he still had a soldier's glint in his eye despite the soft, Buddha-like paunch above the waistband of his track shorts. The three of us often met at a rumshop on the old Tel Aviv corner, across the street from a mural of Michael Manley and Marcus Garvey decorated with graffiti that said SEAGA RAPE JAMAICA. WE WANT NO WAR.

"Seaga was a mon who in them times used to move with the radicals 'pon the street an' kick up pure rumpus," Dixie said. "We called him Blinds on account o' the dark glasses he always wore. An' when Blinds walked, it seemed like he had all the power in the world. You know that since he won the West Kingston seat for the first time in 1962, he has never held a rally in his constituency? He don't need to. That's how sure he is of his people there."

Dixie acknowledged that Dudley Thompson had put his own force, the Spanglers, in the field because Seaga's methods had left the PNP with no other choice. Meanwhile, an even more vicious kind of symbiosis was developing between the politicians and their paladins. As members of Parliament from both parties consolidated power by building housing projects for their supporters, a Mafia-style link was quickly formed between the construction industry and the gangs. The PNP built a housing project in West Kingston called Arnett Gardens—soon popularly rechristened as Concrete Jungle—and it was during the building of this project that two gunmen, Feathermop and Burry Boy, emerged as the PNP's premier enforcers. By the early 1970s, when Michael Manley became prime minister, the ties between contractors and gunmen, between politicians and their outlaw bagmen, were too strong to break. The leaders had let slip the dogs of war, and there would be no leashing them now.

When Jamaicans look back to the beginnings of this tribal warfare in the Kingston of the 1960s, they still argue over who started the fighting. Dudley Thompson and Edward Seaga are universally acknowledged to have been the field marshals, but for many people the first skirmish was a speech Seaga made in 1965. The occasion was a ceremony at Kingston's National Heroes' Circle, where all of the party leaders had gathered to commemorate two men who had led the bitter Morant Bay rebellion of 1865. Alexander Bustamante and Norman Manley were there, both aging and ailing, and Seaga and Michael Manley were each only a few years away from becoming the leaders of their respective parties. Some youths in the crowd booed Seaga, and he faced them down with an open threat of war.

"If they think they are bad," he shouted, "I can bring the crowds of West Kingston. We can deal with you in any way at any time. It will be fire for fire, and blood for blood."

No one doubted that he meant it. But of all the men at National Heroes' Circle that day, perhaps Norman Manley grieved the most. He was then four years away from dying, exhausted by three decades of political struggle and battle with the forces of the JLP, and he lamented Seaga's rising power in "this new era of violence in Jamaica which threatens the whole basis of our national life." Norman Manley had made a speech during the 1966–67 state of emergency prompted by the West Kingston riots, in which he refrained from calling Seaga by name and instead spoke ominously of him only as "this voice alien to Jamaica."

"With what voice does he speak, this highly educated and sophisticated man? What language does he use? Do we recognize the voice of Jamaica, or do we hear a voice alien to our ideals, our practices, and our faith? Our side cannot quiet this ugly turmoil. Both sides must meet and honestly agree. I hate to see Jamaica divided and torn. I hate to see Jamaicans killing and maiming Jamaicans while the leaders roll around in comfort. I hate to see the spirit of nationhood broken and destroyed. Who will join me, for Jamaica's sake?"

But no one was listening. It was already too late.

Endgame

Dixie's emerald-and-ruby inlay glinted in the lamplight when he smiled. He was in a good mood this night, settled on Brambles's veranda to reason about the seventies and his days as the Tel Aviv posse's top ranking.

It was a Saturday night and King Chubby, Central's best dee-jay, had set up a pair of booming speakers on Super-Stud corner for a street dance that would go on until dawn. The sound system was pounding through the neighborhood with dance hall tunes by SuperCat and Ninja, hailing the rule of the dons. And they were no longer just dons; now they were "don-gaddas," veritable gods of the streets.

Brambles pointed out the girls from the Protein posse, the local queens who'd so named their crew because they were eating well, now that their boyfriends—"boopses"—a'foreign were sending down money from crack sales in Miami and New York.

"Them nice-up themself for the dance," Brambles said approvingly. Then he looked at me in my habitual khaki shorts and limp cotton shirt, damp with sweat. He sucked his teeth in affectionate contempt.

"I never see an American daughter dress like you. Why you

no put on somethin' crisp? You all the time look like you some kinda' war correspondent."

"She all right," Dixie proffered. "She dressed fi' work."

Gunshots rang out from the corner and we all thronged to the shard-topped yard wall to see what was happening. The Super-Stud crowd was running up Foster Lane, with police Jeeps in hot pursuit. Brambles's daughter Natalie burst in through the gate, laughing and panting.

"Bwoy toss a firecracker right under the police car," she gasped. "Everyone haffi scatter. Chubby well-vexed!" But his speakers were still cranked up to the max, and soon everyone was back on the corner as if nothing had happened.

"We get so we don't even run from gunfire now," Brambles said mournfully. "We run to see what happen."

Dixie wiped the beads of sweating condensation from his Red Stripe and began to talk, melding his own biography into the days when Manley was prime minister and the power of the gangs reached its crescendo. He had been a major player on the posse stage, and he looked back to his performance with a mixture of sorrow and nostalgia.

"Before there was Tel Aviv," he began, "well before Michael Manley's time, the big massive here in central was the Max gang, an' that was my tribe. 'Massive' is jus' another word for a gang. Well, I did some time, just at the end of the sixties, in the General Penitentiary over there in Raetown, an' while I was in, I kind of lost touch with the runnin's on the street. There was a tailor we called Liniments on Foster Lane, a guy who dressed sharp and got some ranks behind him. When I came out, Liniments was controlling things with the Max."

According to Brambles, the word on the neighborhood wire was that Dixie had "bowed" and become a batty-mon, a homosexual, in the General Penitentiary, and that this was why the youths from the Max had turned against him. But he recouped his former status by killing the man who'd started the batty-mon rumor, another Max member named Buckles. Dixie and Liniments resolved their differences, and together they forged the new gang they called Tel Aviv.

That was around the time when the PNP won its first general election since independence, in 1972, and Michael Manley became prime minister. Central was his constituency, and his victory meant that the neighborhood was finally going to get some housing and development projects. It also meant that Central's posses would start lining up for their share of this patronage gravy.

There were already ominous signals that the gangs were calling the shots downtown. After testing their power during the West Kingston riots, the JLP Phoenix and the PNP Spanglers had begun colonizing other sections of the city. Now that Manley and the PNP were in power, it was clear that the PNP's garrisons were going to carry superior force.

"I can still remember the day when Michael came down here campaigning, just before the '72 election," Brambles said. "He was set to speak at a rally right there on East Queen Street, at the football field where you and I met that first day. He was so proud and happy-like—this was his own constituency, after all—and he didn't expect any trouble here. Well, the mon walked straight into a three-way gunfight between the old Max, Tel Aviv, and the Skull. The Skull was one o' dem lickle JLP cadres that the Phoenix from West was infiltrating Central with, and it was based up on the Laws Street corner."

He shook his head sadly and Dixie nodded in agreement.

"We was all tryin' to demonstrate our power that day," Dixie

said. "It comin' like we knew Manley would be the next prime
minister, so we was all tryin' to muster ranks and show him who
ruled down here."

"When the shots start fire, I went over the chain-link fence
with everyone else," Brambles said. "Everyone haffi' run from
the guns. But I was there to take pictures, so I was close enough
to Michael to see him face, an' I will never forget that. Was like
him never really believe what him see."

After Manley won, the PNP started pouring money and talent
into his constituency, sending some of the party's most progressive men into Central to organize youth groups, sports clubs, and
community development projects. Party member Arnold Bertram
worked out a momentary truce between Tel Aviv, the Max, and
the Skull, whose members were warring in the neighborhood.
A tall, lanky man whose dark face wreathed quickly into a smile,
Bertram had an engaging manner that was part sufferer and part
canny politician; soon after he brought Central's three gangs to
the peace table, the PNP made him minister of information and
culture. By 1973 things were quieter in the constituency, and
the tribal warriors were thinking more along the lines of football
clubs and youth groups than guns. But the Skull gang was still
Central's loose cannon, taking orders from the Phoenix in West
Kingston. Its leaders were two brothers, Roddy and Rockeye
Nesbeth, and the ties between them and Seaga's Labourite gunmen were tight.

"There was always too much tension," Dixie said. "Too many
dogs, not enough bones. You see, Manley was already gettin'
into socialism, and it seemed like everyone got politicized all of
a sudden. So Tel Aviv got bigger after we start call weself social-
ists—the youth dem liked that position. But Roddy and Rockeye
and the rest o' the Skull got vexed with the situation an' jus'
pulled away. They felt like they was left out of the action and

there was more to be had—guns an' such—from the breddas over in Tivoli Gardens. Them mon there didn't want no peace. In the bad-mon bizness, peace is beside the point. How is youth an' youth goin' to set themself up, distinguish themself inna' their area, without violence?"

The gangs in Central Kingston were crucial to the PNP's ability to control its territory there, but the West Kingston posses had the greatest firepower and ranks, because the sprawling slums and shantytowns of the city's west had long been prime spawning grounds for outlaws. The Spanglers and the Phoenix had been contending for jobs and patronage in the west since the mid-sixties, but the Spanglers—along with other West Kingston gangs loosely allied with the PNP—did not really become part of the political equation until their party came to power. When that happened in 1972, West Kingston's gang geography underwent a change. As all of the other posses began lining up behind the ruling PNP, Tivoli Gardens became the only real bastion of JLP gun power in the area. By the mid-1970s, one paladin had emerged in the PNP's Concrete Jungle as the area leader: a top-ranking tribalist named "Red Tony" Welch. His patron was Anthony Spaulding, the minister of housing for the PNP.

"Jungle," as Red Tony's domain was usually called, had been a hotbed of gang activity for a long time. The neighborhood lies north of Tivoli, on the other side of May Pen Cemetery and a ghetto known as Denham Town. Jungle and Tivoli had been fighting each other over politics for years. To make things even worse, Jungle backed up against another shantytown called Rema. The two armed camps faced each other across a no-man's-land that ran along Seventh Street. By the mid-1970s, Seventh Street had become one of West Kingston's worst war zones. The enmity between Jungle and Rema stemmed from the usual causes, but it deepened after Manley came to power because of the patronage lavished on Concrete Jungle. The sufferers of Rema had no patrons; they had been the stepchildren of the JLP ever since Seaga bulldozed Back O' Wall and hundreds of its displaced squatters fled to Rema for refuge. But Seaga funneled all of the money and jobs into Tivoli, and the people of Rema had nothing. Now they were trapped along the firing line between West Kingston's two most deadly political posses: the Tivolites and Welch's Concrete Jungle gang, all but invincible now that Welch enjoyed the protection of Anthony Spaulding. Red Tony Welch was the don of Concrete Jungle, the gangster-diplomat who dealt with Spaulding and got jobs for the Jungleites on work sites all over town.

"You see," Dixie explained, "when you is a sufferer, you cyan' really deal 'pon a level with the big mon like your local member of Parliament. You mus' have a representative fi' deal with the MP. And Tony Welch meanwhile started to make a name fi' himself, doin' battle with Rema and Tivoli, and pretty soon he got into position, got ranks behind him."

So when Anthony Spaulding needed a job done, like the fire-bombing of the tenement yards on Orange Lane, Tony Welch obliged. But even with Welch's dominance in Concrete Jungle, the neighborhood still spawned a string of other, smaller gangs. They sprang from corners named for their toughness—Texas, Angola, Mexico—and each had its own little armed squadron. As Dixie said, too many dogs, not enough bones. As they attached themselves like barnacles to the politicians, downtown Kingston became, in the words of one PNP leader, "a geography of violence."

This violence got worse as Manley and Seaga hardened the lines between their two parties. After 1974, when Manley declared socialism as the platform of the PNP, Seaga went on the warpath. He declared the JLP as a right-wing, freedom-fighting opposition, stonewalling Manley at every turn. And the paladins in turn took their cue from the big men uptown. Now the PNP shootists started seeing themselves as Cuban-style revolutionaries, and the JLP's gunmen thought they were fighting to save Jamaica from Communism. Their gang signals were superficially funny: Labourite youths refused to drink Red Stripe beer because red was a Communist color; PNP sufferers wouldn't touch Heineken beer because it came in a green bottle, and green was the color of the JLP. But some of them died because they ordered the wrong beer in the wrong neighborhood or because they unthinkingly went to a dance on the other side of town.

Michael Manley lamented the theatrical but deadly enmity that was splitting the sufferers and turning Kingston into a battleground. Like his father, he recoiled from violence; he had hoped to mobilize Jamaicans into a conscious vanguard for change, and now the power of the gangs mocked all of his best intentions. But Manley himself was often obliged to rely on the gunmen for protection when he went into sections of the city where he would have been defenseless without their guns. Many people told me that Winston "Burry Boy" Blake, one of the PNP's most notorious enforcers, had saved the lives of Manley and his wife Beverley when a JLP gunman shot at them and Burry Boy threw them to the ground, covering their bodies with his own. That was the reason, they said, why Manley made the decision to pay homage to the enforcer by attending his funeral in 1975.

Even more frightening was the fact that Manley seemed unable to rein in his own ministers. There was no stopping warlords like Anthony Spaulding, and other party members, like Dudley Thompson and D. K. Duncan, were equally besotted with the street power they got from their affiliation with the gunmen. Such ties were a badge of honor in the ghettos, the way a politician earned respect.

There was another side to this courtship, however: the bitter endgame that invariably played out when a gunman got too big and finally challenged the politician himself for supremacy. At that point, the big man quietly ordered the police to lock up the uppity mercenary or gun him down. If he lived, the gunman went to prison, where outlaws from both parties got to know one another and began to see the folly of shedding each other's blood for the politicians.

Men like Tony Welch and Bucky Marshall (another shootist for the PNP) would find themselves periodically cooling off in the General Penitentiary with JLP rankings like Claudie Massop and Byah Mitchell. Or they would be thrown together in Gun Court, the dreaded detention center on Kingston's South Camp Road where those accused of gun crimes went to rot. There they sweated out the days and months, crammed into reeking cells too small to lie down in, eating from the same slop buckets and being beaten with cat-o'-nine-tails by the same sadistic warders. Even though they came from opposite sides of the political fence, jail taught them their commonality. This was a lesson with serious repercussions, as the politicians later found out.

Claudie Massop, Seaga's enforcer in Tivoli, left Jamaica in 1972 for a long stint in England after Manley and the PNP came to power and Massop's fortunes at home were therefore less secure. When he returned in 1977 he was still the don in Tivoli, and he even began thinking about running for some kind of political office. There was an ugly confrontation between Massop and Seaga himself, when Massop accused his patron of being a warlord who cared nothing for the sufferers. Massop's own awakening was mirrored in the prison and street experiences of other gunmen; many of them were then beginning to shift uneasily within the confines of their old political allegiances. The hard line between the PNP and JLP was too constraining, so some of the rankings were teaming up for "bank work" (robberies) and ganja dealing. Claudie Massop had a lieutenant in Tivoli named Byah Mitchell, and Byah began hanging out with PNP gunmen from Wareika Hill and Concrete Jungle. Copper, the Robin Hood renegade from Wareika, had a girlfriend in Tivoli and was often seen there in the company of Massop and Mitchell, his former enemies.

Meanwhile, Bucky Marshall, the PNP shootist, was in jail, having killed a popular youth from Concrete Jungle. The victim was a protégé of another Jungle gunman, Anthony "Starkey" Tingle, and although Starkey was PNP, he too had made some friends on the other side of the fence. When Marshall heard that Claudie Massop was back from England and that he just might be persuaded by Starkey to take revenge for the slaying Marshall had done, the jailed gunman started fearing for his own life after he came out. He began making overtures to Massop's forces through the grapevine that ran from the General Penitentiary to the streets.

By that time the rankings' downtown force field was exerting a gravitational pull beyond the ghettos. They had become authentic cultural voices for an entire nation of sufferers, and their outlaw exploits were the stuff of myth. Everyone knew they were powerful and dangerous; so were the politicians, but the politicians would never belong to the sufferers' true tribe. Reggae stars like Bob Marley and Peter Tosh came from the same roots as the outlaws, and even though the singers had risen to international fame, they kept their old ties to the ghettos that had birthed them and their music. Although Marley had moved far uptown from his old Trenchtown haunts into a breezy greathouse on Hope Road formerly owned by Island Records magnate Chris Blackwell, he was still close with Claudie Massop and Bucky Marshall, burning many a spliff with Massop in the

Hope Road yard and scamming to fix the occasional horse race at Caymanas Park. But the alliance between the reggae superstar and his old friends in the underworld could turn deadly in a heartbeat. When someone shot Marley in his yard just before the 1976 election, Kingston buzzed with rumors that the CIA was behind the attack. But some said he'd been set up by the Tivolites after a racetrack scam went sour.

It seemed as if the rule of the gunmen was just another feature of Jamaica's downhill slide. By 1977 Manley was losing ground in a series of small disasters: protracted, and ultimately failed, negotiations with the International Monetary Fund; a friendship with Fidel Castro that unsettled many Jamaicans—ever prickly where Cuba was concerned—and alienated the United States; an entrenched establishment that was turning against him, and an opposition led by Seaga that was obviously arming itself to the teeth. A rising panic swept through Kingston as Michael Manley and Jamaica's experiment in democratic socialism both began to run on empty.

The sufferers in Central Kingston felt the pressure drop, and some of them were the ones who would soon pay for this political anxiety with their lives. In late 1977 a little cabal of rogue officers from the Jamaica Defense Force—loyal to Manley and convinced that the police force was in Seaga's pocket—hatched a plot to destroy the JLP posse in Southside.

The Labourite Skull crew there was still massed behind the Nesbeth brothers on Laws Street. The posse youths had ingratiated themselves with a formidable Franciscan nun, Sister Benedict, who ran the Holy Family School in Southside. "Sister," as everyone called her, had been living in the ghetto long enough to know the wisdom of keeping cool runnin's in her area, and she pacified the ever-restless Skull men by giving them occasional work at Holy Family. In return they guarded the school and the

Laws Street Training Center next door, but that was hardly a steady source of revenue. Instead they turned for money to the housing project the PNP had started building a few blocks away on Barry Street, but the work ground to a halt because the Skull kept fighting with other rankings over who got work on the site. This dire struggle was an affront to the PNP's ability to control its neighborhood, and the police were doing nothing about it. So the army began putting some of its men into the field; one of them was Major Ian Robinson, a gunslinger who liked showing the police how to do their job.

"He was a small man," recalled *Gleaner* journalist David D'Costa, "quite fearless, and much valued by the army to engage in shoot-outs. There were instances where the police had criminals holed up in some part of Kingston and there was so much gunfire that they were hesitant to go in. Then Robinson would show up with his six-guns blazing and, at great personal risk, go in and shoot to death three or four men. That would put down the uprising."

Robinson knew that the Skull was a thorn in the PNP's side. To infiltrate this Labourite squadron in Southside and eradicate it once and for all, Robinson began to assemble an odd cast of characters from the army's Military Intelligence Unit (MIU). The MIU's Captain Karl Marsh was put in charge of the eradication squad, working under a shadowy Cuban adviser known only as "Montero," a man who disappeared later on. Their infiltrator was a Southside youth named "Junior Soul" Douglas, who started hanging around the construction site on Barry Street just before Christmas 1977—the time of year when the sufferers are especially desperate for money—and putting out the word that the army needed men with guns to guard the work site. The news spread through Southside like lightning, and young men started jockeying for their chance to get the guns. Then the army put its Mata Hari to work: a lieutenant named Suzanne Haik, who lured a dozen Southside Labourites to a hotel, where she received them in a filmy nightgown and promised that they'd soon get their weapons, along with three hundred dollars for their guard work. Everything was ready for the massacre that followed.

On the night of January 4, Junior Soul went into Southside with the drivers of two vehicles and found Roddy Nesbeth, along with nine other suspected gang members. He told the men that soldiers were waiting out at Green Bay, an army firing range west of Kingston, to give them the promised guns. The Southies were suspicious at first but decided to go ahead with the plan, and the little caravan left Southside for Green Bay.

It was still dark when they got there. Soldiers met the crew and escorted them down to some targets set up in the sand by the water's edge. They told the men to bunch up, and before the victims knew what was happening, a dozen hidden machine guns opened fire on them.

Roddy Nesbeth had already gotten down in the sand, and now he started crawling for his life toward the dense macca-thorn bushes that surrounded the cove. He heard his friends dying as he crawled. Glenroy Richards, Southside's champion soccer player, cried for his girlfriend as he bled to death in the sand. "Valerie, Valerie," Roddy heard him moan, "I tell you I never want to go, an' now I dead."

Five of the ten intended victims were killed outright; Roddy and four others miraculously escaped. Norman Spencer, one of the survivors, heard his friend Ian Brown call out his name and beg for him to wait. As the two of them crawled through the sand, another survivor, Anthony Daley, caught up with them. "I-mon eye gone," Daley said laconically. The soldiers had shot out one of his eyes. Delroy Griffiths, the last survivor, made it to the water's edge and swam out to sea. He was rescued by a fisherman.

By then the sun was up and the death squad had radioed back to headquarters at Up Park Camp with the bad news that five men had escaped. Soldiers were immediately dispatched to Southside to hunt down the survivors and execute them; they were told to look for men with cuts and scrapes on their skin. But Roddy Nesbeth outwitted the MIU. He led the wounded survivors straight to the Holy Family School, where Sister Benedict hid them and then called the police. They were glad for the chance to embarrass their army rivals, and they took the survivors into protective custody.

Out at Green Bay, Major Ian Robinson was taking pictures of the five bodies sprawled in the sand. He was still sure the survivors would be found and killed, and then he would give out the army's official story: that soldiers posted to the firing range for target practice had been ambushed by the Southside gunmen and had fired back in self-defense.

Robinson's photographs showed the long shadows of three soldiers standing over the dead men. He took the pictures back to Up Park Camp and, in the excitement of the moment, left them on his desk. Someone brought them to David D'Costa at the *Gleaner.*

"I didn't know quite what to do with them," D'Costa said. "The army's story was that the 'shoot-out' had taken place at midday, but the pictures of the dead men clearly showed the soldiers' long shadows. That meant they could only have been taken in the morning or the afternoon, and by the afternoon the story was already out. So we knew it had to have been in the morning. And slowly the army's story began to unravel."

An inquest into the Green Bay massacre began two months later. Although the jury eventually reached a verdict that "unspecified persons" were criminally responsible for the slayings, no one from the army was ever sent to prison. Criminal charges were brought against eight soldiers; one was freed for lack of evidence in 1981 and the remaining seven defendants were released a year later, after the government entered a plea of nolle prosequi. Most of the officers involved in the plot left Jamaica for other islands in the Caribbean; a few went to the United States.

Manley's responsibility for what came to be known as the Green Bay massacre remains an open question. There are those who think it was carried out on his orders. Others see it as Seaga's brainchild: even though the victims were Labourites, Seaga would not have balked at sacrificing a few expendable sufferers in order to smear the PNP.

Brambles knew all five Green Bay survivors; most of them were still in Southside, living and partly living. Delroy Griffiths was a crackhead, prancing through the streets like a puppet on wires and begging everyone for money to get high. Roddy Nesbeth was more in control of himself, even though he drank too much and liked his cocaine.

"Is Roddy you haffi' meet," Brambles said one afternoon. We were sitting on his porch while Ricky and Natalie did their homework, but Natalie was in a playful mood and we were laughing as she tried to style my hair, even though it was too short to even comb. "But we better find him soon," Brambles mused. "He goes back and forth to Brooklyn. His brother's jugglin' coke up there."

We found Roddy a few days later, perched on a stool in his favorite rumshop. I was tongue-tied with him at first and couldn't think of anything to say except that I felt like I'd met him already, in the *Gleaner*'s stories about the Green Bay inquest, at which he was a star witness. A reporter had described him as "a slender, light-skinned man wearing abundant dreadlocks."

The description still fit, although his locks had been trimmed a long time ago. No description would have prepared me for the rum-bleared, faraway look in Roddy's eyes.

He spoke softly, and it was impossible for me to hear him above the throb of the rumshop jukebox. "We cyan' reason here," he said. "Too much ears 'round this place. Let's go breeze out on the road."

We got into my car and headed out along the Palisadoes toward Port Royal, a good place for a reasoning about piracy and politics. The afternoon sun blazed over the narrow road, making it shimmer, and a hot wind carried the smell of sea wrack from the open water. When we reached the town, Roddy wanted to chill out with some ganja, so we bought a little twist of brown paper–wrapped herb from a fisherman behind the police station. Roddy squatted on the black sand, squinting into the harsh sunlight and looking across the harbor to the city while he rolled his spliff. Then he was ready to reason.

We went to a sidewalk bar, where a gigantic land crab materialized and started clawing its way up my skirt. When I freed it gingerly, without shrieking, Roddy flashed me a wide, approving grin. "Daughter level," he said to Brambles. "She cool." So I just asked him to remember Green Bay, and he put the details together in pieces, like he was assembling a jigsaw puzzle.

"Most o' we was Rastas, you know, not Labourites. That was the thing. We had influence with youth an' youth inna' our area, but we was never really on the political side o' things. We was independent-like, free agents, an' nobody coulda' really an' truly control we. We wasn't in nobody's pocket, an' we would tek money from either side."

Brambles smiled at me across the table and raised one eyebrow. He always said that men like Roddy were nothing but "lumpen capitalists," meaning they were about as far from a political vanguard as anyone could be. Their lives had taught them that loyalty to any politician was pure folly, and anyone could buy them.

"So there was the housing scheme goin' up," Roddy went on. "An' you know, that was the only work theory we 'ave in the area at that time. So when Junior Soul start come 'round, sayin' there was some boss-mon goin' to give we guns and money to guard the site, we jump up."

"But didn't you think it sounded suspicious?" I asked.

"Sis," Roddy answered, his face a weary mask, "it was the Christmas. An' all o' we 'ave we baby-mother, an' them axin' fi' ting-an-ting. Plus, the army bizness was a draw. We see some soldier bwoy start patrol in Southside, an' them deal with we 'pon a level, not like the cops. They finger not so fast 'pon the trigger. So when Junior tell I is the army him a' work for, it sound kinda martial an' militant. I liked that.

"But to this day I don't know what save me, why I drop down inna' the sand before the guns open up. I guess I was in a tactical frame o' mind, an' when the soldiers told us to bunch up by those targets, somethin' told me to stand oblique-like, never to hand it to them."

"Hand what to them?" I asked.

"Myself, sis." Roddy smiled.

I had been out to Green Bay several times by then to walk around the cove, and I'd tried to crawl through the macca-thorn bushes. They look exactly like the crown of thorns on Christ's head. The sandy part of the cove is small; the rest is jagged limestone, and Roddy had been barefoot, wearing nothing but a shirt and trousers. When his girlfriend found him later at Sister Benedict's, she worked for hours to pick the thorns out of his skin.

"When did you know you weren't going to die?" I asked.

"I never begin to feel myself breathe again till I knew I was off that army land. There was helicopters flyin' above an' the sound of soldiers shouting from the range, an' I knew that if any o' them found me in the macca, I woulda' been dead fi' true."

I saw Roddy's survival as a miracle. But to him it was all in a day's work; he had been shot at so many times that escaping from an army eradication squad was just another adventure. He recounted the rest of that morning with a sangfroid that had a certain cinematic flourish.

He crept low through the thorns until he came out onto a dirt road that bordered a sugar estate. Luckily the cane was at its highest, ready for the winter harvest, so Roddy was able to hide from the helicopters among the spiky stalks. He was so drenched with sweat by the time he staggered out from the cane that a young man standing by the road asked him if he had come from the sea. Roddy told him he'd come through the swamp, and there were no more questions. They walked together to a country shop, where Roddy got a steadying draw of ganja. Then he caught a bus back to New Kingston and went down to Laws Street in a taxi.

"I supposed to be a dead mon by then," he said. "But the duppy go home in style!" He laughed and then got serious again. "If Sister Benedict hadna' taken we in, we all woulda' been dead, fi' true," he said.

News of the massacre spread through Kingston's ghettos by the end of that day, sparking a sudden reckoning throughout the gang underworld. It was the outlaws' endgame with the politicians, and everyone—from Claudie Massop and Byah Mitchell to Tony Welch and Bucky Marshall—knew that a line had been crossed. It had been one thing to war with one another over scarce scraps from the bosses' tables, and to take one another's lives in a struggle that had come to resemble some terrifying kind of blood sport. But now they saw how expendable their lives really were. Slowly a gang truce began to take shape in the tribalized ghettos of Kingston. Beginning on the night of January 5, the men from Tivoli and Rema, Concrete Jungle and Tel Aviv began crossing the no-man's-land that divided them, smoking chalices full of ganja and talking peace.

"If you had been there, you might have said it was a miracle," Roddy remembered. "Everyone—Tony Welch and the Jungleites, Claudie's people, Bucky's crew from Matthews Lane, the Southie massives—all start lick chalice pipe together. We keep dance in each other's areas, meet up at National Heroes' Circle an' down at Parade. It was like we rose up as one an jus' say *no more war!* We black sufferers say we not goin' kill one another again so that politicians can stay on top. No, mon. Things goin' change up now!"

I remembered a remark that Bucky Marshall had made to a *Gleaner* reporter as the peace movement spread. "This is not political," the outlaw said. "This is from we who have felt the pangs of jail."

A few journalists, like Carl Stone, were regulars at rumshops downtown, but many had never before been in the ghettos. Once they heard the eloquence of the streets, they started putting the sufferers' words into print. "Let us not sentimentalize them," wrote the *Gleaner*'s John Hearne. "Those that I met were not asking for instant love or trust. They were simply demanding that young black people with few jobs stop killing other young black people with fewer jobs, in the name of the two parties whose chief executives looked after each other very well when it came to the matter of handing out well-paid jobs. Every one of them knows that the five men killed at Green Bay were set up for the killing because they were more useful dead than alive."

Neville Toyloy, a radical journalist with the pro-Manley *Daily News*, put the truce in simple terms. "The youths have made it plain that they will not be turning against one another for politicians. They are tired of being used. The key, as they see it, is unity. For it is they who have suffered and died."

Even Claudie Massop was ready to put down his guns. "The peace will have to last," he said, "because our lives depend on it. The youths have been fighting among themselves for too long and is only them get dead. Everybody I grow up with is dead."

Brambles had taken a slew of photographs during those first, euphoric days of the truce. The night after we talked to Roddy Nesbeth, he dug through the cardboard barrel where he kept his archival stash and pulled out folders full of truce shots. In one Claudie Massop had his arm around Bucky Marshall, and both men were engulfed by a throng of ecstatic sufferers. Bucky wore his usual knitted tam and mugged like a clown. But Claudie, his neck encircled by a silver torque, emanated the dignity of a chieftain.

Manley and Seaga kept their distance from the truce. It caught Seaga by surprise; he was in Miami when it started, meeting with high-ups from his party who had gone into exile and were plotting their return. It was said that he was also parlaying with anti-Castro Cubans in Miami who supplied some of the JLP's guns.

Meanwhile, in Kingston, the Jamaica Council for Human Rights and the city churches were getting involved in the peace movement, setting up a church advisory committee. Manley made a tentative effort by meeting with its representatives, as did several delegates from the JLP, but Seaga never attended any truce meeting with the prime minister. He was talking only with his own gunmen in Tivoli.

In the midst of these negotiations, Bob Marley came home. He had left Jamaica more than a year before, after the shooting in his uptown yard, and had been dividing his time between the

United States and England. Claudie Massop had caught a plane to London and persuaded his old friend to come back; the truce leaders were planning a historic peace concert at Kingston's National Stadium, and they wanted Bob there as its star.

Kingston registered two seismic tremors on the night he flew in. The One Love Peace Concert on April 22 included most of the major reggae artists of the moment: Ras Michael and the Sons of Negus, Jacob Miller, Dennis Brown, Culture, and Peter Tosh, who was then beginning to record with Mick Jagger. Jacob Miller did his new song about how "Green Bay killings a' murder." Peter Tosh lit a spliff onstage and told the crowd, "Me don' wan' peace. Me want equality! I am not a politician. I jus' suffer the consequences."

But the high point of the concert was the moment when Marley summoned Manley and Seaga onstage, making the leaders clasp hands above his head in a promise of no more war. It was the only time during the truce that the two men came face to face, and it took everything Marley had to get them together onstage.

The Central Peace Council, an organization formed by the sufferers themselves, put pressure on Manley and Seaga to keep the police out of the ghettos; the outlaws knew that otherwise the truce laid them wide open to cops who were eager to make a name for themselves by killing one of Kingston's most wanted. The chairman of the peace council was an educated, well-spoken Rastafarian named Trevor Phillips, and I asked Brambles if he knew where Phillips was.

"That bredda haffi' leave Kingston in a hurry," he said, "once the peace collapsed and the guns start fire again. I don't know where he is now, or if he's even alive."

The truce had started to crumble even by the time Marley did the One Love concert. The politicians recognized that peace in the ghettos threatened the status quo, and so they sat back and let the police do their eradication work. And on the national political front, the timing of the truce could not have been worse; Seaga and the JLP were pushing hard for Manley to call an early election, and although he held off until 1980, the gun fever was already building to a crescendo downtown. The JLP had been spoiling for revenge since 1976, and its partisans were eager to fight. The PNP began digging in for what promised to be a bloody election campaign.

Dudley Thompson, the minister of national security and justice, disavowed the truce and distanced the PNP from the sufferers who had called it. Repudiating the Rastafarian community his party had courted since 1972, he said that "I-mon culture" did not represent Jamaica. This was also a dig at the Rastafarian youths gunned down at Green Bay. "No angels died at Green Bay," Thompson said. "I have no apologies for those who shout about human rights and police brutality. We have a definite challenge to authority in the form of terrorism." He called the gang leaders "mad dogs" who needed to be destroyed.

The first to die was Dennis "Copper" Barth, the ranking from Wareika Hill who had begun hanging out with Claudie Massop and the Tivoli posse, lulled by the gang truce into believing that he could cross the line between PNP Wareika and JLP West Kingston. He was killed by police at the Caymanas Park racetrack in May 1978 in an ambush set up by Lester "Jim Brown" Coke, the up-and-coming don of Tivoli. Brown set Copper up to rob the racetrack office and then tipped off the police. He was already jockeying for position as Tivoli's next godfather, the enforcer who would control the JLP's ranks for the coming 1980 election. His rise spelled Massop's doom.

The police executed Claudie in February 1979. He was riding home to Tivoli just before dawn on a Sunday night, returning from a soccer match in Spanish Town. Three motorcycles and a detachment of squad cars trailed the taxi Massop was sharing with two friends from the peace council, and they stopped it on Marcus Garvey Drive. When they ordered Massop to get out of the car with his hands in the air, he tried to explain that they were coming home from a game and had no guns. The lead cop shouted, "*Kill!*"

Massop had time for only one word—"*Wait!*"—before he was riddled with more than fifty bullets. The taxi driver, who ran for his life toward the sea, was the only one who survived.

In the morgue photographs of his corpse, Massop looked a little like Che Guevara, his dark skin pallid in death. Thousands of sufferers lined up to view his body at the funeral home where he lay in state, and mourners, many of them women, wept in the street for the gunman they saw as a Robin Hood; one woman remembered the Christmas season a few months before, when Massop spent more than one thousand dollars to buy shoes for people in Tivoli. The PNP rankings in Concrete Jungle stood at attention as his funeral procession passed by.

The *Gleaner*'s Wilmot Perkins, no admirer of outlaws, was nevertheless moved to write a eulogy for the slain gunman: "Massop is part of the legend of the Wild West. He was by all accounts a pretty rough customer. He faced trial for murder and for shooting with intent. But by good fortune, ruthless management, shoddy police work, or the triumph of truth, he was never proven guilty. He survived to become, in the tradition of Wyatt Earp, Doc Holliday, and Wild Bill Hickock, a gunslinger putting his sinister skills and reputation at the service of peace."

But any hope of peace died with Massop. Jamaica was getting ready for an election that would prove to be the most violent in its history, and a new crop of gunmen was coming up to fight this undeclared civil war. The veterans of the 1970s were either dead or in exile. Byah Mitchell, Massop's best friend from Tivoli, died soon after Massop's murder from a cocaine-induced cerebral hemorrhage. Bucky Marshall fled to Miami, where he started selling ganja and cocaine. He stole a stash from Rockeye Nesbeth, the brother of the Green Bay survivor, who eventually caught up with Marshall in Brooklyn at the Starlite Ballroom and shot him dead.

This migration north was a sign of what was to come, the first wave in the posse exodus to the United States. In my peregrinations with Brambles and his friends, I was already hearing about "notches" who were making a name for themselves in Brooklyn and Miami. One night in Central, a young man in brand-new clothes sauntered up to me and asked if I had heard about a ranking from the neighborhood named Delroy Edwards, who was sending back money and guns for his old friends in Southside.

And everyone was talking about Jim Brown, the man who replaced Claudie Massop in Tivoli. His real name was Lester Lloyd Coke, but no one called him that. He was a big, round-bellied man with a deceptively cheery smile, and he started calling himself Jim Brown after the 1967 epic *The Dirty Dozen* became the movie of the year in Jamaica. The original Jim Brown, one of football's most bruising running backs, starred in the movie—the only African-American in a cast that included famous heavies like Charles Bronson and Telly Savalas. Jamaican gangsters went crazy for this story about a crew of hardened criminals who were let out of prison to assassinate high-ranking Nazis. From then on Lester Coke became Jim Brown.

Now he was running a posse called the Shower, so named because it rained down bullets on its victims. But the island was too small to hold him; by then he was shuttling between Jamaica, Miami, and New York, and the Shower was becoming the mother of all posses in the United States.

"There's nothing for them here anymore," Brambles said one night as we walked back to Central after the Raetown street dance. "Everyone wants to fashionize up north, get rich in a New York minute an' come home big an' broad. But maybe they never come home at all, except in a coffin for the dead-house mon."

Kingston
Farewell

The Green Bay massacre and the short-lived gang truce it sparked were soon forgotten in the nightmare of the 1980 election. There were 889 murders that year, over 500 more than were reported in the previous year, and most of them stemmed from political warfare. In April, thirty men dressed in combat camouflage assaulted a JLP dance on Gold Street, the boundary line between Southside and Tel Aviv, killing four people and wounding eleven. Jamaica's experiment in democratic socialism was coming to an end in what Michael Manley called "a hail of bullets and a river of blood."

The 1980 campaign also brought the first murder of a political candidate. The PNP's Roy McGann and his bodyguard were killed in Gordon Town, a village in the Blue Mountain foothills above Kingston, in a late-night gun battle with a JLP mob. Police were there, supposedly to protect the candidate, but the last words that McGann's bodyguard shouted were, "The police are firing on us!"

Another ghastly riot erupted in Spanish Town, where Manley and D. K. Duncan were scheduled to address a PNP rally. On his way to the town square, Manley was stopped by a detachment of police who warned him that "soldiers" had already fired into the crowd. Although the melee made it hard to tell exactly where the shots were coming from, Manley took the police at their word and was horrified to think the army was now shooting at its own people. But he and Duncan refused to back down, and they drove on to the square, debating what to do next. "The discussion suddenly became irrelevant," Manley recalled in his book *Struggle in the Periphery*. "A new burst of gunfire started. It was coming from every direction." Some witnesses claimed that Duncan drew his own gun and started shooting back, another first for a political candidate.

Late one afternoon on a scorching spring day, just before I left Jamaica in 1986, Brambles took me to a farm near Spanish Town to meet the man who had procured the JLP's guns for that shooting. His nickname was "Billy the Kid."

Billy worked as a caretaker on the farm, which was owned by a JLP councillor for the area, and we found him in the fields at dusk. Like any seasoned veteran of the political wars, Billy was taciturn and evasive, and he hedged about his role in the 1980 shooting until Brambles made one of his inspired moves. He knew that Billy loved western movies with a passion, so he mentioned that I'd come to Jamaica from Wyoming, the legendary territory of many a Wild West bandit. Billy's face lit up, and he considered me with fresh interest.

Billy warmed to me then, sensing a kindred spirit. He began to talk, with an outlaw's engaging modesty, about his godfather role in the JLP and the party's paramilitary organization in Spanish Town. Billy was the JLP's gun hawk and bagman, the one who delivered the weapons and paid the mercenaries. But I was slow to grasp the fine points of this arrangement; I wanted to know where the money came from.

"Well," Billy said, "we 'ave a JLP caretaker for the area, a mon named Williams, an' he is a druggist."

"You mean he owns a pharmacy?" I asked.

Billy and Brambles laughed.

"No, sis," Billy said. "I mean the ganja bizness. Williams got the money for the guns from his weed. You want to talk to the men who shot up that rally? Then mek we go an' find them."

We drove to a shantytown called Homestead, not far from the middle-class neighborhood where Billy lived. Soon we were turning right and left, and right and left again, through a maze I would have been unable to find my way out of alone. Without Billy's constant directions, I might as well have been blindfolded. This was nothing like the grid of streets I had come to know in downtown Kingston: Homestead was a tangle of sandy lanes and narrow pathways, many of them much too small for a car. They were walled off by zinc and scrap board fences, behind which the yards stretched for what seemed like miles. A full moon was rising as night fell, bathing the place in a ghostly light. Although the settlement was quiet, except for the friendly sounds from rumshops and yards, I could imagine the terror that would have transformed it in a night gun battle.

We finally pulled up in front of a tiny rumshop with the requisite complement of young and old sufferers, lounging in the shadows and basking in the evening coolness. "Come out," Billy said. "You two wait here until I come back." Brambles got himself and me two Heinekens—the correct Labourite beer for a JLP neighborhood—and waited for a long time until we saw Billy coming down the lane with five young men, sauntering with the unhurried gait that proclaimed, Is *we* rule here.

"This is the Ayatollah," Billy said, introducing the posse's un-mistakable leader. He was drop-dead handsome, his chiseled fea-tures framed by a mane of dreads, and he was dressed in camouflage pants and a fishnet T-shirt. A few gold chains glittered in the moonlight on his chest. The other men were silent, waiting for their leader to make his move, and the rumshop crowd parted for them like a scene out of the westerns Billy so admired.

The Ayatollah suggested that his crew and I drive to his yard "a few chain" away, to reason. I threw a questioning glance at Brambles, who only nodded, and we left him and Billy at the shop. Now we were moving so deep into the Homestead maze that my claustrophobia went from panic to fatalism until it came to rest at trust.

His home was a small, poured-concrete house with a living room crowded full of plush red-velvet settees. The men sat down with their beers and spliffs and waited politely for me to say something.

"Well," I faltered. "I want to ask you about the 1980 time. Billy told me that some of you . . . played a part in what happened at the rally."

"You is a journalist, or what?" the Ayatollah asked.

Everyone leaned forward when I said that I was working on a book about gangs and political violence; this was their story, and they wanted it to be told. The Ayatollah smiled, but sadly.

"Then I will tell you how it went," he said. "Months before the election, PNP activists start comin' out here, all the way from Concrete Jungle. An' let I tell you, they was one wicked set o' men. They bruck down doors an' shot up yards, demonstrating the power of the PNP. They killed my baby-mother. They was lookin' for her brother, thru' they knew he was a Labourite notch. They found him, and after they killed him, they shot her too. She was eight months pregnant at the time."

The other men nodded in agreement. One of them, a youth

who was probably a child during the campaign fury, spoke up. "You remember the Manley time, miss? You recall the shortages we had? How there was no salt fish, no flour, no rice, no cookin' oil in the shops? Jamaica never stay so until Manley messed everything up." I refrained from saying anything about how the merchants and shopkeepers were to blame, hoarding precious foodstuffs to raise the prices when the dollar plunged. Many of them were paid off by the JLP.

"An' there was Cubans all 'round the place," another man said. "They was buildin' the José Martí School near Spanish Town, an' Manley said we was all to be grateful for their bein' here." He sucked his teeth. "Why Jamaica need Cubans to build ting here? They all the while gwan' like them better than we."

The Ayatollah spoke again. "But it was the violence whey' turn us against the PNP, fi' true. Things just got so bad toward the 1980 time. The Jungleites had guns an' we had nothing to defend ourselves with."

"So what about Williams?" I asked.

"Yes, him," answered the Ayatollah. "Him 'ave the ganja trade well in hand, so him jus' let off lickle money and guns fi' we here in Homestead, an' some o' the other areas like Winter Pen, Gordon Pen, Duncan's Pen, and Spanish Town Central."

"What kind of guns?"

"Mostly M1s," the Ayatollah said. "Them is old, yes, but effective. An' we each got paid two hundred dollars for shooting up the rally. By that time, we was spoilin' fi' revenge."

We rose from the velvet seats and drove back to the rumshop. The huge moon was high by then and the night's pleasures were in full swing; the jukebox was cranked up and I couldn't hear the Ayatollah's voice when he whispered in my ear.

"What?" I said, leaning toward him.

"I jus' axe the daughter if she like to 'ave a lickle coke."

It was the first time anyone in Jamaica had ever offered me cocaine.

Brambles was quiet for a while after we said good-bye to Billy and the Ayatollah. I was concentrating hard on the road, clouded by exhaust thick as fog. He knew that I was leaving the island for good that summer, and neither of us had begun to deal with separating. He read my mind and broke the silence.

"So what we goin' to do to mark your leave-taking?"

He'd talked about taking a road trip to the country, across the island to Negril. He had a friend named Kenty, an ex-corporal from the Jamaica Defense Force, who bought sinsemilla from a ganja grower near Negril and smuggled it out from the Kingston wharves. Kenty had suggested that the three of us go to check his man in Westmoreland and then asked me to carry a hundred pounds of skunk-smelling sinsemilla back to Kingston in my trunk. But I had been in too many roadblocks to oblige, halted by uniformed cops and their sinister-looking friends in street clothes, with their index fingers poised so lightly on the triggers of their M16s that the sound of a passing car's backfire would have been all they needed.

"If you interested in this cocaine bizness," Brambles said, "the way it ties in to politics an' ting, you could do a lickle research in Negril. I 'ave a friend there who juggles coke, an' he could tell you some stories about the white wife."

That was the phrase of the moment, a perfect description of the drug's foreign origins and its power to lay waste. Cocaine was a novelty, a fairly recent addition to the island's pharmacopoeia, but it was quickly becoming the next bad dream, as it always does. Tourists had brought it to Negril in the late 1970s, where it was soon de rigueur for whites and their rent-a-dread consorts. But across the island in Kingston, cocaine made a different kind of entrance.

The drug started showing up in the pockets and noses of JLP gunmen just before the 1980 election. That was a coincidence no one cared to probe. But it was said by Carl Stone, the UWI professor and political scientist, that the drug was partly responsible for the sickening nature of the violence during that time—atrocities such as the killing of children and the mutilation of pregnant women. Stone called 1980 "the reign of the wall-eyed gunmen."

Whether or not Seaga was feeding cocaine to his paladins, the JLP definitely controlled the trade. Jamaica became a major Caribbean transshipment point for the drug when Seaga came to power, and several of his government ministers were said to be involved in protecting its movement into and out of Jamaica. The police—most of them badly paid and poorly trained country boys who were easily corrupted—were cut in on the trade. By the time I moved to Kingston in 1984, cocaine was everywhere. The Chinese controlled the uptown market and the JLP had it to themselves in the ghettos, which was why it was easy to come by in Labourite enclaves like Southside. By 1984 crack was already replacing powder cocaine in the ghettos; since Jamaicans were given to smoking ganja, it was natural for them to take to the smokable (and cheaper) form of cocaine.

But islanders were slow to awaken to the drug's menace. Foreign political consultants and aid agencies had crammed it down their throats that ganja was their country's major peril, and the Americans didn't seem too worried about Jamaica's cocaine problem—it was ganja they were forever spraying with lethal herbicides and burning with flamethrowers. But the Americans would soon have reason to worry about Jamaica and cocaine. In 1984 the Drug Enforcement Administration sounded a quiet warning in its annual intelligence report: "Increasing evidence of cocaine traffic in Jamaica is of concern both because of the threat to the local population and because it involves foreign criminal elements. Some Jamaican traffickers are believed to have switched to cocaine because of the relative ease with which it can be shipped, in comparison to marijuana, and because of the large profits to be made."

What the report neglected to say was that Jamaica's entry into the Caribbean transshipment trade dovetailed neatly and brutally with the island's American-funded ganja-eradication program. As the ganja barons found it harder to get their product off the island, they began to piggyback their shipments on the cocaine trade. And it wasn't long before the local market became a lucrative sideline; the friend Brambles wanted me to meet in Negril was one of the local ganja dealers who had made the shift from the "Weed of Wisdom" to the "White Wife."

Cocaine hit the local population with a force that was not unlike the way alcohol devastated Native Americans in the nineteenth century. As one of Brambles's Foster Lane friends said, "The first time I tek it, it mek I feel dazzled-like." Soon he was hooked on the dazzle, selling every stick of the furniture his mother had left him and pimping his baby-mother for his high.

We left for Negril, with Kenty riding shotgun, on a cool early morning and took the Junction road, the steepest and most beautiful route over the Blue Mountains. The road was no wider than a cart track in many places, empty as a bush path except for country people on foot or riding donkeys. Soothed by the bucolic loveliness of the landscape, Brambles lost his usual edginess and became serene. We stopped so many times along the way, buying roasted corn and paper cups of scalding soup straight from vendors' kettles, that it took us the better part of the day to reach Negril. Kenty wanted to check his grower on the outskirts of town, so we dropped him off at a red-dirt footpath into the hills and then went to find Brambles's friend.

His name was Lyrics; in patois, someone who "flies lyrics" is a genial con artist of the first rank. "I don't know how we goin' to find him," Brambles said. "I mean, what kind of mood he's goin' to be in. Sometimes he licks the pipe for days and days, an' then he's in no shape to reason."

Lyrics's yard was high up in the district called Red Ground, perched on a hilltop with sweeping views of the sea. We parked the car and walked, panting, up a steep, rock-strewn path with hummingbirds darting through the bush and goats trailing their ropes as they browsed. Lyrics was sitting in a porch swing that hung from a huge mango tree, drowsing in the shade. He greeted Brambles as if he had known his old friend was coming.

"You gwan' live long!" Lyrics said, the Jamaican way of saying that you'll have good luck for showing up just as someone is thinking about you. Lyrics was smoking herb, and he was in a mellow mood, but as we began talking, he waxed eloquent about his ups and downs with cocaine. He liked talking about the drug, and he had the addict's classic fascination for his substance: dread of its consequences coupled with no will to quit just yet. He was bitter, but he was still in thrall to the White Wife.

"There was time, not so long ago," he said, "when we here in this island never touched cocaine. What did we know about coke? We don't grow it. But it seem like ever since this Seaga bizness start up, the JLP here in Westmoreland come down hard on the ganja men like punishment. This area been PNP ever since Norman Manley's time—old people here still remember the sugar strike of '38. You know that when Seaga start burnin' the ganja fields, some of the cane workers set fire to the fields in revenge?"

rics laughed.

Comin' like they was sayin', No ganja, no cane. I don't know. Sometimes I think the JLP set this whole thing up. Seem like the seventies belonged to Manley and to ganja, but the eighties now, they belong to cocaine. I see dreads I know from town, walkin' down the road with boards from them own yard fi' sell out, just for coke. It's the freebase thing. Once you start, you cyan' stop so easy again. An' if you 'ave plenty ganja, you can trade it for powder. Right now in Negril, a hundred pounds of good sinsemilla will get you a quarter ounce of coke."

I did some fast arithmetic in Jamaican dollars. Prime sinsemilla was selling locally then for $400 a pound, so a hundred pounds was worth $40,000. Cocaine went for $100 a gram—itself an interesting fact, since the magical $100-a-gram price held in both Negril and New York, even though in Jamaican dollars that same $100 was one-fifth of the U.S. price. That alone told me how arbitrarily the price of cocaine was fixed; the Colombians had such a glut that they would sell it for whatever the local market would bear. And Negril's cocaine, like the drug everywhere, was whacked every time it changed hands, adulterated with anything from ground-up aspirin to foot powder. In a quick computation I figured that a quarter ounce of cocaine (seven grams) was worth $700. This meant that local users were trading $40,000 worth of ganja for $700 worth of coke.

"Lyrics," I said, "that doesn't make any sense."

"You think this supposed to make sense?" he shot back. "Does it make sense to burn a man's fields, to mash up his livelihood? To bring in cocaine at the same time as you destroy our ganja? I'm just telling you what we trade our ganja for, inna disya' time. Since you ask."

Brambles and I were in somber moods when we left Lyrics's yard, so we drove into Negril to roam through its pleasure palaces. We had a drink at Rick's Cafe and watched the local girls hustling the tourists. The prostitutes were working Rick's in droves, and so were the sad-eyed women who begged the white girls to let them do the bead-tipped Bo Derek hair thing. On the winding cliff road outside the bar, rent-a-dreads zoomed by on their bikes with white women clinging behind. The arrangement meant that some of the rented Rastas might take a little money home to their baby-mothers, unless they smoked it first.

We walked through town and stopped in at Hedonism II, the all-inclusive resort that used to be a Club Med. Brambles looked miserable and tried to disappear in the lobby, so I stayed just long enough to pick up a brochure that said, "The pleasure comes in many forms. At Hedonism II, we have everything a body could ask for: you can stretch it, build it, tan it, relax it, strip it, wet it, feed it, cool it, fix it and yes, even abuse it if you so choose."

We walked barefoot along the seven-mile beach, wrapped in darkness and not saying much. A few hustlers passed by us, hissing entreaties: did we want some coke? As I sat on the beach alone the next morning, while Brambles went off with Kenty to do business, a Rasta strolled up to me and issued what he must have thought was an invitation I couldn't refuse. "Daughter 'ave a nice, fat pussy," he said in a whisper that was meant to cajole but only sounded full of menace. When I gaped back at him, struck dumb, he got the message and walked away.

Brambles just laughed when I told him and Kenty about the encounter. "You is fair game," he said.

The trip to Negril made me sad, as Jamaica's North Coast always does. Kingston has its own funky vibe, but its people keep their dignity. The tourist strip, on the other hand, always makes me think of what Claude Lévi-Strauss meant by "tristes tropiques": it is Jamaica at its most forlorn.

My final weeks in Kingston were suffused by sadness too. It

rained relentlessly while I packed up two years of life and boxed belongings to be mailed home. As I unframed pictures, giant cockroaches skittered from their nests behind the glass. Cleaning out a closet, I came upon a spider so enormous that I left the house for the rest of the day. I slogged across the sodden campus lawns for farewell drinks and suppers with friends, envying the casual stoicism with which Jamaicans say good-bye. The centuries of necessary migration have made them adept at farewells, and my own impending departure was less painful because we all knew that I would return. But somehow I knew there were faces I would never see again.

One of them would be Neville Hall's, the history professor who had taken me up Blue Mountain for the first time. As we sat on his jasmine-scented veranda one night, sipping rum liqueur, I tried to memorize his beautiful voice, something no photograph would ever convey. A few months after I left, Neville died in a car accident on the Mona Road near the university gate. It was dusk, and the bus driver who hit Neville's car was driving without headlights, thinking to save his battery.

I had quickened my work pace in those final weeks and did some last interviews. One was with Keith Gardner, the killer cop known as "Trinity." I had not expected him to see me, but when I reached him on the phone at the Halfway Tree police station, he seemed to like the sound of my voice.

"How do you spell your last name?" he asked, evidently writing it down in his appointment book. The spelling is curious to Jamaicans, accustomed to English surnames.

"It's 'guns,' sir," I answered. "Guns, with a t."

He laughed and said he would meet me the following morning.

I parked my car in the lot at Halfway Tree and walked past the lockup, where prisoners put their eyes to the tiny windows and begged in a chorus for food. Trinity did not keep me waiting; he ushered me promptly into his office, where he had pictures of himself with Nelson Mandela, Jesse Jackson, and Queen Elizabeth. I asked him how he had gotten his nickname, and he explained that the original Trinity was the hero of a spaghetti western.

"The name came from my alleged dexterity with a gun. It started in '73 or '74, while I was stationed at Olympic Gardens. My style was different. I liked to achieve and maintain the element of surprise. So those were the days when I used to carry up to ten, eleven prisoners at one time, by myself. I used to walk them on foot. I had a reputation then and I commanded a lot of respect."

He spoke of the impact that westerns and gangster movies had on Jamaica's cult of badman-ism, but he said that when he was a boy, his mother, a fundamentalist Christian, refused to let him go to movies. They were "worldly things."

He remembered growing up in Trenchtown and listening to Bob Marley harmonize with the original Wailers at dances. Brambles had told me that Trinity had a brother who became a notorious outlaw, and that Trinity shed no tears when he was gunned down by police; they said he spat on his brother's body as it lay in the street. Trinity was a child of the ghetto who got out, and his career led him to kill the grown men he'd once played with when they were all children in Trenchtown.

I asked him what it was like to be in a gunfight.

"It is a phenomenon," he said, looking down at his hands folded gracefully on his desk. "There's a feeling of high that you get. Your adrenaline is running and your heart is beating fast, because you don't know what is going to happen in a split second, between the moment when the guy reaches for his waist and all hell breaks loose. You don't want to shoot him before you know, because you haven't seen the gun yet, but you don't want to wait either, because just a split second will decide whether you are going to die."

He reckoned that he had been in some ninety-seven shoot-outs, too many to still be counting. "I think the moment you start counting, you are becoming degenerate," he said.

I thought about the affinity between cops and criminals, how like each other they finally became, and remembered the sufferers' stories about Trinity showing up at dance halls dressed all in black, with a brace of pistols on his hips like a gunfighter.

A news photograph hung on the wall behind him, taken during the 1980 election when he was Seaga's bodyguard. He was crouching, under fire from an invisible sniper in a West Kingston street. I asked him what he thought of Claudie Massop and the other rankings he'd rubbed shoulders with. Trinity leaned forward with an eager glint in his eye, but then he checked himself.

"There are many things I would like to talk about," he said graciously. "But you will understand that I cannot. Perhaps at another time . . ."

"Yes," I answered, baffled by how unexpectedly likable this man was. "I hope we meet again."

The following day I said good-bye to another beloved friend, a journalist from Trinidad. He had covered the Caribbean for forty years and had known the founding fathers of every island's movement for independence; the men who were historical figures to me were memories to him. I'd always told him about the work I was doing, and although he admired it, he also thought I took foolish chances. He never even went to political rallies in Jamaica anymore, unless he could find a spot way at the back of the crowd and get out fast if he had to. He was bitter about what had become of a Jamaica he had once loved.

"This is nothing but a tiny island ruled by two thugs," he

said as we parted. "Why do you care so much what becomes of it?"

My good-byes downtown were harder than the ones with university colleagues; I had a sense of closure as far as teaching was concerned, but I was beginning to realize that the posse saga was unfinished. Kingston was only a prologue, an orientation for the journey that lay ahead. "Everything change up now," Brambles said one night as we walked through the neighborhood. "If you want to follow this posse bizness, is New York or Miami you haffi' penetrate. An up-there-so, you is on your own."

One June evening, two weeks before I left, we were sitting on the bench over the gully on South Camp Road, talking with an older man named Joseph Manning. His nephew, Delroy Edwards, had gone north to Brooklyn and was running a crack posse there. Joseph had raised Delroy from a child and was resigned to what the youth had become, now that his exploits were being sung all over Southside. Joseph himself was something of a don in the area, but his money came from a welding business he'd built up over many years. He was still a sufferer at heart. Every day when work was over, he'd get barefoot, put on a pair of track shorts, and drive back down to Southside in his silver Volvo. When his friends saw it parked by the gully bench, it was a signal that Joe was around and available for favors. He was the one who could be counted on to drive a woman in hard labor up to Jubilee Lying-In or to bail someone out from the Central police station.

Brambles and I settled on the bench with Joseph and his little group of friends, watching the action at a shop across the street. Everyone called it "Brooklyn Corner"; it had a bandooloo (illegal) telephone hookup for unbilled overseas calls, and at night there was always a line of people waiting for their turn at the phone. "You see that place?" Joseph said. "The phone rings all the time with calls from one youth or another, in Miami, in New York, wherever. An' all o' them seem like they gone down into posseism an' the drugs bizness."

Joe wanted to check out the midnight show at the Palace Theater, so we walked over there and looked at the posters, which advertised *Rambo*. Brambles sucked his teeth in derision. "The old movie posters here used to say, 'Drama!' " he stage-whispered. " 'Suspense!' It was mostly those two words there. Everybody woulda' wind up 'pon the edge o' them seat and wonder who killed who an' all them type o' question. An' we come outta' the cinema, go home, an' talk 'bout the plot all night long.

"A show like *Rambo* don't hold inna' my time. Nobody woulda' wan' go see him back then. When I was a youth comin' up, we used to like see some heavy westerns. Not a whole heap o' shooting, but a story, a serious detective story. We wanted dialogue! Like Hamlet, Prince of Denmark. Weren't no fool-fool actors in them days neither. We had Anthony Quinn, Burt Lancaster, James Mason. Those guys could talk! Rambo cyan' even talk. He's too stupid. Now is all words o' one syllable an' that kind o' thing. An' who's this other guy? This one they call Schwarzenegger?"

Brambles made another rude sound.

A few days later he reminded me of one last person I should talk with, an older man named Custom whom he'd mentioned many times. Custom lived in Tivoli and had been close to Claudie Massop, whom he called "a human rights mon" and had loved as a brother. So he came to Brambles's yard one night and the three of us walked down to the seawall at Victoria Pier.

I was tired that night. My head was crammed full of images: the Ayatollah's face in the moonlight that night at Homestead, eager for his cocaine; the sad-faced hookers at Rick's Cafe in

Negril; Trinity talking laconically about his ninety-seven shoot-
outs. I was hoping that Custom would tell me something noble
from Massop's career; maybe he had been there the day Claudie
confronted Seaga in Tivoli and accused him of being nothing
but a warlord. But all he talked about was murder after murder,
in loving detail: how many men Massop had killed to get his
ranking as a don. The one that broke me was a story about his
shooting some youth off his bicycle.

I flew into a rage, vibrating between anger and tears. My voice
seemed to come from somewhere else, ringing down the empty
waterfront. I was shouting about not wanting to hear any more
stories of sufferers who got big by killing one another. Didn't
these men see that this was nothing to be proud of?

Brambles and Custom sat like statues. Custom finished his
beer, got up slowly, and sauntered off into the west, back to
Tivoli. Brambles was too angry to say anything.

"Mek we go back a' yard," he muttered.

We walked through the streets without saying a word, but
when we reached his yard he took my tape recorder and turned
it on.

"Orientating statements," he said, speaking into the microphone. This was to be a lesson in what I had obviously failed
to learn; despite his year of careful teachment, his pupil had let
him down. Instead of speaking in patois, he used the painstaking
English he'd learned as a schoolboy, back in the colonial days
when his teachers made him recite Shakespeare and read the
dictionary. Brambles loved words for their power, and that night
he wanted me to feel it.

"To enter into the study of this ghetto society requires a certain kind of courage," he began. "It is an enormously variegated
and complex subject. Those willing to take on the task must
have an active, energetic mind capable of putting together seem-

ingly infinite numbers of observations and events into something approaching a meaningful whole.

"To think and work in such a manner requires intellectual openness. Agility. Or the person must face the distinct prospect of being overwhelmed by the breadth and depth of social and political phenomena. I must emphasize scholarly courage and mental agility. All previous preconceptions and biases must be eliminated.

"I have seen the incipience of intellectual arrogance in you, and sometimes you question the credibility of events. You are entering a new experience. You are writing something unique. You are white. It is difficult for a white person to simulate a black experience. And it is even more difficult to express or interpret something you have never experienced before. Be calm.

"The people in the ghetto are not the masters of their own destiny. People can use them because they don't have any money or security. They are not surrounded by the amenities they require. They are anxious. It is for these reasons why they are so susceptible to all these kinds of exploitation.

"You take things for granted, for to a certain extent you are very pampered. But these people who you talk to are professors in their own right. And regardless of your education, you could not survive one week in this ghetto without prostituting yourself. These people don't get any protection. They are strong. They are resilient. They are only the victims of circumstance. They are the professors of poverty, and the pawns in the game of power politics."

There was nothing left to say. He turned off the tape recorder and went into the room where Natalie and Ricky were sleeping; I heard him rummaging through his picture stash. When he came back out onto the veranda he made a black-and-white patchwork quilt of photographs, his farewell gift for me to keep. I had seen some of them before, like the one of Claudie Massop and Bucky Marshall at the start of the 1978 truce, standing in the midst of a smiling crowd of sufferers with their arms around each other. I had seen the one of Dennis Barth, the gunman called "Copper," who was killed by police in the purge that followed the truce. Brambles had gone on assignment to photograph Copper in jail, and he captured him wearing a black beret, looking out at the camera in near profile, his chin in one hand and a pensive, wary look in his eyes.

But there were other pictures, from 1980, that I had not seen. One was taken on Foster Lane and showed a crowd watching an open army Jeep pass by. The soldiers had machine guns propped on their knees, and one had beautiful hands with an index finger poised ever-so-gracefully on the barrel. There was just enough light under his helmet for me to see his eyes, narrowed into slits. The driver was glancing at a nearly naked boy standing in water flowing down the gutter, his mouth open in a frozen, silent shout.

There was a picture of the dead gunman who'd been killed in Brambles's yard, trying to hide behind the refrigerator on the veranda. The man's eyes were still open; blood dribbled from his mouth onto a shiny polyester shirt with flowers. It was a playful pattern, something you would have found on Carnaby Street in the sixties. Absurdly, I started to cry.

"Don't weep fi' him," Brambles said. "He was one wicked ras-clot bredda."

But then he spoke gently, the way a Jamaican parent tells a child to stop sniffling. "Stop yu' noise."

We sat listening to the night sounds on Foster Lane, the roosters and the dogs and the music from tinny radios.

"You are not here to say who is good and who is bad," Brambles said. "You should only be committed to reality."

PART TWO

New York

Meeting in
Rikers

I n October 1987 the Bureau of Alcohol, Tobacco and Firearms (ATF) launched a nationwide series of raids on Jamaican
posses called Operation Rum Punch. By then the posses were
linked to 625 drug-related murders and ATF director Chester
Higgins called them "probably this country's most violent" organized crime gangs. The raids brought 124 arrests in 11 cities:
New York, Miami, Boston, Philadelphia, Cleveland, Dallas,
Denver, Detroit, Kansas City, Los Angeles, and Washington,
D.C. For the first time, I saw the familiar names of Kingston
posses in the *New York Times*: Tel Aviv, the Spanglers, and the
Shower.

But Operation Rum Punch was not the first time the posses
made news. Had I been living in New York in the summer of
1985, I would have seen the story about a shooting that August
at a Jamaican picnic in Oakland, New Jersey. Gunmen from the
Shower and the Spanglers opened fire in a crowd of Sunday
revelers, killing two people and wounding nine others. The
Spanglers were then selling drugs on Edgecombe Avenue in Harlem, and one of their soldiers had died in a gunfight with some

interlopers from the Shower; the New Jersey shooting was a reprisal, another episode in their ongoing blood feud. One injured survivor, a woman in her eighth month of pregnancy, posed a rhetorical question to a reporter from the *Times*. "What is the PNP doing this for?" she asked. "We are in the USA, not in Jamaica fighting politics."

"This feud has being going on for years and years," said another shooting victim. "It didn't start at this picnic. This whole thing is because political leaders have lost control."

A year later a New York City policeman died in a Queens shoot-out with a Spangler, who cornered him in a stairwell and put a 9 mm automatic to the officer's head while he was desperately trying to reload his six-shot service revolver.

The arrival of the posses and their rapid entry into the streetlevel crack trade caught American law enforcement by surprise. There had been Jamaican "gatehouses" in cities like Miami and New York since the 1970s, little storefront operations where Rastafarians sold ganja along with crafts, vegetarian food, and reggae records. Violence was rare around the gatehouses, but now the relative peace of the ganja trade was shattering as crack took over, bringing a younger generation of outlaws onto the streets. They were the children of Jamaica's nightmare years, seasoned by the ruthlessness of its small, dirty war.

The posses' American debut, deadly though it was, was a serendipitous windfall for the Bureau of Alcohol, Tobacco and Firearms. The drug crisis had engendered a struggle for supremacy and funding in the federal law-enforcement bureaucracy, and the Justice Department, under Attorney General Dick Thornburgh, was winning. The Bureau is part of the Treasury Department, with a colorful history that goes back to Prohibition. By the mid-1980s, however, the ATF seemed to have outlived its purpose and there was pressure from the Justice Department to terminate it. Then the Jamaican posses arrived on the scene and gave the embattled bureau a new reason for being. Besides murder, their major violation was interstate gunrunning, an offense that clearly came within the ATF's historic domain; its agents hoped that Operation Rum Punch would give them some good, flashy publicity. Unfortunately, the raids were bumped from the front pages by news from Wall Street: they coincided with the week that ended on Friday, October 16 and the following Black Monday, when the Dow Jones plunged a total of 716 points and signaled the end of the Roaring Eighties.

But the ATF stayed with the posses like a rodeo bronc rider. Its agents had been tracking them since 1984, when Interpol asked the bureau to trace the shipment of twenty-two Shower guns that Lester "Jim Brown" Coke had sent to Kingston from Miami. They discovered that these guns were only a fraction of the 210 automatic weapons bought by the Shower in Florida and Ohio, and some of the guns began turning up in drug and murder cases in Washington, D.C., New York, Detroit, Miami, Chicago, and Los Angeles. "It was an amazing scenario," said the Miami ATF agent J. J. Watterson. "We had murders everywhere."

I was in New York at the Columbia Journalism School when Operation Rum Punch took place, and I called the ATF's Manhattan office as soon as I read about the raids. Special Agent Robert Creighton asked me to come downtown that afternoon for a talk with the team of agents assigned to the posses. They had been piecing together the story of the gangs, mostly from interviews with suspects, but they were learning more about homicides in this country than about the Jamaican background of the posse phenomenon, and they were eager to talk to someone who knew the political geography of downtown Kingston.

Creighton, in his impeccable white shirt and shoulder holster, reminded me of Eliot Ness. Before we sat down to talk on the black Naugahyde couch in his office, he showed me the gun case in the front waiting room, with its array of sawed-off shotguns and a 9 mm pistol labeled "the favorite weapon of drug dealers." Two other agents, John O'Brien and Bill Fredericks, soon joined us. Both had been working on the posses since 1985.

O'Brien was rotund and sandy-haired with a laconic sense of humor. He was getting a master's degree in Irish history at Columbia and was fascinated by the parallels between the fratricidal politics of Jamaica and Northern Ireland. He'd known about the Spanglers since the 1985 shooting at the picnic in New Jersey, and he mentioned a recent Harlem killing after which some Spanglers cut up the victim's body like a serving of jerk chicken. "Have you heard of this practice?" he asked me. "I think they call it 'quartering.' " Then he shook his head. "Yes, the posses do have a certain flamboyance within their world."

Bill Fredericks seemed to be the one with the lion's share of posse experience to his credit. He was the ATF's liaison with Scotland Yard, which was then tracking "yardies," as the posses are called in England, and he had a working knowledge of Kingston's major players, past and present. Short and stocky with graying, tousled hair that looked like it had last been cut with a kitchen knife, Fredericks was part ruffian and part rogue; an attorney later likened him to "a short Nick Nolte in the movie *48 Hours*." He was a Marine Corps veteran whose experience with the posses had given him a measure of respect for their toughness; they were worthy adversaries. But, like many of the police and federal agents I later came to know, he also felt a sadness about their wasted lives. "You confront them with what they've done," he said, "and sometimes they just break down and cry. They talk about being raised as good Christians, and you can see they could have had another life."

"When did you first realize that the posses were here?" I asked Creighton and his men. "How did you become aware of them?" Fredericks remembered the call from Interpol and said that at the same time, police in New York began to notice a sharp rise in homicides within the Jamaican community. It was also apparent that crack, the new street drug, was being sold by Jamaicans quite unlike the Rastafarians whom police were familiar with as ganja men; it seemed as if these new dealers had known about smokable cocaine before.

The Caribbean origins of crack are still under debate, but drug researchers believe that the Bahamas was one of the first places it showed up, around 1980. By the end of the 1970s, Colombians were shipping a vast share of the powder cocaine destined for the United States through the thousands of islands and cays that make up the Bahamas, and some of it was being diverted to the local population. It was there that residents began cooking the powder into freebase, an elaborate chemical process that uses ether to "free" the base cocaine from cocaine hydrochloride powder. American cocaine cognoscenti already knew about freebasing—it was with this chemically volatile operation that Richard Pryor set himself on fire in 1980—but it was a designer drug. It was simpler and safer, though less pure, to use baking soda and water to make a cheaper form of freebase, and this was the recipe that came to be used in the Bahamas and elsewhere in the Caribbean to make crack.

Jamaicans have always traveled frequently between their island and the Bahamas, where no visa is required for Jamaicans. So they may have learned about crack there and introduced it to Kingston well before the drug made its appearance on the streets of New York and other American cities. Whatever its murky origins, it was clear that by 1984–85, Jamaicans were cooking and selling it all over the United States, sometimes in the hinterlands, where local law enforcement never expected to find it. In 1985, for example, police raided a string of crack houses in the little town of Martinsburg, West Virginia; they were run mostly by Jamaican apple pickers who had come to the state on a visa program for agricultural workers.

In big cities the posses were soon muscling in on the crack trade, using high-powered weapons and earning a reputation for fearlessness. They bought guns by the dozen from dealers around the country—Florida, Virginia, and Ohio were some of their favorite sources—and began using interstate highways in the South to ferry guns from Florida to New York. Bill Fredericks recalled that one of the first posse wake-up calls to ATF came from West Virginia. "I remember getting this frantic phone call from a state trooper down there," he said. "He had pulled over a carload of Jamaican guys for speeding, and when he did a routine check of their trunk, he found some very serious guns."

Then Fredericks did an excellent, drawling imitation of a southern lawman: "I've got some guys here who . . . well, they speak English, but I can't understand 'em. And, Jesus—you should see these guns. Y'all up there know anything about who these people might be?"

That afternoon with the ATF agents was the first time I asked anyone in American law enforcement for what I wanted more than anything: some official corroboration that the posses were working for politicians. I had heard this from countless sufferers in Kingston but never on the record from any official source. "Oh, yeah, absolutely," Fredericks said. "The people we inter-view will tell us flat out that the Shower supports Seaga and the Spanglers support Manley." But he still thought that the gangs had relinquished their political loyalties once they migrated to the United States. "They're more interested in buying Mercedes-

Benzes than in sending money home to the PNP or the JLP," he said.

I didn't say anything about what I had heard to the contrary. We talked for the rest of the time about the posse geography of downtown Kingston—which streets spawned which gangs—while I kept the names of living gunmen to myself, sensing that the ATF was already on their trails.

Six days later the *Daily News* reported yet another posse shooting at a Brooklyn disco called Love People One. A policeman was wounded in the crossfire, and his partner remarked that "the place is like Vietnam. The young toughs show up there to show off their gold and their BMWs. Three things interest these guys: guns, drugs, and cars."

Love People One was the place where Southside's Delroy Edwards and his Renkers posse gathered to drink, dance, and snort their coke; the disco had once been a funeral parlor, but now it was one of Brooklyn's hottest clubs. I told Brambles about the Renkers shooting when he made his weekly phone call to me from Brooklyn Corner in Southside.

"That bredda get too-too bad now," he said, speaking of Delroy with a trace of rueful admiration. He'd recently seen Delroy in Southside when the don came back for a visit and brought money and guns. Brambles described the treat Delroy staged for the Southside people, a street dance and a carnival the sufferers called a "Coney Island," with rides for kids. The money for the treat had come from crack; Delroy and the Renkers were having their brief run with glory, selling as much as $50,000 worth of the stuff on a good day, and lately there had been a lot of good days up in Brooklyn.

But they were numbered. By the autumn of 1987, police and federal agents were closing in on Delroy and the Renkers because the posse was killing too many people. As Brambles woefully put it, "Sometimes you can find men who just think reasonable-like and mek money." But the posse entrepreneurs were not known for their business skills alone; they were all too fond of firepower and murder, and this always brought down the heat.

Violence went with the territory of the drug world, a nasty, necessary strategy for controlling ever-fractious troops and defending turf from other dealers. The temptation of fast money meant that the soldiers themselves—like the corrupt cops who shook them down—were always looking for a chance to go out on their own. Loyalty was a scarce commodity within the posse ranks. And when the dons resorted to violence to discipline their troops, some of the soldiers started going to the police with information; if they informed, they might get a lighter prison sentence in return for cooperating. Once the cops were able to flip one or two gang members it was only a matter of time before they could rope in the don.

The Renkers gang, though vicious, was nothing like some of the other Jamaican posses—bigger syndicates like the Shower killed many more people—but in the pantheon of New York street gangs the Renkers were unusually violent. Delroy and his henchmen killed six people and wounded seventeen others in three years. The first assault was in the spring of 1985, when Delroy stabbed a man in a subway stairwell. In November 1986 he shot three gang members near a Renkers crack house on Pacific Street after the men stole his money and drugs. In January 1987 Delroy and his troops laid siege to a rival posse's crack spot and set it on fire, shooting and wounding a woman inside. The month of March 1987 was outstanding for its violence. On the eighteenth police found the frozen corpse of Norman Allwood in a garbage bag; Allwood was the seventeen-year-old Renkers soldier who'd been beaten to death months before, after Delroy accused him of stealing money. A week later the Renkers shot two men from a rival posse as they sat in a parked car. Then they went on a drive-by shooting rampage on Saratoga Avenue in which, miraculously, only one man died. There were six more shootings in Brooklyn that spring.

By the summer of 1987 Delroy's ambitions were moving beyond Brooklyn. He wanted to branch out to Washington, D.C. His uncle, Kenneth Manning, had the same idea; he started stealing crack from Delroy and giving it to two Renkers soldiers in Washington to sell. Delroy never suspected Manning of this treachery, but he knew that the two men in Washington were fouling up. So he ordered Manning to kill them, and Manning obeyed. He murdered one of his erstwhile partners himself, then got another Renkers man to kill the other.

Delroy's last killing was at Love People One on a night in September 1987 when a youth named Sean Thompson accidentally stepped on Delroy's foot. The teenager didn't know who he was dissing, and when the don ordered him to apologize, Thompson just walked out of the club. Delroy shot him on the sidewalk.

By then this litany of violence had become so familiar in city ghettos that it had taken on a trancelike quality. To the police it was business as usual, an inevitable by-product of the drug world. But in February 1988 another kind of homicide—a drug-related assassination, in Queens, of one of their own—galvanized the New York police into a brief war on crack dealers around the city. Delroy Edwards had nothing to do with this slaying, but it coincidentally brought about his own downfall.

The victim was a rookie officer, Edward Byrne. He was killed as he sat in a parked squad car, guarding the home of a witness in the upcoming trial of an African-American drug lord named Lorenzo "Fat Cat" Nichols. Delroy Edwards knew Fat Cat—he sometimes bought powder cocaine from the Queens dealer—and he also knew Fat Cat's associate, Pappy Mason, who was later indicted along with Nichols for the Byrne killing. Mason had grown up in Brooklyn and done prison time in the late seventies with several Jamaican dealers; he thought of the borough as his own turf, and he'd tried at one point to invade some drug territory that was controlled by another Jamaican posse, the Gully.

By the time of the Byrne killing, detectives from Brooklyn North Homicide had been tracking Delroy Edwards for years and hearing about his exploits from a string of informants. They were also familiar with Delroy as one of the drug dealers who had been shaken down by rogue cops from Brooklyn's 77th Precinct. This story broke in 1986 after several of the 77th's "buddy boys" had been poaching in Edwards' territory for some time, stealing money, drugs, and guns from his apartment in Crown Heights. All things considered, it was time to take Delroy out.

Bill Fredericks said later that the SWAT team—two dozen federal agents and New York police officers—"looked like the Third Marine Corps division hitting a street corner." Delroy surrendered without a fight and went into custody at Rikers Island.

The Southside sufferers knew about the bust by that evening. Joseph Manning told Brambles the news, and he called me from the corner. Brambles had no particular fondness for Delroy, but he was nevertheless bitter about his downfall; he thought Delroy was small game.

"Why them never arrest Jim Brown?" he shouted into the phone. "Why them never arrest Vivian Blake?"

"But they've tried," I said. "You know the reason—they're Seaga's men."

Miami's Metro-Dade police—along with ATF, the Immigra-

tion and Naturalization Service (INS), and the Drug Enforcement
Administration—had been after Lester "Jim Brown" Coke since
1987, after authorities finally linked him to the 1984 murders of
six people in Miami; they learned who Jim Brown was only after
they'd arrested another Shower accomplice in Miami who flipped
and told them about the 1984 slayings. At the same time, they
realized that Brown was the man who had killed twelve people
in the 1984 attack on the Rema ghetto in Kingston. So he was
picked up by the INS and deported to Jamaica, but Seaga was
prime minister and his protection made Jim Brown untouchable.
Soon after he returned to the island, Brown killed the driver of
a Kingston minibus; when it looked as if nothing was going to
be done about this, the city's bus drivers went on strike. Their
protest brought about Brown's arrest, but he was soon acquitted
because no one was foolish enough to testify against him.

Vivian Blake, meanwhile, was shuttling back and forth between Miami and New York, running drugs for the Shower.
Federal agents estimate that between 1984 and 1987 the posse
moved roughly 300,000 pounds of ganja and 20,000 pounds of
cocaine north from Miami. Most of it went to New York, where
some was then redistributed to the Shower's branches in Toronto, Philadelphia, and Maryland. But Blake also had his hands
full in Miami: there was an ongoing war between the Shower
and the Spanglers in South Florida, just as there was in New
York. The Spanglers were based in Fort Lauderdale, under the
leadership of Tony Welch—the former don of Concrete Jungle—and a man named Kenneth Black, who had donated
$100,000 to the PNP in 1986 at the party's annual conference
in Montego Bay.

Blake had so far evaded arrest; he was more polished than Jim
Brown and looked like a businessman in his silk suits with a
neatly folded white handkerchief in the left breast pocket, over

his heart; Kingston people said the handkerchief was a talisman against obeah. Blake and Brown were strange bedfellows and their alliance was an uneasy one. Brown was pure "ragamuffin," as Jamaicans put it—a sufferer born and bred in the ghetto—but Blake came "from good table." His father had been a trusted adviser to the PNP, and part of Blake's legend has it that he went to Columbia University to study and play soccer but soon left to sell drugs. He was the Shower's financial brain, and although the Tivolites saw Jim Brown as their "don-gadda," the truth was that without Vivian Blake, Brown would have had nothing. Despite his privileged background, Blake moved easily in Jim Brown's world of terminator-terrorists. Two of his half-brothers were executioners for the Shower, Kirk "Black Tony" Bruce and Errol "Kong" Hussing. Bruce alone confessed to a staggering total of eighty-seven murders when he was finally arrested in 1988, after he and two other men from the Shower killed three men and a woman in Landover, Maryland.

So Brambles had a point when he said that Delroy Edwards and the Renkers were nowhere near as deadly as these Shower men. On the phone that night he was simply closing ranks with a fellow sufferer who'd been roped in by cops. "Delroy's nothin' but a fryer," he said. "Him never reach the heights whey' them say." When I told him that Delroy and the Renkers were charged with six murders, he refused to believe this was true. But I was in no mood to fight. I missed him, and I missed the work we'd done in Kingston.

I went back that summer for a few weeks, but it wasn't like the old times. Brambles was poorer than ever; the Jamaica Information Service wasn't giving him assignments anymore, and he wondered if this was because he had associations there with the Manley years. Seaga's press corps was full of new faces: American-trained media experts who were skilled at public relations and knew how to hype the economic "miracle" that Seaga was working on the island. Brambles was a different breed of photojournalist.

Without a steady income and with two children to support, he talked that summer about leaving Kingston and finding work in the States. He didn't want to join his brother, a drug dealer in South Florida; he wanted to try New York. "There's nothing for me here on the Rock," he said. "Mek I go a' foreign like everyone else with any sense."

The streets of Southside bore him out; Renkers graffiti covered every bullet-pocked wall, proclaiming Delroy as the ghetto's godfather, and the sufferers were smoking crack in sullen witness to the drug's deadly power. It seemed that a fresh sense of hopelessness had claimed the streets, now that Seaga was in control and the police were executing sufferers like pariah dogs. The drug dons wheeled through Southside in their flashy red rental cars, their well-fed bodies hung with gold "cow-rope" necklaces, and the boom boxes thundered the indomitable rule of the gunmen and the guns.

Delroy's uncle in Southside, Joseph Manning, asked me if maybe I could write "something positive" about Delroy. I told him I had to wait until he came to trial. He was going to be prosecuted under the federal RICO statute, the first Jamaican posse leader to receive that honor; the feds were serious about this case. But Joe didn't wait for the slow wheels of the justice system to turn. Just before Christmas he bought Brambles a ticket to New York. All of our hopes converged: Brambles was looking for work, Joe was thinking I could redeem his nephew with some friendly reporting, and I wanted to start penetrating the posse underground in Brooklyn, ideally with Brambles at my side.

He landed at JFK on a freezing night, and I met him with an armful of warm clothes. He gave me a quick, tentative hug, making light of what I thought was a momentous reunion. Both of us hunched our shoulders when we walked outside into the assault of a New York winter night. "Jesus-peace," Brambles muttered against the icy wind that blew off Jamaica Bay. "Is nuff-nuff respect I 'ave now fi' disya ras-clot climate. You people up here mus' haffi' be strong fi' survive."

Brambles had an aunt in the Bronx whom he stayed with that first winter, in an overcrowded apartment where a floating array of Jamaican relatives bunked on the floors. But he quickly found a job at a Madison Avenue graphics sweatshop that ran on the labor of Caribbean illegals. He worked twelve-hour days for a hundred dollars a week, his blood pressure soaring and his back slowly getting wrecked from operating the heavy presses, but he managed to send most of his money home to his children.

After a few weeks I realized that he wasn't going to take me under his wing as he had in Kingston. I wanted to start moving with him through the Crown Heights territory in Brooklyn that Delroy had ruled, but Brambles refused to go to various posse hot spots. He was rightly afraid of getting caught in crossfire or in trouble with the New York police. But he'd promised Joseph Manning that he would go to Rikers to see Delroy, and that was a promise he kept.

The day of that first visit was so bitter that our feet were stung into numbness as we waited for the prison bus, on Fifty-ninth Street under the cables of the Roosevelt Island tramway. The other passengers were mostly sad-eyed women and their children; one of the younger women happened to be Delroy's girlfriend from Brooklyn. She told us that her name was Janice and that she was born in Barbados. "Look like the daughter come from good table," Brambles said, quietly so that she couldn't hear him. "Is a pity she get mixed up in this bizness."

Her face tried to be pretty, but it was too hard. She was all dressed up despite the cold, wearing enormous gold door-knocker earrings and a headful of ringlets. On the bus Brambles began teasing her about Delroy's many baby-mothers in Kingston, and she turned her head away in silent rage. When we were halfway to Rikers he gave me a little warning about Delroy.

"You is not to go in there an ax question like you know him is guilty, you hear? Or he won't say a word. I don't care what you read in the *Daily News* or what you know from Joe an' me. Jus cool, understand?"

He gazed out the window at the Greek delis and gaudy clothing stores of Queens.

"He was a fryer, that's all," Brambles said. "And the Renkers was never a posse like Seaga's Shower massive. You see, posse is a political thing. When you say posse, is like you 'ave a drugs bizness goin' on in America, an' so you send for your political affiliates. All the original posses have them political links. And then you 'ave people who come up here, like Delroy. Yes, them is PNP or JLP and them organize in a drugs bizness. But that is just a syndicate, a crew.

"The reason I know Delroy never run a direct posse is because him never send for none of the key people in South. So him cyan' be that big, really. Him never reach that stage. Yeah, some o' the men in the Brooklyn Renkers crew came from South, but most o' them was Yankee boys, and some even come from PNP areas like Dunkirk and Franklin Town and Matthews Lane."

He thought back to the days when he first knew Delroy, before the JLP gave him guns, and he called Delroy "an impressionist," meaning that he was just a charismatic thug who had a sufferer's camaraderie with those around him.

"But he turned into a monster in the 1980 time," Brambles said. "And when him come up here, was like him could never really get enough. Him haffi' prove himself all over again. There was always an agonizing frustration. Seem like some o' the things them say he did in Brooklyn, he did them fi' get back fi' the way things was at home."

I asked him whether he believed that Delroy had done all of the killings he was accused of. "Delroy don' haffi' kill nobody," he answered, dismissing my credulity with a withering glance. "Me tell you how the killin' really goes. When you is a don, inna' your work, a youth might hear some lickle joke 'pon you. And without you even tell him to go an' kill the joker, he will jus' do it, jus' fi' big-up himself in your eyes. Jus' fi' mek himself into a notch."

Brambles paused to screw up his face and suck his teeth in a dazzling imitation of rude-boy viciousness. "An' then he will come to you an' say, 'Boss, disya' bumba-clot bwoy *dead!* The stinkin' blood-clot bwoy *dead!*' So you see now how it really a' go? If you is a coke don an' a nex' mon come rob your stash, your soldier will jus' kill him fi' defend you. So most o' them killin' where you hear go on with Delroy, him nah' even haffi' tell him youth fi' do them thing. When you is a don, a youth jus' go kill fi' you, fi' please you. Delroy wouldn't want to hot-up himself personally."

We were crossing the arched bridge across the bay to Rikers and his voice was all but drowned out by the roar of jets taking off from LaGuardia. We were herded into a dingy waiting room that was not much warmer than the island outside; prison guards and hyperkinetic children went in and out, bringing gusts of cold air with them. The room was blue with cigarette smoke and it echoed with coughs and crying. An hour passed before we heard our names called. Then we walked through metal detectors and onto a bone-rattling bus that took us out to the maximum-security compound where Delroy was. His girlfriend mentioned that he'd just been hurt in a knife fight with another inmate.

The guards made us open our mouths to check for drugs, and then they let us through clicking metal doors into a small visiting room. There was a joyous reunion going on in one corner between Larry Davis and his family. After being accused of a murder, Davis had single-handedly held off an assault by police in Harlem. By the time he was arrested, his stature on the street rivaled Mike Tyson's. He was the don of Rikers.

Delroy was sitting by himself at a table, watching Larry Davis like a jealous hawk. But his face broke into a smile when he spotted his girlfriend and Brambles. The two men greeted each other with such cool style that it seemed like they'd just parted the night before in Southside. Brambles introduced me as a journalist who knew Joseph Manning, then said that I knew the Southside runnin's and was writing a book about the posses. Delroy gave me a quizzical stare, but he seemed not to mind that I was there.

He was thirty-one then and handsome, in a baby-faced way; he had small, pert features and dark skin. The only clues to his warrior's life were a face flecked with dozens of tiny scars and a wariness in his eyes, the same look I saw in the photograph Brambles had taken of Copper in prison. Even when he smiled, Delroy's eyes had the faraway, affectless gaze of a gunman who got old when he was still young. His body was thick with prison weight lifting and his forearms bulged out of the standard gray jumpsuit. It looked even more drab because he was wearing jewelry: a gold cuff bracelet and a diamond stud in one ear. I imagined how good he must have looked to women on the dance floor at Love People One, and how terrifying to Norman Allwood as he cowered in that cold Brooklyn basement a few hours from death.

Brambles and I turned away for a while so that Delroy and his girlfriend could talk and kiss. When we came back, the three of us began talking casually about Southside. Soon Delroy was reminiscing, with gallows humor, about 1980 and the day when he and Trinity were shot at. They had been riding in a JLP motorcade up South Camp Road when someone started shooting from the PNP housing project. Delroy's eyes sparkled at the memory of this excitement. He was thrown from the Jeep when Trinity ordered the driver to put on some speed, and Joe Manning took him to a hospital uptown; Delroy said it would have been crazy for him to go to Kingston Public Hospital, where gunmen sometimes shot their enemies as they lay in bed.

This turn in the conversation made me bold. Despite Brambles's warning not to ask Delroy anything about his criminal career, I brought up the 1980 election. To my surprise, he volunteered the information that it was Ryan Peralto, the JLP's candidate for Southside, who had paid him sixty dollars a week (about ten American dollars) to fire shots for the party.

I let my breath out and said that sixty dollars didn't sound like much money for such dangerous work. Delroy shot me the same nonplussed look as the one I'd gotten from Roddy Nesbeth, the survivor of the Green Bay massacre, when I'd said that the three hundred dollars he was supposed to get from the army wasn't much either. I kept forgetting how little it took to hire a paladin in the ghettos.

"Is the politicians who first bring the guns into that place," Delroy said of Southside. "But all they ever did for us was tell us where to throw stone and lick shot." Then he laughed. "You'll never get the big-men-them to talk about their part in the political wars. But just know that Seaga is the biggest gangster of them all."

Before we left, Brambles told Delroy that I would cover his

trial. He didn't seem to care, one way or the other; he knew that his chances for acquittal were nil. He'd beaten many raps, including murder, and the only prison time he'd done was in 1985, after police in Penn Station caught him with a gun on his way to Philadelphia. But now he knew that the cops had all of his former Renkers men in custody, and every one had flipped.

"When they see a Jamaican come through the system so many times and they never hold him yet, they're bound to get him one day," Delroy said philosophically.

His luck had run out.

The Anatomy
of a Posse

That winter faded reluctantly into a typical New York spring, dreary months when the dream of warmth only teased. Brambles got sick again and again, coughing through one siege of bronchitis after another. When his boss refused to give him a raise, he started moonlighting for his friend Rockeye Nesbeth from Southside, who had an apartment in Crown Heights where he sold crack. His spot was up the street from Delroy's former base on Rogers Avenue, and it was doing a brisk business now that the posse don's arrest had opened up the street to other dealers.

"We took out his competition," sighed Harry Malone, a dark-haired, mustachioed detective from Brooklyn North Homicide working on the Edwards case. Malone explained that the Renkers had fought what he called "a war on two fronts," contending for drug turf with a troop of African-American dealers called the Wild Bunch and another Jamaican outfit, the McGregor Gully posse. The Gully was based on the corner of Sterling Place and Schenectady Avenue in Crown Heights, a few blocks west of Delroy's corner, and it was still going strong. The posse came from a PNP neighborhood of the same name in Kingston, and its political affiliation made it a natural enemy to the JLP Renkers. The war between the two posses turned the corner of Sterling and Schenectady into a battleground.

The constant competition for drug turf not only raised the level of gun violence on the street, it also lowered the price of crack. Malone remembered the early days when a vial sold for twenty dollars, and Delroy started competing with his rivals by offering two-for-one specials on weekends and holidays. Now Rockeye was selling vials for three and five dollars. Crack often replaced money as a medium of exchange: Brambles sometimes traded a few vials for things that buyers had stolen, like Walkmans and videotapes. For a woman in dire need of a smoke, the price of a vial was a blow job.

On the freezing stairwells of derelict brownstones along Rogers Avenue, the dealers hunkered down in sweatshirts and goose down trench coats. Inside the buildings, crackheads loaded their stems and beamed up for a few seconds of euphoria. But even with its grimness, Rogers Avenue somehow reminded me of Central Kingston, perhaps because it had the same aura of faded gentility—a fresh layer of despair laid down over former dreams. The neighborhood had been home to generations of newcomers: Jews from Eastern Europe, African-Americans from the South, and West Indian immigrants. They had taken loving care of the brownstones and turned some of them into elegant homes. But now Crown Heights was bursting at the seams with the children of other diasporas. The Lubavitch Hasidic Jews sequestered themselves on the southern side of Eastern Parkway and the northern side was posse territory.

Delroy had lived above a grocery store on the corner of Rogers Avenue and Lincoln Place, a block north of the parkway. The windows were empty eyes now, but its second story of faded yellow siding reminded me of a dwelling perched above a downtown Kingston rumshop. It was there that Delroy's father, a tailor nicknamed "Lloyd-Pants," had lived when he came up from Jamaica and began selling ganja from the back room of the store, and it was there that someone murdered him in 1982, soon after his son arrived from Southside. Delroy was tried and acquitted for the murder of a man who he said had killed Lloyd, but the word on the street was that Delroy murdered his father and then took over his ganja business.

From the grocery store you could look straight down Rogers Avenue across the East River to Manhattan, where the art deco corona of the Chrysler Building glittered in the pale winter sunlight. "The Land of Oz," Brambles said one afternoon as we stood gazing at this view by the pay phone on the corner that served as an outdoor office for the Jamaican dealers. Their "Yankee-boy" competitors worked the corner a block north; the two cadres coexisted most of the time, but not always.

It was almost time for Brambles to start the evening shift at Rockeye's, so we got some chicken, rice, and peas from Joy's Restaurant and headed for the crack house. A steel door opened off the stairwell into the second-floor apartment, where every window was boarded over; the only light came from bare ceiling bulbs and votive candles that flickered on the mantelpiece, tables, and windowsills. They were meant to ward off obeah and the police—a gesture from Rockeye's wife, who was intensely superstitious. "You ever see so much candle inna' your life?" Brambles asked, shrugging off his jacket and checking to make sure that the 9 mm was still under the couch cushions where Rockeye kept it. "Tall candle, round candle, square candle. You wonder how is any oxygen left in the place fi' breathe."

The walls were decorated with religious iconography from Woolworth's. There was a picture of a blond Jesus praying in

Gethsemane and a Catholic image of the Virgin with her blue robe opened to a heart on fire. A funeral parlor calendar was turned to a photograph of Martin Luther King, Jr., with part of his "I Have a Dream" speech printed beneath.

Jesus, Mary, and Martin gazed down on the little table by the couch where the crack vials sat in plastic bowls. The steel door to the hallway started pounding with a buyer's knocks; Brambles slipped the vial out and took the money in through a peephole. He said business was good—the place sometimes made as much as one thousand dollars a day—but of course none of this was his to keep. Rockeye paid him when he felt like it, maybe ten or twenty dollars for a night's work. Brambles hated what he was doing.

"I haffi' bleach now like a crackhead," he grumbled. "An' then they thank me, so mannerly-like, when I sell them this poison."

He filled the hours with reading. He loved *The Nation*, and he also pored over New York's dailies and the African-American papers. But his glaucoma was getting worse, and he dreaded the day when he might be unable to read.

Across Brooklyn and Queens, on the other side of freedom, Delroy Edwards was languishing in Rikers and waiting for his trial. I went to see him often, without Brambles now, and took him body-building magazines and hair-care kits. He was wearing his hair in the style of the moment, a jheri-curled "fade" shaved close on the sides with short curls on top. He was always glad to see me and would give me a broad kiss, for the benefit of the other inmates. But we never got into any deep talk, because his lawyer had ordered him not to discuss his case.

In Brooklyn Federal Court, Judge Raymond J. Dearie was hearing pretrial testimony from fifteen Renkers men who had flipped for the prosecution in hopes of lighter sentences for themselves. Judge Dearie was a slight, puckish man who was learning some new things on this case: how to decipher Jamaican patois and how to stay unprejudiced when Kenneth Manning told him that he'd paid an obeah woman fifteen thousand dollars to put a death curse on the judge. Manning's pretrial testimony was chilling enough anyway.

"Mr. Edwards' uncle is my brother, so we is like family," Manning told Judge Dearie, speaking of his relationship to Joseph Manning from Southside. "I never really got a job. I just around Mr. Edwards. Like, if he wanted to make drugs, I help him make drugs, and if somebody need a driver to shoot somebody, I say let's drive together."

Detectives from Brooklyn North Homicide were shuttling Renkers inmates back and forth between upstate prisons and Brooklyn to testify before the judge. The price of their information often included late-night dinners of jerk chicken, with the detectives buying, and conjugal visits to girlfriends while the officers waited in their cars. Not surprisingly, friendships sometimes developed between the detectives and the posse men. "I've never had a bond with a gang like I do with these guys," Harry Malone confessed during a lull in the proceedings. "I'd have a hard time remembering they were going back to jail."

Malone got especially close to a young man named Elvis Mortimer, one of the Renkers soldiers whom he called "Delroy's push-buttons" because they did whatever the don said. But now the don was as good as dead, and his soldiers were facing the justice system on their own.

"Elvis would call me, just to talk, at two and three in the morning," Malone said. "My wife asked me when I was going to adopt him." He shook a cigarette out of a crumpled pack and lit it. "You know, that's the thing about these Jamaicans. They're very winning. If you had a chance to alter their lives, with the personalities they already had, they would have been nice guys. Unfortunately, Delroy got to them first."

Malone sat forward on the hard wooden bench and took a color photograph from his wallet. It was a picture of the corpse of Devon Steer, one of the cousins Kenneth Manning executed in Washington after he'd set them up to sell the drugs he had stolen from Delroy. Steer's head was blown apart by the point-blank shot Manning fired from the rear seat of the car in which they were riding. I winced at the photograph, and Malone looked gratified. "This is what these guys were ultimately about," he said. "I guess I have some trouble remembering that sometimes."

A flurry of publicity surrounded the posses as Delroy's trial approached. The Treasury Department had drawn up a list with some twenty thousand names of Jamaicans living in this country, some of whom had been arrested for nothing more serious than a traffic violation. District Attorney Robert M. Morgenthau was using the list to help prosecute suspected posse members, and Jamaicans in New York were infuriated by this stigmatization of a primarily law-abiding and hardworking people. They sought help from the American Civil Liberties Union, which argued that the list violated the civil rights of all Jamaicans in this country.

"What we object to," said Una Clarke, head of the newly formed Jamaican Committee on Civil Rights, "is using the word Jamaican in front of drug gangs. No one says Italian Mafia or Irish Westies"—the name of a notorious Irish gang in the Hell's Kitchen district of Manhattan's West Side—"so they shouldn't say Jamaican drug posses either."

But others were probing the links between Jamaica's highest-ranking politicians and the island's drug posses: in April 1988 Edward Seaga's name was called in a Congressional committee investigating Caribbean drug trafficking. The name-caller was a convicted marijuana smuggler, Michael Vogel, who said, "You can't operate like the people I know were operating without the head of that island knowing what's happening." Vogel's testimony brought a flurry of denials from Seaga and other Jamaican officials.

Less than a year later, Michael Manley became prime minister after a relatively peaceful election in which only about two dozen people died. He had come to New York before the election to drum up support from the Jamaican community there, and I spoke with him after he'd given another one of his charismatic speeches at Columbia University. We sat down on a rickety classroom table that kept threatening to break, and he joked about the world slipping out from under us. When I asked him about the posses, though, he lowered his mellow voice to say that they were "terribly real" and not just some figment of the American imagination. But he was obviously hoping to avoid this subject; his most pressing task was to repair the breach between Washington and the PNP by declaring that he was no longer the fiery socialist of the 1970s. He went to visit George Bush at the White House and proclaimed that "socialism is dead."

Washington responded by cutting the repentant Manley some slack, and federal authorities backed off from their earlier statements about links between the posses and Jamaica's politicians. "Nobody in Jamaica is benefiting from the posses' activities in the United States," said James A. Williams, an attaché with the Drug Enforcement Administration in Kingston. "The money made by Jamaican narcotics traffickers in the U.S. stays in the U.S."

The New York press wasn't quite as restrained about the posses when Delroy's trial opened in the summer of 1989. The *Post* ran a story under an inch-tall headline: JAMAICAN GOT CITY HOOKED ON CRACK. Federal prosecutors Jonny Frank and John

Gleeson—who was second seat in the 1986 trial of Mafia don John Gotti—told the jury that "Delroy Edwards deserves a special place in history as one of the first drug dealers to introduce crack to the streets of New York."

The defendant listened glumly, wearing a dark gray suit and a maroon tie, which looked strange with his haircut. His court-appointed lawyer, David Gordon, stood up after John Gleeson finished and instructed the jury not to find Edwards guilty just because his associates were "vicious, ruthless, horrible people." With admirable understatement Gordon acknowledged, "This is an upsetting case."

I was sitting between the *Newsday* columnist Jimmy Breslin and a powerfully built Jamaican with a cleanly shaved head. He was wearing paint-splattered work clothes and told me that he'd come to hear the opening summations from his contracting job on Long Island. He introduced himself as Conti Thomas; the "Conti" was short for "Continental," which meant that he was a ladies' man with style.

Whispering from time to time, Conti said he'd been a close friend of Delroy's father and that he knew Delroy had killed him. "I didn't come here to support Uzi," he said. "I come to watch him meet his doom. Everything they goin' to testify to in this court, we knew it 'pon the street long time now. That posse was nothing but scavengers. I'm here to listen 'bout how these guys squandered what they had."

One of the first witnesses was Paul Taylor, Delroy's brother-in-law, who testified about the day when three officers from the 77th Precinct raided the apartment on Rogers Avenue and stole a .38 pistol, a large bag of marijuana, and fourteen hundred dollars in cash. Prosecutor Jonny Frank asked Taylor if the police had given him a receipt, and his "no" was lost in the laughter that erupted in the courtroom. Then Taylor described how Delroy had cut his face with a knife when Taylor tried to tell him that he wasn't the thief. "Edwards didn't treat his employees well," John Gleeson had advised the jury in his opening remarks. "He didn't pay them. He beat them. He shot them."

The litany of beatings, shootings, and stabbings became monotonous after only a few days of testimony. Sometimes the sheer monotony had an impact of its own, however, coupled as it was with a cool affectlessness that stunned the jury. When Kenneth Manning described killing Devon Steer, one of his soldiers in Washington, it sounded like the steps of a recipe.

"I shoot him in the head," he told John Gleeson.

"Where in his head?" asked Gleeson.

"Back of his head."

"How many times did you shoot him?"

"Once."

The driver of the car panicked when Steer's corpse got wedged in the front seat, but Manning managed to dislodge it as they drove and dumped it down an incline. Then he told the driver to set fire to the car.

"What did you do after you found out that the evidence was burned?" Gleeson asked.

"I don't do nothing. I go to sleep," Manning answered.

After the trial was over, a female juror told me that this remark had frightened her so badly that she couldn't sleep for three days.

The jurors had a similar response to testimony about the murder of Norman Allwood, the African-American teenager who was beaten and tortured to death in a crack house basement. Both Kenneth Manning and Conroy Green were there that night and they described the murder in grisly detail: how Allwood had begged for mercy while Manning poured boiling water over him, and how Conroy Green had stood off to one side, trying not to listen to his pleas. The lawyers held a sidebar conference with

Judge Dearie about the photographs of Allwood's corpse; by this time the jury was so rattled that David Gordon requested they not be shown the color shots.

There were very few Renkers victims who were still alive to testify; one of them was a soft-eyed Jamaican named Rudolph Simms. He wheeled himself to the stand, paralyzed from the waist down by a bullet from one of Delroy's gunmen. Simms had made the mistake of going to a grocery store near the corner of Sterling Place and Schenectady Avenue one night for a "hot dragon"—unchilled stout. He had hung out with the McGregor Gully posse, who controlled that corner, but he happened to be there at the wrong time. The Gully had just done a drive-by shooting on the Renkers, and Delroy wanted revenge. So he ordered a soldier named Stanley McCall to go to the Gully corner and shoot "anyone who looks Jamaican." That was Rudolph Simms.

"I shot him two or three times," McCall said coldly. "Then I turned around to where Delroy was watching from across the street. When I got back to the car, he said, 'You see that man you shot? When he fell, you should have gone up and put the gun to his head.' "

Someone from the Gully posse later told me that Simms's nickname was "Pleasure." His brother is the reggae singer Sugar Minott, and he used to do the soundboard at Sugar's performances. At the end of his testimony, Jonny Frank got him to admit, in a voice just above a whisper, that because of his injury he would never be able to make love again. A collective sigh rippled through the courtroom and the woman next to me groaned.

I went upstairs to the district attorney's office with Simms and his sister. He sat in his wheelchair, mopping sweat from his brow beneath a jaunty leather cap of red, gold, green, and black cut into sections like a soccer ball. I asked him whether he could still work the soundboard for his brother. "Sometimes," he said, a tired smile momentarily lighting up his face. Then he looked down at his crumpled legs. "But nuff-nuff things pass me by now."

The trial lasted more than a month, but David Gordon called only one witness for the defense—an expert who testified that the voice on a certain tape recording made by undercover police might not actually have been Delroy's, setting up a Renkers drug deal. By the time the trial concluded, the jury had become accustomed to the grisly details of a posse's world.

"In the opening phase, that courtroom was so tense you could almost sense the jury stopped breathing," Judge Dearie later told a reporter. "The sharpness got out of it real fast, and we adjusted to the violence." The reporter said the judge "compares the adaptation he perceives in himself and the jurors to the adaptation the defendants must have made to actual events."

The jury found Edwards guilty on all forty-two counts of the indictment, and they were so nervous after delivering their verdict that the foreman asked if anything would be done to protect them from reprisal. Judge Dearie later sentenced Delroy Edwards to 501 years without parole and, for good measure, gave him a federal fine of over $1 million. The rest of the Renkers defendants went to jail.

One of them was Conroy Green, the soft-spoken posse enforcer who was present at the Allwood slaying and also confessed to killing three of the Renkers' other victims. After the trial was over, Harry Malone gave Green my phone number, and he started to call me from the prison in upstate New York. He put me on his list of visitors, which took some time to be cleared by the prison authorities, because Green was in the federal witness-protection program. Just before Labor Day he called to say that I could come meet him.

The guards left us alone in an empty visiting room, its windows tilted open to the sound of birdsong from the yard. We began talking about his youth in Kingston and what it had been like to grow up in the PNP neighborhood of Dunkirk. Brambles had a brother who lived there, so he and I used to drink in its rumshops from time to time.

Conroy remembered the neighborhood as a fairly peaceful place, until the 1970s, when it started fracturing along the usual political fault lines. He had watched his Dunkirk friends get sucked into the violence, but his hardworking parents had done their best to keep him out of trouble. They saw what was coming before the 1980 bloodbath, so they left Kingston and went to Albany, New York. Conroy joined them just after the election and finished high school and a year of community college then. He had two children with a woman there, and the first serious fight he got into was with a man who had made a pass at her. He came back with a gun.

"Even the youngest youth comin' out of Jamaica, he might never have held a gun," Conroy said, "but if you put him in a situation where he's threatened, he's gonna retaliate in a way that's real cold, like a ragamuffin."

Conroy joined the ragamuffin ranks with a string of arrests for assault and armed robbery; to escape prosecution, he left Albany for Brooklyn in the summer of 1986. His cousin in New York was tight with an executioner from the Shower posse named Karl Dunstrom, also known as "Fabulous." No one knows how many people Fabulous killed, but one ATF agent estimated that it was close to a hundred, after tallying Dunstrom's election-period homicides in Kingston with the murders he later did for the Shower in the United States. Fabulous was finally sentenced to life without parole for his part in killing four people in Landover, Maryland, in 1988.

Although the Renkers posse was distinct from the Shower, both came from the same side of the political fence, and the old ties between Southside and Tivoli Gardens meant that men from these two posses moved easily with one another. So Conroy saw Fabulous from time to time in Brooklyn, and he got to hear Fabulous brag about his work. "Some Jamaicans are truly crazy," Conroy mused. "They think that when you murder, you get big an' broad. Some of them really get high off of it. Some of them do it just for the intimidation."

Conroy's cousin knew Delroy Edwards too, and he introduced Conroy to him in the summer of 1986. At that first meeting Conroy saw only a young Jamaican like himself, who was already a don in Brooklyn, and figured that it wouldn't be that hard to do what Delroy did. He soon joined the Renkers and became the man Delroy relied on to help discipline his unruly soldiers. This discipline sometimes meant murder.

His first killing came when Delroy ordered him to snuff a Renkers worker who'd been selling fake crack and stealing the real thing. "I shot him and I saw him fall," Conroy remembered with a faraway look in his eyes. "Then I was going to shoot him again, but I said 'nah' and got the hell out of there. I drove up to the store to tell Delroy, and his fuckin' face lit up—all I saw was teeth."

I asked Conroy if he felt remorse for what he had done, and he floundered with the question for a while. Then, by way of an answer—and perhaps to convince me and himself that he had not always acted without decency—he told me a story that turned out to be even more chilling than the chronicle of violence he'd already set forth. It was about a robbery in Philadelphia in the summer of 1987, when Delroy had heard about a Jamaican ganja dealer there who supposedly had a huge stash of weed. He sent Kenneth Manning and Conroy Green to steal it.

"We went into this house, and the guy was home. So we tied him up and beat the hell out of him, and still he wouldn't talk. All we got was five bags of marijuana and some guns. The guy kept saying he didn't have any money.

"There was a lady there with a baby, and Kenneth wanted to rape her. Real young baby, maybe six months old. I kept telling Kenneth no, that the police would be on us if he did it, and so we held him back. That was the only thing that stopped him. I was holding that baby the whole time, because his mother was tied up. And he was screaming and panting, and the mother was sitting. Just sitting."

Conroy's dead-cool description of the terror of this mother and her baby was more unsettling to me than the scene itself. "So why did you feel like you had to stop Kenneth from raping her?" I asked, knowing that fear of the cops was not the reason.

"I don't know," Conroy answered, showing some emotion for the first time that day. "Her baby was a boy, a nice little baby. He looked just like my son."

The afternoon shadows were lengthening on the prison lawn and a guard came in to say that our time was almost up. I was still thinking about the effects of living with violence, remembering the reporter who said that perhaps the way Judge Dearie and the jury adapted to hearing about the Renkers viciousness mirrored the defendants' own adaptation. I was struggling to reconcile the stories Conroy had told me with the quiet, reflective man who sat next to me now. So I asked him one last question: if there was something unique about Jamaica's political violence that had conditioned him for the killing he did later in New York.

"Being from Jamaica, you see it growing up," he answered,

"You see it all your life. Even before I killed somebody, I felt like I killed before. . . . When I shot at people, I felt like I did it before. It wasn't like I was trembling and asking, What is this I'm doing? It was like I was into it all along. And I think that's just from social settings, from growing up around all that violence, the way Jamaica was with politics. The way it was when I was just a youth comin' up. And once you get up to New York, you find that being affiliated with Jamaican politics, you get stronger because of the reputation it carries. People respect you more and don't mess with your territory."

The guard returned and I began collecting my notes and tapes. "You know," Conroy said as a parting thought, "the police wouldn't have bothered with us so much if it wasn't for the murders we did. They have this big charade 'bout the war on drugs, but it's only that—a charade."

We hugged good-bye. Conroy mentioned that the West Indian parade down Eastern Parkway was coming up next week. "Go for me," he said.

I went with Brambles, who had never seen the annual Labor Day carnival that draws more than a million revelers to Eastern Parkway. Conti Thomas, the Jamaican boulevardier I'd met at the Renkers trial, called a few nights before the parade and told me to come check him at the basement social club where he played dominoes and drank with his friends. Brambles was overwhelmed by the crowd-bath on the Parkway, so packed with people that we were lifted off our feet and carried along by the throng pressing forward with the floats and the dancers and the steel-pan throb. Fearful about guns in a crowd of such size, he was glad to take refuge in the Hole, Conti's basement spot.

It was cooler down there. Conti was nursing a white rum, pacing himself for the night that lay ahead. There was only one other woman in the room, and I caught her eye. She was arguing passionately with an old Jamaican about the novels of Charles Dickens. "No, mon," she cried above the sounds of a boom box and several domino games. "You're wrong on that, you know. Pip is in *Great Expectations*, not *Oliver Twist*."

I walked over to her and said something disingenuous about A levels in English literature.

"What you mean, A levels?" she said, tossing her elegant, fine-boned head. "I went to the University of the West Indies at Mona."

"When?" I asked.

"I got my degree in 1975," she answered, breaking into a grin, "before you were born."

Her name was Shenda and she was just six years younger than I, but the years in Brooklyn had aged her. Conti tried to draw me aside and say something about her crack smoking, but Shenda gave him a shove and pulled out a chair for me at the table where she was sitting. I asked her where she'd grown up, and she said that her people were Maroons from Moore Town, a village in the Blue Mountains, but that her parents had brought her up in the "sleepy green parish of Hanover," halfway between Negril and Montego Bay.

Moore Town is one of the villages founded by the slaves who ran away with Nanny, the legendary chieftainess of the Maroons. Shenda laughed joyously when I repeated the story about how Nanny took the British cannonballs into her pum-pum and fired them back. She had wrapped her head in a traditional bandanna for the parade, and the bare lightbulbs in the club's ceiling were glinting off her high cheekbones. When I told her that she looked very much like the way I imagined Nanny, she stopped laughing. "Let me tell you something," she said softly. "If those ship captains who stole my people out of Africa had had to deal with me, there would have been no slavery. No, mon. Slavery would have died right then and there."

Shenda was living with her Jamaican boyfriend in his mother's brownstone a few blocks away, and she gave me her phone number before Conti motioned Brambles and me over to his domino game. The men were talking about the Renkers trial; they had all known Lloyd Edwards and they were glad that Lloyd's son had gotten his comeuppance at last.

"Delroy Edwards," Conti said, studying the lay of the dominos before he made his next move. "Everybody forget about this guy already. All they want to know is, why all the killing? What did they get out of it? Anywhere you turn—at the racetrack, in the bars—there's nobody to give him sympathy. There's not one man or woman in the street have one good thing to say. Everybody was afraid of them. They destroy more people life than they ever help anybody."

He whacked the wooden table hard with a domino and smiled; he and his partner were going to win this game.

"If you gonna go bust shot, you gonna bust shot 'pon your own brother an' sister. If you gonna make war, go somewhere else. Why black haffi' make war 'gainst black? Why Jamaican haffi' make war 'gainst Jamaican? This whole posse thing is so blind an' dumb an' ignorant. We not dealin' with slavery now. We in America now."

Sesame Street

A few months after our first encounter, Shenda got her marching orders from her boyfriend's mother. The elderly woman had put up with Shenda until her crack habit got in the way, making her volatile and quick to pick a fight. So she started living in her boyfriend's car, a late-model sedan with plush blue-velvet upholstery and a spider-web crack in the windshield. Shenda packed her own heat—a 9 mm—and I thought that she had made the hole with a bullet until she told me she'd put it there with a high-heeled shoe during a fight with her boyfriend.

She parked the car on Rogers Avenue, which she called "Sesame Street," "for the unpredictable theatrics of its inhabitants." Some of the cast lived or hung out in a crack house across the street from Delroy's old base, and Shenda had nicknamed it "the Paupers' Graveyard"; it did seem like the end of the line. But she always considered herself superior to the Graveyard crew, because of her West Indian background and her university education. She thought of her crack smoking as a detour, never a destination—a temporary indulgence that would pass like a fever once she was ready to give it up. "Too much ambition plus not enough education equals disaster" was her formula for explaining Sesame Street.

The Paupers' Graveyard became her base in the bitter winter that followed Delroy's trial; she slept there sometimes and stayed inside during the day to smoke and be warm. The crack house was a four-story brownstone that had once belonged to a prosperous woman from the South who earned her living as a music teacher. She had long since gone into a nursing home, and her grandson had turned this formerly genteel residence into a derelict shell inhabited by a floating array of squatters. But relics of the music teacher's occupancy were everywhere in the Graveyard: ornamental woodwork that was warped now with cold and damp, and two battered pianos that still stood in the upstairs front room. Shenda had taken music lessons as a child in Jamaica, and when she was inspired she played snatches of Mozart and Beethoven on the baby grand. Sometimes a squatter named Dread interrupted her to cook his crack on top of the piano.

Dread lived in one of the upstairs rooms and earned a few dollars by renting it out to girls who gave blow jobs for smoke. But Shenda and I hung out in the garden apartment downstairs; it belonged to a couple, Natalie and Sinclair, who marshaled the Graveyard troops into something that resembled a family. Natalie was a spectral presence, rail thin and hollow-eyed, and she coughed all winter long from pneumonia. She spent most of her days in bed, tucked under a faded red-satin coverlet that gleamed against the dark gray walls of the room. Shenda used to call her "the den mother."

To augment Natalie's welfare checks, Sinclair brought in a little money by fixing electrical appliances for people in the neighborhood. He had wired their apartment with a bandooloo hookup to a light post outside, and it was the only part of the building that had electricity. There was no plumbing either, so everyone relieved themselves in plastic buckets that Natalie kept in a curtained alcove off the bedroom. The back of the Graveyard faced a courtyard behind the Lutheran church around the corner, and sometimes the buckets were emptied there. The bedroom was warmed by a single heater, and on cold days the place was a refuge for dealers who came in to get warm and smokers who needed a place to get high.

"If you call this street by its real name in the book," Shenda said on a very cold afternoon while sharing some crack with Natalie, "the cops are going to shut the whole place down." But she was only joking; we all thought the outside world was past caring what happened on Sesame Street.

Ten or twelve smokers were gathered in the Graveyard that day, huddled around the heater and an elegant old coffee table, topped with smoked blue glass, that had been left behind by the music teacher. They were cooking their own crack in small vials of water and baking soda, looking up every now and then to watch the color television that was tuned to "America's Most Wanted," an afternoon favorite in the basement. The Jamaican posses often turned up on that show, and someone joked that its title referred to us all. Suddenly the wooden door to the hallway outside began pounding, and we heard shouts of, "Open up!"

Everyone froze. I looked at Natalie on the bed, and she gestured for me to open one of the sliding wood panels. They were badly warped, so I had to get down on my knees and push from the bottom. I looked up from the floor into a slit of light from the hallway and the barrel of a gun.

The three cops crashed into the room and held us all at gunpoint. They were undercovers, dressed in acid-washed jeans and grubby sweatshirts, but the bullet-proof vests gave them away. They took in the scene and spied the little piles of crack on the blue glass table. One of them sighed. "OK," he said. "We're not looking for drugs. We heard you're stashing guns here."

Everyone laughed and eased their bodies down into slouches as the cops tore Natalie's bed apart and ripped the cushions from the couch. No guns. They seemed relieved but chagrined, and backed out the door mumbling threats about coming back. The crackheads were lighting their glass stems before the cops were even out on the street.

"We get the message loud and clear," Shenda shouted into the empty hallway. "You see that these are all just black people smoking and blowing their fuckin' minds. No gun people here! So we niggers can just go on smoking ourselves to death." She waved her stem in the air as if she wanted someone in the world to take it away from her.

The police raid united Shenda and me in a kind of conspiratorial bond. Our friendship deepened after that afternoon, and soon she began confiding the story of her life. It came forth in shards of memory, through months and finally years, as I learned to understand her as someone who specialized in the loss of things that were irretrievable: love, family, and homeland.

We had our best talks in Shenda's car, cruising around Crown Heights. We were sitting in the front seat on a raw, rainy day, parked in front of a take-out place with boxes of food on our laps, when she told me about losing her virginity to the only man she had ever loved. "We were childhood sweethearts, Robert and I," Shenda began, almost in a whisper. "I never wanted anyone else. I can still remember the first day he touched me. It was summertime, and nobody was at my house but us. And he just said, 'Today we're going to do this.' And we did."

She went to the university in Kingston and got a degree in English literature; when she and Robert married, Shenda began teaching at a private school in Hanover. Those were her ripest years. Her son was born in 1977, and it seemed like his birth meshed with the promise that Jamaica held in the mid-seventies.

"We had a country that wanted some serious attention," Shenda said. "God, I was idealistic then. . . .

"I was going so good. I was twenty-two years old, I had a house, I had an education, I had a husband and a son. And Robert and I had four years together—we had four beautiful, wonderful, fantastic, unimaginably dreamlike years together. It was a hell of a thing when he died."

He was in a road accident that killed everyone in the car but Robert, who survived with serious injuries. He loved soccer and refused to obey his doctor's orders not to play while he was recovering. One afternoon he was at the field near their house when a ball went out of bounds and he couldn't resist kicking it back in. His spleen ruptured and he died in the hospital in Montego Bay. Shenda was pregnant with twin daughters when Robert died.

"You know, I talk it now, and it's only when I remember the poems I wrote after he died that my pain starts to sting again. It smarts, but it does not burn. I've learned to resolve myself to the pain. But I never got over it, really. It's affected my entire life."

She recited a passage from one of the poems:

I'm going to smash up the schoolhouse where he would play.
I'm going to pray God bring down fire and hail.
I'm going to take out the Bomb, destroy the world.
I'm going to sit in the kitchen, under the shelf
And cry a little, and die a little, all by myself.

We ate our jerk chicken and looked out at the rain peeling down the windshield. "I think a lot of my problems stem from his death. I became bitter about life, saw that it don't have nothin' to offer, so what am I tryin' for? And you know me, with my words! I was flashin' out, trashin' out at everyone. I was cursing God and they tried to stop me from doing that, my mother especially. She said, 'Never question God's goodness, there's a reason in everything.' But I said, '*Reason?* Where could you find a reason in this? I got two babies in my belly and a son who's barely four months old? *Where* is the *reason?*'

"So I said, 'If He's got a reason for this, I don't want to hear it from nobody else. I want Him to come, put Himself in some form so I can hear it live and direct from the source. And if He don't come, I will tell you that He be wicked to me, He hates me.' "

Shenda stayed with her mother until the twins were born. But she had lost the will to "walk good." She stopped teaching and drifted over to Negril, where her genteel manners stood out in the crowd. Soon she was meeting Americans who wanted to smuggle ganja, and she cut herself in on their deals by hooking them up with growers.

Cocaine was already trickling into the sleepy little town, and Shenda met two coke-running American women. One lived in New York, "with trust funds upon trust funds," and she introduced Shenda to a wealthy businessman from New Jersey who paid her way up to New York in 1981. She lived with him for only a few weeks before she moved to Brooklyn and briefly shared a place with the trust-funded cokehead. Shenda's stories about this woman were laced with wild humor; her mother lived at the Dakota, the landmark apartment building on Central Park West, and they used to have long conversations every morning about what to wear.

" 'Should I do the red dress with the gray shoes?' " Shenda trilled. " 'Or the white one with the beige shoes?' I'm sitting there listening to this, wondering where on earth I was. And all

I could think about was my kids. God, I just wanted to hug my kids."

She found jobs as a temporary office worker and stayed with them for a couple of years, until she started to smoke cocaine. "And the rest is history," Shenda said with a bitter laugh.

I admired Shenda for her unapologetic anger at life's indifference, at the way it can deal blows from which some people don't recover. She had no self-pity about her own current predicament; she had chosen this life, and she never doubted that her strength would one day pull her out of it.

When the spring came, we left her car parked in front of the Paupers' Graveyard and walked around Crown Heights—ducking into reggae record shops on Nostrand Avenue to check out the cases full of Ethiopian paraphernalia and stopping at the Korean greengrocers to buy clusters of lime green guineps, which we sucked on as we strolled. Vendors on the corner of Eastern Parkway sold jelly coconuts and tamarind balls rolled in sugar, tall stalks of cane, and sliced pineapple in plastic bags, which made Shenda homesick.

Our route took us by a tiny store where Rastafarians sold goatskin drums and huge leather crowns, big enough to stack dreadlocks underneath. "You see this spot?" Shenda asked. "Well, it used to be a restaurant. The woman who ran it was named Magie, and she was my best friend.

"Everyone on the street knows Magie's story. She came up from Kingston and did fine for the longest time, running this cookshop. Until some dealer showed Magie 'bout cocaine. She fell in love with him and let him stash the stuff at her place, and soon she started dipping into it.

"Well, you know how when you eat one slice of cake, and then another, and then another? And pretty soon you figure you might as well just nyam-up the whole damned thing? So it went. Magie went through seven ounces of this guy's coke, and when he came back he just tied her hands behind her back, stuffed her into a black plastic garbage bag, and threw her off the roof."

Shenda paused to wonder whether Magie could have survived that fall. "If he'd thrown her free-handed, maybe she wouldn't have died. Could have just broken her bones. But if your hands are tied behind you and you're in a bag, you don't see how far you have to go to the ground. Plus, the fear. When you're in a bag, you're disoriented. It's like you're going up a down staircase.

"That was almost four years ago. But I still see Magie's face sometimes like it was yesterday. I remember her, all fat and shiny-eyed, sweating and singing in her restaurant. She was my best friend."

There were so many deaths in the neighborhood that every streetcorner carried the memory of a shooting. On our way back to the Paupers' Graveyard, we passed a corner adorned by a mural with the names of young men and women who had died there. Some of the names were accompanied by dates and faces, surrounded by flickering candles, rainbows, and doves.

There was a killing that spring on Rogers Avenue. One of the Jamaicans in front of Delroy's store shot an African-American dealer who had intruded on their turf. Just before we heard the shots, Shenda had opened the Graveyard's iron gate to one of the Jamaicans from the corner; his name was Luke, and he had sensed trouble and was getting off the street. We stayed in Natalie's room until long after dark, when the police had left and the coroner's van had picked up the body.

Luke was philosophical about the slaying. He had been a soldier in the Jamaica Defense Force in the late 1970s and had seen so much shooting in his Kingston neighborhood that nothing in

Brooklyn fazed him. "We're all here to find a living," he said. "Every mon must eat bread. But is rough out there all the same." Luke's military training gave him disdain for the posse shootists who sprayed bystanders with gunfire; he liked to think that, if the need ever arose, he would have the skill to kill whomever he was after and leave the innocent out of it. The first story he ever told me about the political warfare he had experienced in Kingston involved the shooting of an innocent man.

"It was in 1977, right before the Green Bay killings. My brother was the JLP caretaker for our area, and he had this pair of green Bally shoes that he loved. You know, that was the party's color, but he was the only one in the area who had such fine slippers. There was a guy named Clinton who was getting into all kinds of trouble, breaking into houses and robbing people. So my brother stopped him from doing that and told him he would help him look for work. Clinton asked to borrow my brother's Ballys."

A squad car full of PNP police was just rounding the corner when Clinton walked from his yard. The cops saw him in the green shoes and took him for Luke's brother, the JLP activist they were after. They shot Clinton dead.

"I ran down to the corner and there is this cop from the eradication squad standing over the body and shouting, 'Who him is? Who him is?' So I say, 'You kill the fuckin' mon an' you haffi' turn 'round an' ask who him is? An' he don't do nothin' to you!' "

Luke saw more than his share of such killings. "You don't have to do anything for the cops in Jamaica to kill you," he said. "I saw a friend of mine from Rema die one night. The cops shot him, but he didn't die right away. So they threw him in the car trunk, and he knew they were gonna take him to some other place fi' finish him off, so he was shouting, "Don't let them put me in the trunk! Don't let them put me in the car, 'cause I don't die yet!" But they carried him off and then everybody start to run, from police station to police station, from hospital to hospital. And we didn't find nobody, until the morning came and we heard that he had died."

Luke went into a downtown Kingston club a few weeks later and found the same policemen drinking there. He was about to throw a firebomb into the place when a friend dragged him away.

"So many things like those, it's hard for people to forget. And even if five or ten years go by, and the person who did that killing is not dead, you must do something. Because every time you see him, you remember your friend, or your brother, or whoever it was they killed. It keeps riding you until you got to do something."

I saw Luke often after that day; whenever I went to check Brambles at his spot or Shenda at the Graveyard, Luke would be selling his crack in the stairwell next-door to Delroy's old place. One night a little party of us went down to a posse bar called the Bucket to eat the spicy boiled lobster that the chef there cooked every Tuesday. Brambles and Shenda were in high spirits, warmed by white rum and music, but Luke was under a cloud. He owed his supplier two thousand dollars and was worried that he might run into him at the Bucket.

Luke's man did catch up with him a few weeks later. It was closing time at a bar where Luke was having a nightcap with Jerry, the owner. After he locked up for the night, the two men walked down the street to where Jerry's car was parked. Jerry saw a black sedan idling by the corner, and he heard the five shots just after he called good-night to Luke.

Shenda called me the next day. "I waited with the crowd

around his body until the cops came," she said. "They knew Luke anyway. They'd been watching him for a long time. But it was terrible to see the way they just dumped him so unceremoniously into the coroner's van. Two of them took each leg and dragged him like a dog."

I hadn't listened yet to the last tape I'd made with Luke, that night at the Bucket. I transcribed it after Shenda's call, hearing the voice of a ghost: "I'm not thinking about sitting down up here and selling drugs for the rest of my life. I try to get legal jobs but I don't succeed. And I have a woman and a baby to take care of down in Kingston. Someday I'm going home."

A few days later, Shenda and I were sitting on the front steps of the Graveyard, turning our faces greedily up into the spring sunlight. We were both thinking about Luke, glancing now and then at the empty stairwell across the street where he used to stand. Shenda spoke some lines from John Milton's "Lycidas," a poem she'd memorized as a schoolgirl.

"In memoriam, Luke," she said. "I can see him over there. I can't believe he's dead. Oh, God. It's a long road. It's a long road to where we are now."

Bones and
the Gully

A few blocks from the Paupers' Graveyard, headquartered in a gray apartment building at 1367 Sterling Place, there was another posse whose fiefdom was briefly enlarged by the Renkers bust. The McGregor Gully gang had been in Crown Heights since the early 1980s, and it had formed a loose alliance with the Forties, a posse that hailed from the Rockfort section of eastern Kingston and shared the same PNP affiliation as the Gully. The men from these two posses had fought a war of attrition with Delroy Edwards, and they were gladdened by his demise.

The Gully's don was Eric Vassell, a man in his early thirties who was known as "Chinaman" because he was light-skinned and half-Chinese. He was Delroy Edwards' contemporary and, like his rival, one of the young outlaws from Kingston who joined the posse exodus after the 1980 election. But Vassell had grown up on the other side of the political fence: McGregor Gully, where he grew up, had been drawn into the PNP's orbit by Manley's victory in 1972. Vassell was only a kid then, but he was old enough to run with the crew of gun-loving youths who apprenticed themselves to the party's older enforcers.

The Gully had taken its name from the drainage canal that ran though its heart, along the western flank of Wareika Hill. The settlement had stayed aloof from political warfare until the seventies, when the PNP began funneling money into the area for a Ministry of Works project to clean and rebuild the gully. This project soon became a magnet for gangsters who wanted their share of the work theory, and McGregor Gully turned into a robbers' roost for tribalists from the PNP. Burry Boy and Feathermop were its earliest enforcers; they had already extorted money from works projects elsewhere in Kingston, and now they began converging on the Gully with a younger tribe of sufferers.

Tony Brown, the leader of the Hot Stepper gang from Wareika Hill, and Tony Welch, the dreaded lord of the Concrete Jungle posse who worked for the PNP's minister of Housing, both began hanging out in the Gully. Dennis Barth, the Wareika Hill gunman known as "Copper," also became part of the Gully crew. Copper was already loved and protected by the sufferers from Wareika Hill because he gave them flour whenever he robbed the nearby Pillsbury mill. These gunmen were getting money by robbing banks and homes uptown, but the McGregor Gully project was easier prey; as Brambles explained, "Them get paid without lifting so much as a gravel."

But a dog-eat-dog struggle was the price of this patronage, and by the mid-1970s it had escalated to such a pitch of violence and corruption that Michael Manley ordered a government investigation into the Ministry of Works. The luckless official who led it, Edward Ogilvie, was gunned down at the gate to his home in 1977 by a gunman from the Gully.

Meanwhile, the PNP Youth Organization (PNPYO) was trying to mobilize young men from the Gully into a conscious vanguard. The leader of the PNPYO was a popular leftist named Paul Burke; he moved easily with the sufferers and, like many other party officials, looked to Cuba's revolution as a blueprint for change in Jamaica. The PNP initiated a work-exchange "Brigadista" program with Cuba, and some of the Gully youth went there to learn about socialism while they built houses and schools. (Years later a few of the local gunmen returned to Cuba for good; Tony Brown of the Hot Steppers took refuge there after Seaga won in 1980.) Despite their best efforts, however, Paul Burke and the PNPYO fought a losing battle against the overwhelming power of the gangs.

Eric Vassell was no Che Guevara. He was too young for the Brigadistas, but he was old enough to know that the PNP's days were numbered and that a victory for Seaga would spell doom for lesser gunmen like himself. He hunkered down in the shadows during the 1980 bloodletting and then left to make a name for himself in New York.

Within a year or two Vassell was selling ganja and a little cocaine in Crown Heights and bringing up a few colleagues from McGregor Gully. The deadliest were three brothers, Danny, Fitzy, and Winston "Balla" Reid. Balla Reid was the mastermind behind the 1977 murder of Edward Ogilvie, the official who tried to probe the gangs' infiltration into the Ministry of Works. His younger brothers were experienced gunmen—Danny had been a policeman in Kingston—and they knew their way around. So did the two other trusted allies whom Vassell enticed to Brooklyn: Desmond Brown, whose brother was Tony Brown, the leader of the Hot Steppers, and Trevor Williams, the ne'er-do-well son of the great Rastafarian drummer Count Ossie. These men formed the nexus of the McGregor Gully posse in Brooklyn.

Vassell was a canny businessman. He soon branched out from ganja and powder cocaine into heroin—the first Jamaican posse leader to sell that drug. His timing was excellent: in the mid-

1980s the New York police initiated Operation Pressure Point to drive smack dealers out of Manhattan's Lower East Side, and Vassell reaped the whirlwind as buyers moved elsewhere for their connections. Vassell got his heroin from a Nigerian, and he marketed it with entrepreneurial savvy, packaging it in dime bags stamped with catchy brand names like "Obsession" and "No Way Out."

Vassell himself had a string of colorful aliases. Besides "Chinaman," he was also known on the street as "the King," "the Don," "Brooklyn Barry," and "the IRS." That one was bestowed because Chinaman taxed his soldiers for revenue and then used the money to buy clothing, Walkmans, VCRs, and guns for the McGregor Gully sufferers in Kingston. The goods went down in cardboard barrels all year long, but most of them were hoarded for the annual Easter treat that Chinaman put on every spring. These potlatches made him a true godfather, the Gully's equal to Tivoli's Jim Brown and Vivian Blake. Many of Chinaman's guns were bought in Florida at a shop in Pompano Beach where Chinaman's brother Donald sometimes got as many as thirty at a time. Chinaman called the guns he sent to Kingston "vote getters" for the PNP, part of the Gully's election-time arsenal. But even without the pressure of elections, Gully people still had to defend themselves not only against Jim Brown's JLP terrorists, but also against Seaga's police.

By 1986 Vassell's posse had taken over most of the apartments in the building at 1367 Sterling Place. When the Jamaican landlord complained to police about all of the dealing and shooting inside and on the street, Chinaman had him killed. Sterling Place then became the Gully's flagship, open twenty-four hours a day, seven days a week. It was only one of the posse's drug spots, but it alone could take in as much as fifty thousand dollars a day.

Chinaman sold much of his crack through the Gully's new

branch in Houston; there was less competition in Texas, and the price of crack was then slightly higher than it was in the saturated New York market. Like Chinaman's move into heroin, this proved to be a wise shift: in 1988 the New York police formed a special street-enforcement unit called the Tactical Narcotics Team (TNT)—another response to the murder of Officer Edward Byrne in Queens—which focused almost exclusively on crack. So Chinaman began using Houston as his primary market for that drug and concentrated on heroin and powder cocaine in Brooklyn.

At that point the only fly in the Gully's Crown Heights ointment was Delroy Edwards and the Renkers, whose drive-by shootings and executions of disloyal soldiers were bringing down too much heat. But the Renkers bust in the spring of 1988 was a mixed blessing for the Gully; it took out their major competitor, but it also brought intense police and federal surveillance into the neighborhood. Between 1988 and 1989, undercover agents made close to forty separate buys at 1367 Sterling Place. There were frequent raids now, including an especially picturesque TNT operation when police went into the candy store next-door with welding torches, cut a hole in the steel door, and dragged out two of Chinaman's soldiers. As law-enforcement agents began roping a few Gully suspects into custody, they got that much closer to taking out the whole posse. So the Gully was running on borrowed time; the agents were only waiting to get Chinaman himself.

In the summer of 1989 I wrote an article on the posses for *The Nation*, and it went through the requisite fact checking before going to press. One of the people asked to read it was Basil Wilson, the Jamaican-born chairman of the African-American

Studies Department at New York's John Jay College of Criminal Justice. I did not meet him until just after the article was published, when we had coffee at John Jay and I realized how deep an understanding he had of Jamaica's gang history. Basil grew up in eastern Kingston, wrote a doctoral dissertation on Jamaica's urban violence, and has since become an expert in Caribbean affairs. In the course of that afternoon's conversation, I asked him if he knew anyone in the Brooklyn posse world.

"Does the name Trevor Phillips mean anything to you?" Basil asked. "He comes from McGregor Gully. Trevor was a PNP activist, and he was involved with all the rankings in the gang truce of 1978."

I remembered who Trevor Phillips was: the leader of the Central Peace Council, and the man whose name had been in so many *Gleaner* stories about the truce that I had asked Brambles if he knew him. But Brambles could only vaguely remember that Trevor Phillips had long since left Jamaica for good.

"He's somewhere in Crown Heights," Basil said. "He still moves with the men from the Gully posse."

Basil had known Trevor since 1978, when Trevor came to New York to be a guest on WLIB radio's "Carib-Beat" talk show, which Basil was hosting. This was just after the gang truce and Bob Marley's massive Kingston concert in its behalf; New York's large Jamaican community was hungry for news about the political crisis at home, and Trevor Phillips was an expert witness. He and Basil had become friends after Trevor left Jamaica in 1979. Two years later Trevor wound up in prison in New York.

"What happened?" I asked Basil.

He heaved a weary sigh.

"Something about a gun. The police arrested him with a pistol that had been used in a robbery at a reggae club, and they sent him up for five years. He started out in Attica, where he had a very hard time because of his dreadlocks and his Rastafarianism, and he fought hard to make the prison authorities respect his beliefs. He wrote me a lot of letters from jail.

"Trevor is a ranking," Basil said sadly. "He has been a ranking from mornin', as they say, and he will never change. That is indelible. But he's one of the most intelligent men I know. Had he grown up somewhere other than McGregor Gully, there is no telling what he might have become.

"Go back through your files on the '78 truce," he said. "And meanwhile, I'll see if I can find Trevor in Brooklyn."

I hadn't looked at those files since 1985, when Brambles and I were working together in Kingston on the Green Bay massacre that sparked the gang truce. But I found Trevor Phillips in a story headlined PEACE COUNCIL AIMS TO UNIFY THE MASSES. There was a grainy photograph of Trevor, with resplendent locks, addressing a crowd at Headquarters House, the downtown Kingston building where the Central Peace Council held most of its meetings.

"We as youths and dispossessed people have come of age," said this distant voice, full of the rhetoric of the 1970s. "We are demanding for all equal rights and justice. We are asking of the well-thinking people in Jamaica to understand the bitterness, the hatred, and the frustration built up in the minds and attitudes of a transplanted African people."

Another picture focused on the crowd at Headquarters House that day. The rankings from West Kingston were slouched in the front row, looking distracted and bored.

A few weeks later, Basil found Trevor in Brooklyn and asked him to come to John Jay for a meeting. He agreed but never showed up. This kept happening, and finally Basil gave me Trevor's phone number so that I could call him myself. We began an attenuated telephone courtship dance. He would call late at night, when he was in the mood to talk, but always in a guarded fashion that tested us both; he was waiting to see whether he could trust me. It was not until the fall of 1990 that he agreed to meet me in Brooklyn. I did not know it, but by then the police and the FBI were almost ready to bust Chinaman and the entire Gully posse.

Trevor was skittish about where to meet; he didn't want to come anywhere near the old Renkers territory, but he finally chose a bar near Rogers Avenue because I said I was familiar with the spot. It was almost empty that night, but Trevor was sitting at the far end of the bar, flirting with the Barbadian woman who tended it.

He had told me over the phone that everyone called him "Bones," and now I could see why: Trevor was thin as a reed. He had a melancholy expression in his soft eyes. The dreadlocks he'd fought to keep in prison had been trimmed a long time ago. But even though the years between Kingston and Brooklyn had battered him, he still had the bearing and dignity of a man who had tried to convince his generation of outlaws to put down their guns.

"Don't even bother trying to understand some of these men out on the street," Trevor said after we left the bar and were walking to the apartment of his Rastafarian friend Khadaffi. "I've known them for too long, and they've turned savage now."

Khadaffi's girlfriend was in the kitchen, cooking up a pot of vegetables in coconut milk, and the dread was in the living room with a few of his brethren, smoking herb and building a delicate pagoda-shaped lamp out of red, gold, and green Popsicle sticks. They drifted into the kitchen for supper, but Trevor and I stayed on the couch to talk. We discovered that we were exact contemporaries, both of us born in 1949, and so Trevor began at the beginning: the 1960s, when we—and Jamaica—came of age.

He told me that his political awakening had come with the
bulldozing of Back O' Wall in 1966. He was seventeen then,
with a father he scarcely knew and a mother far away in England,
so he had embarked on the search for surrogate parents—a Jamaican boy's classic quest. He was drawn to the Rastafarian brethren
in Back O' Wall, and he was in the shantytown on the day
when Seaga's bulldozers rolled in. The memory of that day
abided, even as he grew up and was seduced into political activism by the hopeful message of the PNP. Trevor's activism warred
constantly with his Rastafarian conviction that "politricks and
the shitstem" was a Babylon thing that no dread should touch.

Kingston's thriving musical culture became Trevor's other path
to self-discovery. He began hanging around an older musician
named Carlos Malcolm and his band, which played a blend of
ska and Afro-Cuban sounds. The group was popular with Norman Manley and often played for parties at Drumblair, Manley's
uptown Kingston home. It was there that Trevor first met PNP
politicians like Dudley Thompson, who was then trying to unseat
Seaga in West Kingston.

In McGregor Gully, music unified the young sufferers who
were Trevor's own age. There was a group of very talented
youths who got together in the Gully's yards and at Coxsone
Dodd's recording studio downtown. One of them was a kid
named Robbie Shakespeare, who gave Trevor rides on the
handlebars of his bike; within a few years Robbie was playing
bass guitar for Bob Marley and the Wailers. Trevor got to know
Marley from sessions at Coxsone Dodd's Studio One, and he
got sweet on a shy girl named Rita around the time when Bob
himself started courting her. Even though he lost Rita to his
new friend, Trevor still remembered those times with joy.

But the cult of badman-ism was part of this world too, and
Trevor got caught up in it before he was out of his teens. He

was arrested in 1967 for a robbery at an uptown Kingston club; although he protested his innocence, he had no money for a lawyer and was sent to the General Penitentiary for five years. There he endured the same kind of punishment meted out to the character played by Jimmy Cliff in *The Harder They Come*. He was lashed to rum barrels and beaten with a cat-o'-nine-tails. But he had a chance encounter with Bob Marley during that time, a vivid moment of shared sufferation that strengthened Trevor's faith.

"Alan Cole, Bob's manager, grew up with me in the Gully," Trevor said. "We called him 'Skill' because he was a terrific footballer. One day he and Bob came out to the beach at Port Henderson, where it happened that I was with a prison work crew chopping wood, and they saw me. I was ashamed, being there in prison clothes in front of Bob. But they made me feel like a brother. Skill said, 'Bwoy, everybody out here fight for you, Bones.' And then he turned to Bob and told him I was the man who was sent to prison for something I didn't do. And Bob was looking real pitiful, and I could see that he was feeling my pain."

Although the General Penitentiary was hell, it was a hell with a library. "I loved philosophy and could read it easy," Trevor recalled, "maybe because I'd had it right up through secondary school. One of the first things I read in prison was Bertrand Russell. And then H. G. Wells—I think it was his *Outline of History*. And then someone gave me a book by Nelson Mandela, *No Easy Road to Freedom*.

"And that book really took me into my own life. Mandela talked about how the British in South Africa set the East Indians against the blacks, just like they did in Jamaica. My father was East Indian, and I had a stigma about that growing up. Rastas used to call me 'Coolie' and they would say, 'Coolie-bwoy, what you goin' to do when we all go back to Africa? Where you goin' to go then? You ain't black, you ain't white—they goin' to have to chop you in two!'

"So right then and there, reading Mandela, I saw how colonialism was the same everywhere, how these things all fit together. And I just started reading like mad. Like Eldridge Cleaver said, I read to save myself."

But all of Trevor's reading could not save him from what was happening in McGregor Gully when he came out of prison in 1972. "We used to have a saying in Kingston, 'The wise men come from the east.' And up to the time I came out of GP, this was true—eastern Kingston was never drawn into the kind of warlordism that Seaga kicked up in the west.

"But I will never forget the scene in the Gully on the very day I came back. It happened to be a Friday—payday—and I just saw all these tough guys hanging out: Tony Welch from Concrete Jungle, Tony Brown from the Hot Steppers, this outlaw from West Kingston who we called Starkey. And these guys were all getting fat contracts from Feathermop and Burry Boy for their share of the Gully works project."

As McGregor Gully became another gang hotbed, the police started doing night sweeps and eradication missions through the area. The terror this engendered among the sufferers made them turn to the PNP for protection, and soon the neighborhood became another garrison constituency. Trevor began to see Trinity cruising through the Gully in his Jeep and was astonished that the killer cop left him alone. He thought that maybe it was because he had gotten to know Trinity's outlaw brother Dukie in prison.

"A couple of nights after I saw Trinity for the first time in the Gully, I was at a dance down by the waterfront. I'm carrying a thirty-eight and I see Trinity come in, searching everyone for guns. He's got two pistols wrapped around his legs like a cowboy, and he's in full black, with an M16 in his hand.

"I'm dancing with this girl named Lorna who I want very much to take home. 'Jesus,' I say to Lorna, 'I got nowhere to run, baby. If I drop over this wall outside, it's right at the sea.' And I know by then that Trinity kills anyone he finds with a gun. So I pull mine up between me and her and just kind of slide it between her breasts and tell her to drop to the floor if he comes up, that I'll shoot him first. Lorna is trembling. I can feel her shivering against me. And do you know that man just looks at me and walks on by?"

Things didn't usually turn out this way for the sufferers who went up against Trinity and his colleagues on the police force; too many of the Gully youths were dying in gunfights with the cops and one another. Paul Burke and the PNPYO were meanwhile trying to turn them away from violence, and Burke persuaded Trevor to bring a youth group he'd started into the PNP. Trevor had seen Eric Vassell around the Gully and knew him as one of the kids who were already apprenticing themselves to gunmen.

"There was one of Chinaman's early killings that really broke me apart," Trevor said. "A kid I loved named Rats-and-Bats—we called him 'Batsy.' He had broken away from Tony Brown and the Hot Steppers because of a murder they'd done that Batsy knew was wrong, and Tony ordered Chinaman to kill him. He was just a teenager then, and Chinaman wasn't much older either.

"Batsy had made a tape for Tony Brown, pleading for his life, and on the night they killed him he'd sent a message for me to meet him down in the Gully. But Chinaman intercepted it, and by the time I got it, it was too late. I started running down to

Batsy's yard and I heard the shots. I hid in the shadows, and later I overheard Chinaman bragging about how he saw Batsy fall.

"I just went to my girlfriend's house and broke down. That was the night when I knew how vicious all these guys had become, that they were nothing now but real-life killers."

From then on, in Kingston and later in New York, Trevor and Chinaman kept an uneasy peace. They were almost a generation apart, and separated as well by a different kind of sufferation. Trevor had grown up poor, but he had a good education and a strong dose of Rastafarian culture. He had come of age when political violence was only just beginning. Chinaman was a child of the generation that grew up with Kingston's outlaws as their role models, and they were his distant gods. Trevor knew these men as friends and saw them die in Kingston's endless warfare; his contemporaries were rankings like Copper, Claudie Massop, Bucky Marshall, Tony Welch, and Byah Mitchell. So Trevor was always the Gully's "old head," the man who could move through the city's tribal battlefields and, when the time came, speak for the gang leaders.

Because Trevor saw the shifting configuration of the rankings—that they were caught between their desire for peace and the politicians' plans for war—and because he knew that the truce had no chance of lasting once the preelection frenzy laid siege to the ghettos, he could feel the peace crumbling by the spring of 1978. Bob Marley's One Love concert on April 22 was supposed to be the beginning, but it was really the beginning of the end.

Trevor brought some photographs of the concert to Khadaffi's that night, pictures of him and Bob Marley with their gangster friends. The rankings all looked exuberant. There was Bob clowning around backstage with Bucky Marshall and Tony

Welch; Trevor and Bob holding aloft a photograph of His Imperial Majesty, Haile Selassie; Trevor onstage with Bob at the concert. Their faces were only inches apart, and they looked like brothers. Marley's face was streaming with what must have been sweat but looked like tears, and Trevor's fingertips were pressed together in the Rastafarian gesture of prayer.

Midway through the concert, Marley summoned Manley and Seaga onstage—the one and only time that the two leaders came face to face during the gang truce—and Trevor had shots of that moment too. They were joyless. With Claudie Massop hovering in the background and a tribe of grim-faced bodyguards surrounding them, the two politicians clasped hands over Bob's bent head. Their gesture of peace was a sham. "You can read the fate of the truce in these pictures, can't you?" Trevor asked.

Marley didn't know it that night, but his One Love Peace Concert had been used as a cover for Seaga's forces to smuggle guns into the country. They were hidden inside a shipment of lighting equipment used for the show. "Those guns came in right under the noses of the customs people," Trevor said. "And I was so naive and gullible that I had no idea of what was going on."

On the night of the show, Chris Blackwell—Marley's producer at Island Records—sent someone to the stadium to tell Trevor that this equipment was on the wharf waiting for clearance; Blackwell had no idea what else was inside the metal cases. Trevor made an urgent call to Dudley Thompson, the minister of national security, to clear the containers. It was not until a few days later that Trevor found out about the guns at a post-concert meeting of the Central Peace Council. Byah Mitchell, the gunman from Tivoli Gardens, threw him the warning. "Mr. Chairman," Byah growled to Trevor, "is not peace we dealin' with. Is pieces."

And then Bucky Marshall set Trevor straight.

"Bucky asked me if I knew what was going on, warning me that Seaga was already getting guns for the coming election. 'Whole heap o' guns come down in the equipments,' Bucky said. 'An' me see one me want.' "

As Trevor's erstwhile friends began scrambling for firepower, he watched the truce unravel before his eyes. But he told me that night at Khadaffi's that the worst was yet to come. He knew the man from Tivoli Gardens everyone called Jim Brown, a gunman who'd been around for years and now appeared to be displacing Claudie Massop as Seaga's chief enforcer. Trevor ran into him at Central Peace Council meetings, where Seaga had sent Jim Brown to spy. But it was not until a few weeks after Marley's concert that Trevor realized how dangerous Jim Brown had always been.

"Bob had a spare office at his house on Hope Road, and he was letting me use it. Jim Brown had some money from the concert, so I told him to meet me up at the Hope Road yard. When Bob saw him, he threw me a look like daggers. After Jim left, Bob said, 'Who was that bredda?' And I told him that was Jim Brown from Tivoli, didn't he know who Jim Brown was?

"I'd seen Bob angry before, but never like that. 'Bones,' he said. 'I seen that bredda before. He was here the night I got shot.' "

Ever since that attack in 1976, Jamaica had buzzed with rumors about who had set it up. The timing showed a certain brutal intelligence; the botched attack came just before the December election and made it look as if internal security under Manley's regime was so shaky that it could not even ensure the safety of the island's most important citizen. So Jamaicans always assumed that Seaga and the JLP had been behind the shooting. No one believed that Claudie Massop, Marley's close friend,

would have gone along with such a treacherous move. But Jim
Brown would have done it, to show Seaga that he could be a
trusted assassin.

Trevor asked Bob if he was sure. "Yeah," Bob answered,
shaking with rage. "I'm sure."

It was not long before Trevor saw Jim Brown's calling card
in the deaths of other friends. And the new don from Tivoli
Gardens wanted Trevor out of the way too. Brown convinced
Claudie Massop and Bucky Marshall to steal some footage of
Marley's concert and try to sell it in Toronto. Trevor followed
them to get the film back, unaware that Brown was behind the
theft. Trevor told the Central Peace Council that he would stop
in New York on his way back to Kingston. Brown dispatched
Byah Mitchell from Tivoli to kill Trevor in New York.

"I have nine lives," Trevor said. "And I used one then." He
decided at the last minute to go to Miami instead, where one
of his sons was living. When he got to the Miami airport, he
called his friend Schoolboy, one of the Kingston rankings who
had moved to Florida to sell drugs.

" 'You don't know you is supposed to be dead?' Schoolboy
yells into the phone," Trevor said. "Then he tells me that Byah
Mitchell is there in Miami, over at the yard of this deejay we
called King Sporty, bragging 'bout how he shot me in New
York. And Schoolboy says that everyone is over at Sporty's yard
snorting coke and being happy I'm dead. Byah felt sufficiently
sure he'd killed me to have called a reporter back in Kingston
with the news.

"So I say, 'Schoolie, you got any guns in the house?' He has
a Thompson submachine gun and he gives me a nine, and we
forward over to Sporty's yard. Schoolie knocks at the front door
and I work my way 'round the back like the cops do. Sure

enough, I hear Byah's voice inside. I come through the back door, gun in hand, and shove Byah up against the wall.

" 'You son of a bitch,' I say. 'You killed me, right? Well, I don't know which dread you gunned down in Brooklyn, but it wasn't me.'

"Sporty was begging for Byah's life. So I just put my gun away and told Schoolie, 'Come, mek we get outta this place.'

"And this was supposed to be peace," Trevor said, relishing his bitterness. "We're supposed to have a truce, and meanwhile Jim Brown sends Byah Mitchell all the way to Brooklyn to gun down an innocent man."

Within a year, by 1979, every one of the rankings involved with the truce was dead. Jim Brown got rid of Copper, the man Trevor loved most of all, by setting up a robbery for Copper at the Kingston racetrack and then betraying him to police, who ambushed him there. Police gunned down Claudie Massop in February 1979—probably with Brown's connivance—and his death lifted the last barrier to Brown's control in Tivoli Gardens. Byah Mitchell died shortly after Massop, from a cocaine overdose, and Bucky Marshall was shot dead in Brooklyn by a JLP supporter who caught him without a gun at the Starlite Ballroom.

"I saw which way the wind was blowing," Trevor said. "Seaga was getting ready to shoot the PNP clear to hell, and I could see that one of the first to die would have been me. Everyone I knew was dying. All my friends were getting killed."

So Trevor left Jamaica for Brooklyn, after burying Copper in a five-thousand-dollar funeral paid for with money from the peace concert. He never went back.

It was very late by the time Trevor finished talking. Khadaffi and his girlfriend had long since gone to bed. As I rose to leave, Trevor asked me if I wanted to walk over to the Gully's place on Sterling and Schenectady. But then he reconsidered; he wasn't sure that he could trust me yet.

"That's OK," I said. "I ought to find a gypsy cab back to Manhattan."

Trevor had said nothing that night about the Gully's current runnings or about his own tangled history in New York. But the story of his struggles in the Kingston gang world of the 1970s were a motherlode, an essential preface to the bitter history of the 1980s and the Jamaican gang diaspora in New York. I was grateful to have met him at last.

In the taxi going home I thought of Bob Marley's anthem "No Woman No Cry" and its lament for "good friends we have lost, along the way." Trevor's stories were a requiem for his own lost friends, and for the merciless decade that bore them away. It was this same ruthlessness that spawned the posses, with a grim inevitability.

But Trevor's stories left me to wonder if the 1970s might have birthed a different Jamaica. Had the powerful not been intent on war, had the powerless miraculously been able to turn away from the guns they were given, had the hopeful ones like Trevor not been run to ground, then the sufferers might have found a way out other than this underground railroad into exile and death. But that was tantamont to saying, Had the history of Jamaica not been what it was.

Trevor and I parted with a promise to meet again soon. Neither one of us knew that it would be almost a year before we saw each other again and that we would not meet in Brooklyn.

A Soldier in
the Field

B rambles was still living in Rockeye's crack spot, reconciled to his own protracted exile in New York. He was caught in the catch-22 of a Jamaican sufferer lost in the promised land: the unwritten cultural law that says, If you can't come back from America with your pockets full, then don't come back at all. Jamaicans assume that anyone with the right stuff will come home rich, and any other scenario is so humiliating that it is unthinkable. So Brambles stayed doggedly on, sending his meager earnings home to his son and daughter and freezing through one winter after another. He never relinquished his dreams.

Shenda's fortunes, meanwhile, were improving. She had stopped smoking crack every day and had moved out of the Paupers' Graveyard and into the basement flat of an older man named Mack. Mack was a Jamaican landlord with an array of decrepit buildings scattered around Crown Heights. He was also a fierce anti-Semite, convinced that "Jew lawyers," not the drug dealers who didn't pay rent, were bilking him out of his profits. I got a slug of Jew-baiting whenever I went to see Shenda; it ranged from the good-natured to the vicious, depending on

Mack's mood and how much rum he'd had that day. But he respected me for my learning and called me "Doc."

A few months before Trevor Phillips and I met, I was at Mack's for an afternoon visit with Shenda. They were waiting for a young Jamaican named Courtney to show up with a gun that Courtney was trying to sell to Mack. Shenda said that Courtney was a gun hawk for the Shower posse, a small-time dealer of stolen weapons and drugs.

Courtney strolled in right on schedule, wearing a black leather windbreaker with the gun nestled in his pocket. He was sloe-eyed and very dark, and his hair was sculpted into a fade with a razored hash cut on one side. He reminded me a little of Delroy Edwards, and when I told him so he preened at the comparison.

"You remember that body they found over on Rogers, with a bullet in his head and his two balls stuffed in his mouth?" Courtney asked. "That was one of Delroy's. Savagism. Uzi was a savage. I know, because I worked for him and I stole from him too. When I sell something for fifty dollars and somebody come for a ten-dollar vial, I just cut a piece offa the fifty and sell it for the ten and still sell the fifty. So I 'ave ten dollars inna me own pocket, and the next thing you know, I have a thousand."

He grinned engagingly. "Uzi's comin' out of jail one of these days," he nodded.

I mentioned that it would be hard to come out with a 501-year sentence and no parole, but Courtney had his own ideas.

"You know how I know? Because he has the strongest obeah, and obeah works. I know Mother B., the Haitian woman Delroy used. If you get a hair from somebody's head and put it in a jar and bring it to Mother B., she say, 'Kiss-kiss-kiss-That-that-that.' You dead, you go mad, whatever—and the doctor cyan' tell you why. Mek a coconut tree grow inna your belly and come out through your mouth and you don't know why. Yeah, Delroy go a' Haiti fi' him obeah, and that is why I tell you Delroy gonna come out one of these days. Ain't no motherfuckin' judge can stop no voodoo."

Mack asked to see the gun, and Courtney produced a dull-black Glock 9 mm. He said it came from Texas, one of the posses' favorite states (along with Virginia, Florida, and Ohio) for buying guns. There were retailers who would arrange a "theft" for posse men if they bought in bulk; then the dealer could write it off on his insurance. This meant that the guns sold for less than retail prices on the street. Courtney was asking Mack only one hundred dollars for the Glock.

"My guns come up from Houston," he said proudly, showing Mack how to insert the clip of hollow-headed bullets into the gun's grip. "Greyhound drivers bring them up, tractor-trailers bring them up. The Glock runs things now."

Courtney couldn't resist bragging. "When you have a name as a gun hawk—somebody who is well into the business and don't fear police, detectives, whoever comes upon you—then you get to move with anybody you want to. You move under the ground. I have certain people who I am like a son to, because they can rely on me. If they give me a gun and say, 'Go out there and kill that mon,' I would do it. I wouldn't feel nothin' 'bout doin' that. I'd kill a person in a quick second if the money was good."

Mack and Shenda didn't say a word. I just stared at Courtney.

"For a mon to kill a mon, it feel good," he went on. "You understand? 'Cause when you kill a mon, you get . . . you get *hot*." He said the word in a breathy stage whisper. "You get *bold*. You all right when you kill a mon, 'cause you got it made."

Mack decided that maybe he didn't want the gun that day.

But Courtney was undismayed. "If you no see me wih a gun inna' me pocket, you know I is a fuckery," he said cheerfully and tucked the gun away. He and Shenda were hungry, so we drove to Ashanti, one of her favorite restaurants. On the way we passed the corner of Sterling and Schenectady, with Courtney keeping up a running patter like a guide.

"The Gully right now is the roughest," Courtney said. "Nuff respect you better 'ave fi' dem mon there. They jugglin' kilos. They not fuckin' around. Chinaman runs the thing. You ever see Chinaman yet? Light-skinned bredda, that's how come he get his name. Moves like a ghost."

Courtney made Shenda slow down so he could point out the brightly colored mural above the Crown Heights Soccer and Domino Association, the little video parlor and social club next door to the Gully's apartment building. One side of the mural was a soccer game and the other was a foursome playing dominos. One of the players was Chinaman.

"That's him up there, on the right," Courtney leaned forward from the backseat to point. "This here is the killing fields. Ain't no corner in Brooklyn you can tell me is rough like this."

Courtney had a boom-box voice that turned the car into a sound chamber, and when we got to the Ashanti he felt no need to simmer down. He talked so loud that the other customers eyed us with great interest, and Shenda kept plucking his sleeve to quiet him down. So he tried a stage whisper like the one he had used to describe how it feels to kill.

He said that he had come to Brooklyn as a teenager. He'd left Jamaica to go to West Virginia on an apple-picking contract, but he knew plenty of Jamaicans in New York and they urged him to bail out of his work contract. Some of his Brooklyn friends were running with the Shower posse. "But sometimes I don't even really consider myself as Shower," Courtney said between mouthfuls of chicken, rice, and peas. "I just consider my-self as one young man, confused in this society by the way my leaders made me."

He did what he did for the money, not because he had any great love for Seaga or the JLP. "Why should two white men like Manley and Seaga be runnin' a black country? It don't make no sense. There is gonna' be mix up, bound to be. They only givin' black youth an' youth gun an' gun. So Seaga is bullshit. Manley is bullshit. Jamaica don't have no right leader. It's just, 'You is PNP, me is Labourite. You bring down gun, me bring down gun, and we kill one another.'"

He got up to order a drink, hesitating between Irish moss and another roots tonic called Front End Lifter. Irish moss is a gelatinous concoction made from seaweed, and, like the Lifter, it is supposed to be an aphrodisiac. Courtney decided on the Irish moss and sat back down.

"So I consider myself as a young man who is trying to get something out of life, any which way I can. But I see that I can't really do that in Jamaica or here. In Jamaica it's because of the way the leaders make things. They give all the money to the war people and stir up everyone's mind. But you see, we are still in slavery inna we own country. And you know who puts us under slavery? Our own, that's who. Not the white man, but our own ras-clot kind. JLP, PNP—all o' dem is one. They are all pure gangsters now."

The customers at the Ashanti were listening raptly. It made Shenda nervous, so she suggested that we cruise around for a while. It was still early on a Friday afternoon, and the sidewalks along Kingston Avenue, the main shopping street in the Hasidic section of Crown Heights, were crowded with women shopping for the Sabbath. They trundled their strollers and shepherded large flocks of children, careful to ignore the African-Americans who sauntered by with big tape decks blaring rap and dance hall music. The Hasidic men congregated on the corners in earnest discussion, wearing black frock coats and fur-trimmed hats. They looked as if they had stepped out of a shtetl in seventeenth-century Russia.

This was the year before the 1991 riots in Crown Heights, three days of wrath between the Hasidim and their African-American and Caribbean neighbors. The riots came after a child from Guyana, Gavin Cato, was struck and killed by a Hasidic driver. An ambulance swept the uninjured driver from the scene, while Cato bled to death on the sidewalk.

The ensuing riot was yet to come, but the tensions that fueled it were already present; enmity between the races was old. Courtney stared hard at the Jews. "I don't check too much for white people," he muttered. "I see certain things go down in this neighborhood in my days and this is the way I become. I harden my heart and say, 'Me is a soldier.' "

Shenda threw him a warning look from the driver's seat. Courtney ignored her. "I'm going to be straight with you," he said. "Don't hate me for what I'm going to say. I come over here and fling bottle at the Jew-them. And if me catch one o' dem and me 'ave a gun 'pon me, me would let off bullet inna them too. The reason why I would do it is because I love black people, and this is a black-Jew thing.

"You see, I never forget where I come from. And I never forget my anger. A rebel attitude in black people come up from the time you enslave us. That is our nature ever since you start to separate us from our families. I know everything about this world. This is my world. I know how to struggle and I know how to survive. The only thing you haffi' understand about Jamaicans is that we no 'fraid of nothing. We think we cyan' dead. We have nine lives, like a cat."

Shenda sucked her teeth in disgust. "What you mean, Court-ney, 'struggle and survive'? How black people goin' to survive if them all the while kill one another? How that supposed to raise up we people?"

Courtney went into a full flush of rage. "The black race will never rise!" he shouted back. "Never! Because black people is out to get what's theirs. If white people like the Jews can still move good with one another, it's only because they not livin' by the drugs bizness, and that is where black people find them-selves now in this ras-clot country. Is a tightrope we walk all the time.

"When I see the Gully men war with Delroy's posse, is just a tightrope them a' walk. One night is pure gunshot and mon drop dead. Police come, line off the body with yellow tape, pick it up, go put it in the deadhouse. Body gone. Next morning, everybody cool. Back to square one."

"So what's going to stop the violence?" I asked.

"The fighting will never stop," Courtney answered, slouching back into his seat. "No. I don't really understand what all the fighting is for neither, but I know that it will never end. Because if I have a son, I'm going to grow him up under one condition. Me will tell him, 'Star, you is a Shower mon. You haffi' do what your general says.' Me will grow him up and sometimes kick him down. You understand? Do him some cruel thing just to make him get tough, to make him get cruel. Like how Delroy kill his own father."

Courtney didn't stop to consider the patricidal implications of this child-rearing theory. It was getting late and he had to go pick up his daughter at school.

The three of us met a few nights later at a bar called the Turntable, a popular posse watering hole. The owner's son had recently been killed by a gunman from the Gully, and Courtney described the slaying as we sat down with our beers. "When they shot him, they destroyed his back. You know what that mean? The hole in his back come clear through his chest. He died with half a kilo in his pocket. That mean the killers did not want his drugs.

"This here is the Wild West, you know," he grinned. "They could film 'Bonanza' over here. Little Joe Cartwright."

A friend of Courtney's soon came in and joined us at the table. Courtney introduced him simply as Dread, the generic nickname for a Rastafarian. He wore an enormous leather hat over his locks. Dread crossed his arms over his chest and sat, in absolute, sullen silence, while Courtney talked. His subject was the collusion between drug dealers and corrupt cops, so I was paying close attention and ignoring Dread. But there was something about him that made me very uneasy; I just couldn't tell what it was.

"You remember when the 77th Precinct thing blew open?" Courtney was saying. "That hurt a lot of the guys who were selling for the cops. Certain police would go on a raid and certain things they find never surface again. You see? If them find you with, say, six kilos, they only need one to hold you. Where does the other five go? One alone will put you away for fifteen years.

"So the cops will come to one of us with the rest and say, 'Help us unload this.' And when we hear 'bout five kilos, we say, God! You know how much money we can make offa that? And right away we will pay the cop before we even sell it, because it's an investment. So now the cop is hooked on the money, same as we. And they must get a black mon to sell the drugs for them, every time, because they know that if a white mon goes into our territory, nuff-nuff eyes gonna be upon him."

Dread smiled enigmatically. Courtney described how he had even imitated the cops and done his own raids on dealers. "You ever see police play Tarzan? Go up on the roof, swing through a window feet-first with them Plexiglas shields and break down the whole motherfuckin' thing?

"Me like see that! I have one of them shields myself. Me and a couple of Jamaicans went 'round bustin' crack spots as police— something we see on 'America's Most Wanted.' "

His voice was booming again, but the deejay was playing full-decibel dance hall that almost drowned him out. *"Freeze!"* Courtney bellowed, imitating the police.

Shenda and I caught each other's eyes, both of us flashing back to that day at the Paupers' Graveyard when we'd heard the same command.

"Don't move!" Courtney continued, holding us hostage to his drama. *"Get against the wall! Get the fuck down on the floor!"* He sat back, folded his arms over his chest, and grinned maniacally. "So then we get their stuff, handcuff them to the radiator, and say, 'Bye, folks. See you all later.' "

After that night, Courtney and I started meeting on our own, in Central Park; he liked the open-air privacy of the park's terrain. It was cold, but we would bundle ourselves in warm clothes and meet on the benches underneath the gothic turrets of the Dakota. From there we usually walked to a massive rock on the edge of the boat lake.

In the park, free from his need to keep the bravura mask that he always wore in Brooklyn, Courtney would hum some of the rap songs he had written. They were about violence, and they did not sing its praises.

"How they give us guns to shoot our brothers down," one of his songs began. It was about a Jamaican who comes to Brooklyn, goes on drugs, and "uses up all his thoughts" in the quest for power.

"Ghetto struggler want me to take this brother down," Courtney sang, "for the money that he owes."

Put the gun in my hand and the money in my pocket.
When I knock on Henry's door with tears in my eyes,
I see Henry with his baby on his side.
I close my eyes. Two shots outta the nine.
Henry drop to the floor.
Ghetto struggler, I kill my brother now.
Now I'm feelin' the pain, but who's to blame?
The rich man sit down upon his stone,
And he's not black, he's white.
But who is to blame?

"They keep us in bondage," Courtney said, wiping his running nose on his jacket sleeve. "The chains are off my feet, still my mind is in captivity. I don't know when black people will wake up and see that the chains are gone, but our minds are gone also."

Seagulls wheeled over the lake and a few mallards slapped down on the water, quacking softly at their mates. Behind us on the bridle path a beautifully turned-out rider cantered past, a vision of the other New York. She was wearing an elegant black jacket, fawn-colored breeches, and glossy black boots; the flanks of her chestnut horse gleamed from many brushings. Courtney squinted at her and said she looked like a movie, but not one of the ones he would pay to go see.

I asked him what he thought about the connection between movies and violence.

"Is like these movies hype pure badness," he answered. "I see since *Scarface* come out in the seventies how every one o' we want to play Scarface! Certain movies seem to turn people wicked same time. Things like *Scarface, Rambo, The Godfather* mean something very different in the ghetto. Is like white people can watch them film and not turn killer same time, but in the ghetto we see so much killin' that the films are like real life.

"Me remember one time me was watching *Scarface* with my lickle crew and the whole o' we wanted to be just like him, wanted big dollars, and is big-big we a' think. We want to go rob mon and take away all his cocaine, just like in that movie. Snort up nuff-nuff cocaine and get well-paranoid and go catch nuff-nuff girls and shoot up a club full o' people. Then we would run things! Every mon goin' to hear 'bout our syndicate. We goin' to be just like the *French Connection*!"

We were walking to the subway on Seventy-second Street and stopped to say good-bye across from the Dakota. "Yeah," Courtney said. "Just like *Scarface*. But a pity we nah know that all o' we would get dead."

The next time we met, Courtney brought Dread. He was just as quiet as he'd been at the Turntable, sitting sphinxlike when Courtney mentioned that he had an older friend from the Shower, a man he called "Nines"—short for "Nine Millimeter"—who wanted to meet me.

"Right now, a shipment of guns is comin' from Ohio, and Nines is receivin' it," Courtney explained. "But him is against it, still. He sees the way . . . it's like him sick an' fed up with it. All these guns is just for youth an' youth. So Nines was talking that way to me, saying, 'Why can't mon wake up an' smell the coffee?' You understand?"

The Shower was still going strong in New York, Miami, and Los Angeles; Jim Brown was in Kingston and Vivian Blake was traveling back and forth. But now that Michael Manley had become prime minister again (in 1989), federal agents were hoping that Jamaica's PNP government would finally deliver Jim Brown to them. They had begun extradition proceedings against him, but Brown was playing for time by appealing the extradition order to the British Privy Council, Jamaica's court of last resort.

In the meantime, he was still on the loose in Tivoli Gardens. In July 1990 the Kingston police tried to arrest him there with a force of eighty men. They were caught in a gun battle that killed four policemen. The word on the street in Kingston was that if the Americans roped in Jim Brown, the Tivolites would go over to Montego Bay and start killing tourists. The State Department didn't like the sound of that, so American embassy officials in Kingston told the Drug Enforcement Administration and the Bureau of Alcohol, Tobacco and Firearms to leave Jim Brown alone for the time being.

Whoever this man Nines was, he had to be very brave and very disenchanted with the Shower if he was considering talking to me.

"Nines is an older mon," Courtney said. "Been in this thing since his Kingston days. Been shot thirty-six times. And he is confused right now. Because them is pushin' up the licklest youth to run things, and that is why Nines is sick of the bizness. Him 'ave kids. Him 'ave one big son right now who is a dealer, and it hurts him. Him haffi' hide from him own son right now because him son want to kill him."

Courtney called me on the run from a pay phone in Brooklyn a few nights later. Someone had shot at him on the street in front of the Bucket and then trailed him home, firing a few rounds through the window of the room where Courtney's wife and daughter lay sleeping.

"The worst part of it is, I know who talked," Courtr¿y said, choking with fear, all of his bravado gone. "It had to be Dread. He was the only one who knew 'bout me an' you an' Nines being ready to talk. My worst mistake was gettin' involved in certain things where when you wish you could back off, it's too late. That's what Nines says. When you want to back off, it's too late. You haffi' stay steady, stand firm, and not leave your headquarters till death do you part. Is like a marriage certificate you sign. If you leave, you know too much and a nex' mon goin' to kill you. That is part of a syndicate. Ain't no leavin' but to die."

We saw each other one last time, a meeting on our bench in the park. He had already put his wife and child on a bus to Chicago, where her parents lived, and he was about to follow them. But he had a letter for me from Nines. "Dear Lori," it began, with a heart drawn around my name.

> *I have heard a lot of things that impress me about your book from our friend. We have so much in common. But I only have a short time to let you know all the things going on in Jamaica and with the Shower crew. From last week, I was not careful of what I was doing and the wrong man got to know things. This note might cost me my life.*

Courtney had told me that Nines had grown up in Trench-town and that before he linked up with the Shower he had been on the other side in the political wars, running with the infamous Tony Welch and the Concrete Jungle gang. Nines's letter continued:

> *But I want you to keep on with your book, because it's got to get out to stop the violence that is in Jamaica. I remember the days when Tony Welch and the Jungleites was trying to teach us that we must love one another and defend our areas. I was much younger then, and I was the leader of my pack at the time. But the love we were spreading was a bloody love. Killing our own people for foolishness. At the time I didn't realize what I was*

doing. I was much too deep into it to get out, so I just kept on killing.

Courtney told me that you wanted to know how the Shower got started. Jim Brown and the rest of the Shower was like Robin Hood, taking from the rich to give to the poor. But politics seemed to break up everything.

I was holding the fluttering pages of Nines's letter as a strong wind threatened to carry them off.

There is a lot of things going on in the street along with the guns. Manhattan is the headquarters for the Spanglers and the Shower, and a lot of Colombians are involved in the runnin's.

It has been said that Colombia's Cali cartel, which has surpassed its Medellín competitor as South America's preeminent cocaine organization, handpicked the Shower to distribute the cartel's cocaine in England, where the posses were establishing a second frontier by this time. But Nines was only saying what everyone knew: that the Jamaican gangs had to deal with the Colombians, simply because the cocaine was theirs and theirs alone.

The letter ended:

There is innocent blood shedding down in Kingston. Ladies are dying, families are suffering, and the leaders are laughing, giving youth and youth guns and drugs to fight against their own brothers and sisters. Courtney is trying to get out of badness, I wish him the best of luck. At this time I will let my words. . . . One love Jah Rastafari 9.s.

I never got to meet Nines. He was killed a few nights later in front of a grocery store in East New York. Courtney made it to Chicago and called to let me know that he was all right and to ask me to attend Nines's funeral in Brooklyn; he wanted someone to represent him there. But he understood when I told him that I didn't think that was a good idea.

"This thing they call posseism is the dreadfullest thing in the world," Courtney said. I never saw him again.

.

Reprise

I was haunted by the thought that I might have been responsible for Nines's death. He was the second person who had been killed around me—Luke, the Jamaican dealer, had been the first. Although Shenda and Brambles reminded me that posse vendettas are endless and that the guilt for a death belongs to the person who squeezed the trigger, I took no comfort from their words.

Brambles dismissed Nines's murder with characteristic cool. "Them things is norms," he said.

In the aftermath of Nines's death, I went to upstate New York to meet David D'Costa, the Jamaican journalist who had broken the story of the Green Bay massacre. He has lived in the States since the late 1970s, although he returns often to Jamaica to see old friends. David proved to be as thoughtful and compassionate as the stories he had written suggested: a man whose work as a journalist took him from a privileged background into a deep familiarity with the sufferation of the ghettos.

I told him that years ago I had read an opinion piece he had written for the *Gleaner* after the inquest into the Green Bay affair. I had copied out a passage, and I brought it with me. David said something modest and self-effacing about his writing, but I assured him that this article had stayed with me for a long time.

"Behind Green Bay," he wrote, "lies the deepest fear in our national psyche. It is the one fear that has been passed from ruler to ruler, it is the link which connects the plantocrat and the politician, and it is based on simple arithmetic. From the beginning it was there: so few of us, so many of them. 'Us' in the beginning was readily categorized: white, light, and propertied. 'Them' remain today what they were three hundred years ago: black and unpropertied. The disproportion between rulers and ruled makes terror the ruler's special temptation."

David's memories of the 1970s were vivid, and we spent the better part of two days talking about that deadly decade in Jamaica. He said that anyone could have predicted the posse exodus to America, calling it the "inevitable next chapter" after Kingston. In the course of our conversation I told him about the recent death of Nines, confiding to a fellow journalist conflicts I faced as a participant-observer in the posse world.

He recalled a story of his own that was very like mine, and he offered it as consolation. It was about the murder of a source of his in Kingston, a soldier from the Jamaica Defense Force named Anthony Williams. He had come to David at the *Gleaner* after being tortured by superiors at Up Park Camp on suspicion of stealing guns. The officers were threatening to kill him. David urged Williams to tell his story to the *Gleaner*, mistakenly believing that this would protect the soldier. Williams's strangled corpse turned up a few weeks later in a West Kingston gully.

"He may have been killed for talking to me," David said. "Or he may have died because some ganja or gun deal went sour on him. I won't ever know."

Before I left he asked me if I knew a poem by William Butler Yeats, "The Stare's Nest by My Window"; it was the poet's ode to a young soldier killed in Ireland's civil war, and David said it had always reminded him of Jamaica's own fratricidal war. He fetched the book from his library and read me the lines:

We had fed the heart on fantasies,
The heart's grown brutal from the fare;
More substance in our enmities
Than in our love.

A few months later David sent me a recent *Gleaner* story about the funeral of a gunman named Natty Morgan, a ranking from the sprawling shantytown of Riverton City. He had kidnapped and murdered a lecturer from the University of the West Indies, and the Kingston police had gone after him like bounty hunters in a western movie. But the Riverton City sufferers hid Natty and it took months for the police to track him down. By the time he died, in the proverbial hail of bullets, the poor had claimed him as their hero.

Natty was buried with full honors as his weeping girlfriend put a wreath of flowers in the shape of an M16 on his casket. The Catholic priest who officiated at the rites tore the wreath off the coffin, but she put it back before her lover's body was committed to the dust.

"This is what we have come to," David said sadly. "These are the fantasies we feed on."

Meanwhile, in Brooklyn, the murderous fantasia of the McGregor Gully posse was drawing to a close. Chinaman was at war with the three Reid brothers, the same McGregor Gully men he'd brought to Brooklyn to work for him. But now these foot soldiers wanted to become generals. Consequently, the posse split into two factions: Chinaman and his brother Donald against the Reids. Fitzy Reid had already been blown to pieces in an execution, and his two brothers were out for Chinaman's blood. The police and the FBI were closing in on the Gully.

Trevor Phillips, the gang member whom I had only just met, called to say that he smelled trouble and that he was staying away from the corner of Sterling and Schenectady. His ranking's instinct for survival served him well.

The Gully was busted in the first week of December 1990, less than a month after Trevor and I met. The SWAT raid was like the one that nabbed Delroy Edwards, a massive show of local and federal force. Dozens of Gully suspects were dragged out of 1367 Sterling Place, almost half of the forty-two people who were named in the federal complaint. Trevor was not among them; he'd been laying low at his girlfriend's place and at Khadaffi's apartment, where he and I had talked that first night. Chinaman, too, had gotten away.

The police, foiled again, said that the don was simply nowhere to be found. But the sufferers had another version of Chinaman's escape: he was such a master of disguises, they said, that he walked right by the two hundred cops and federal agents, who didn't even recognize him. Now no one knew where he was. Some said London, others Kingston; Trevor figured that he'd left Brooklyn for McGregor Gully well before the raid, going back to his old ground, where he was untouchable.

The Associated Press quoted James M. Fox of the FBI, who claimed that the Gully posse had made more than $100 million and carried out at least ten murders; the revenue figure was wildly exaggerated, but the murder estimate was on the conservative side. Fox's men seized a batch of incriminating documents in the raid; there were notebooks with the names and addresses of drug suppliers, and there were videos of Chinaman's Brooklyn parties as well as the ones I saw later of the Easter treat in McGregor Gully. The agents also found a photograph of Chinaman with Paul Burke and other members of the PNP. This prompted the usual angry denunciations from Kingston: Manley's press secretary said that party records had been checked for any mention of Eric Vassell, and "no evidence can be found of any personal or official association with anyone by that name."

The Gully bust put Trevor in jeopardy. Having violated the terms of his parole ever since he came out of prison in 1986, he would be guaranteed another long stint in the system if the cops caught up with him now. And he was frightened for his friends from the posse. He felt no loyalty to Chinaman, whom he had always despised, but he knew what the other soldiers' fates would be now that Chinaman had deserted them all, and he knew what their prison lives would be like from now on. One of the youngest Gully soldiers, a youth named Modeler, whom Trevor knew and loved, was only days away from taking his own life. Modeler hanged himself in his cell at the Manhattan Correctional Center after writing a farewell letter begging his family to forgive him.

The weeks after the Gully bust also threw Trevor into a terrifying personal quandary. For years he had dreamed of finding someone to tell his story, knowing that his own part in the posse saga was also a chapter in Jamaica's untold story. Now, despite his friends' insistence that I had to be a police informer, he had finally met someone he thought he could trust. But he was afraid for his life. As Courtney had said about the Shower, there was no way out of a posse—"Ain't no leaving but to die."

Trevor called one night in early January to say that he was leaving New York. "I haffi' make a move," he said. "Leave and chill for a while until things settle down." He wouldn't tell me

222 BORN FI' DEAD

Trevor's disappearance felt like a small death. As the months went by without a word, I began to give up hope of ever seeing him again. Then one night, almost a year later, he called from Miami. His voice was as mellow as ever, but I heard a certain urgency.

"I want to see you," Trevor said. "I want to talk."

"Has something happened?" I asked.

"No," he answered, "I'm just fed up. There's all this stuff in the Miami papers about Jim Brown and the Shower, and it's just so much garbage. No one really knows what's going on."

Trevor was talking about the latest news from Kingston. The police there had recently tried to arrest Jim Brown for the Americans, who wanted him extradited. But they had unwisely gone into Tivoli Gardens to do it and had lost four men in the ensuing firefight. So a small detachment of U.S. marshals went down to Kingston and convinced Jim Brown's lawyer to try another method: he persuaded the gangster to come into a Kingston police station to refute some charge or another, and Brown, unsuspecting, showed up. He was put in jail while he appealed the extradition order to the British Privy Council.

"So why don't you come down to Miami?" Trevor said. "I want to pick up where we left off." He told me that he had a new girlfriend, Crystal, and that things were going well. That was "lyrics," shorthand for telling me that he was surviving, which I knew had to mean that he was juggling weed. He and Crystal were living in a motel called the Shalimar, in Liberty City; he gave me directions and told me to come there from the airport.

I landed in one of those apricot-and-lavender tropical twilights that I remembered from Jamaica, a sky shot with ribbons of darkening colors. It would be years before Miami became a dangerous place for visitors in rental cars, and I drove through Liberty City with the windows open to warm air, listening to the Haitian Creole and Jamaican patois on the streets. The Shalimar turned out to be a shabby two-story building with a Chinese owner whose eyes I could feel boring into my back as I climbed the stairs to Trevor's room. But the place was homey, in a run-down southern way; there were palm trees waving in the back-draft from the motel air conditioners and a few roosters crowing from nearby yards.

I called Trevor's name from the other side of his door and heard his voice above the sound of a television. He opened the door with a gun in his hand but smiled when he saw me. Crystal uncurled herself like a graceful cat from the bed, where she'd been watching *The Bonfire of the Vanities* on TV and came forward with a wide, shy smile. She was half Trevor's age and looked even younger: a tall, elegant girl-woman with soft brown skin and almond eyes.

Trevor put the Glock away in the nightstand drawer and gave me a hug.

"Why the gun?" I asked.

"Excuse me." He smiled wanly. He launched into a story about some Guyanese dealer who was after him for a hundred-dollar debt. The day before, which happened to be Trevor's forty-third birthday, this dealer had caught up with him and stuck his gun in Trevor's stomach. It didn't fire.

"Another one of your nine lives," I said.

I asked to see Trevor's gun, since I had never held the weapon of choice that was killing thousands across America. It was a cheap plastic model, manufactured in Georgia, but with its clip of hollow-headed bullets in place it felt heavy as lead.

"Not a lady's gun," Trevor quipped. "My American Express card—never leave home without it."

Crystal went back to *The Bonfire of the Vanities* and Trevor and I sat at the table by the window, its curtains closed against the gathering darkness. As he'd promised over the phone, we took up the thread of the conversation we'd begun almost a year before in Crown Heights, knitting a word trail that took us from Kingston to New York. I reminded him of what he had said about Jim Brown and the Shower over the phone and asked whether the Shower was selling cocaine in New York when Trevor got there in 1979.

"At that time it was mainly weed," he answered. "The Jamaican cocaine thing didn't really get going until Vivian Blake and the Shower started selling it in the Bronx.

"I remember being in Vivian's house up there in 1980, with a guy named Danny from the Gully. This was just around the time when the posses were shifting from ganja to powder cocaine. They had kilos in these Ziploc bags, and I didn't even know what it was. But they were weighing it out. And even though they all were snorting it, they tried to hide the fact from me because I was a very strict, orthodox Rastafarian and a lot of them were dreads too. So they knew they shouldn't be doing that shit."

Although the police and many Americans associate Rastafarians with the posses, most of the brethren despise cocaine; they see it as the cruelest of the white man's snares. I remembered a powerful poster I'd seen in a Rastafarian home in Kingston: a black man's face bent low over a pile of white powder, and as it rose into his nostrils it became a white-linked chain.

"I came in one night and Danny had these aluminum foil packets and straws," Trevor said. "He rubbed a straw under my nose and said, 'Try this.' And it burned like hell."

"Did you ever get into cocaine?" I asked.

He told me that he'd started smoking crack soon after he came out of prison in 1986 and hooked up with the Gully again in Brooklyn. The drug wracked him so badly that he wanted to die, and one night, when he thought he was alone in the bathroom at Chinaman's place, he began talking to his face in the mirror above the sink. He swore he was going to kill himself. At that moment, the shower curtain peeled back to reveal a kid from the posse who'd heard every word.

"No, Bones!" he cried to Trevor, grabbing him by the shoulders. "Don't talk like that, mon!"

That night was Trevor's reckoning with the drug. He started struggling to come off it, and eventually he won. But without his Rastafarian's conviction that cocaine was an evil thing, he said he didn't know if he would have had the strength to quit.

"You got me ahead of my story," Trevor said. "Anyway, back in '80, Vivian Blake was up there on Grant Avenue and 167th Street in the Bronx, selling weed and cocaine. But he didn't call himself Shower quite yet. The posse then was just Tivoli guys linked up with Rema guys. It was around '83 that we started hearing about crack, and by the next year the name Shower came up because these guys were talking about how they showered everybody with bullets. And the name stuck."

The ones who were showered were the dozen victims of Jim Brown's 1984 rampage in Rema; perhaps that was the massacre that gave the Shower its name.

"There was always a tight bond between Vivian and Seaga," Trevor went on. "Vivian's men in the Bronx worked strictly for him, and they all came from Tivoli and Rema."

I thought back to Brambles's remark about Delroy Edwards: that the distinguishing trait of a true posse was its don's ability to bring up his own people from Kingston, and that of all the posses, only the Shower had that kind of organization and power. "That meant that Vivian had to be big to get his men up from Kingston," Trevor said. "He was receiving all the weed shipments from Jamaica and it was rumored that Seaga himself was getting the stuff out. By the time Vivian started trafficking in cocaine, he had established the necessary contacts with Colombians up here. He was coming into clubs all dressed up, hung with gold, and when Jim Brown came to town they drew plenty of attention."

Chinaman was in Brooklyn by then, living in an apartment close to Sterling Place that everyone called the White House. He was already selling ganja and began to deal heroin as well. "The first time I ever touched heroin and knew what it was, I was at the White House with Pablo," Trevor said. Pablo was a friend of Trevor's from McGregor Gully. He is paralyzed now from the waist down, crippled in one of the Gully's shoot-outs with the Renkers. "Pablo told me that someone was coming by for the ten-dollar packets that were in the mailbox downstairs. When I went to check it out, I knew this thing wasn't coke.

" 'Pablo,' I said, 'what is this?' 'Dope,' he answered. 'That's what they call the heroin.' I went upstairs to my girlfriend's and said, 'Jesus, Chinaman is selling dope!' And she just laughed at me because I was so naive. This blew me away. I'd seen movies about people going through withdrawal shakes and being destroyed by this stuff."

Chinaman's heroin selling further alienated Trevor from the Gully's inner circle. "He never let me in on the drug runnin's or the murders, because he knew I would plead for the guy's life. And he tried to keep secrets from me. One of my friends in the posse said, 'Bones, you is the only man that Chinaman never diss physically outta the whole o' we.' He would slap them up, kick them, whatever. But he never laid a hand on me, because he knew I'd fight back."

The other Gully men saw the enmity between Trevor and the don, and there were times when a few of them urged Trevor to kill him. "I had a friend from the Gully named Rockers who came to me one night and told me that I'd better kill Chinaman before he killed me. We were in a little weed spot in Brooklyn, and when we came out, there was Chinaman standing by the door. Rockers said, 'There he is. Shoot him.' You could see Chinaman start shaking. I could see his knees buckle. And Rockers was clinging to me, whispering, 'Kill him! Kill him!' But I couldn't get it in my heart to do it."

Trevor drew the curtains from the window and looked out into the night. "What I wanted was not what surrounded me in life," he mused. "I don't know if it was my early education or what, but I had developed a social conscience. I was around people who glorified killing, but I couldn't find the glory in it."

By the time Trevor came out of prison in 1986 and went back to Brooklyn, the Gully was at its height. Chinaman had made a deal with an African-American passport examiner at New York's Rockefeller Center office, a man named Kenneth Weatherspoon, who also procured American passports for Delroy Edwards and the Renkers. Chinaman paid Weatherspoon twenty-five hundred dollars for each passport, and this was how he brought up soldiers like the Reid brothers.

"Until he started getting those passports, Chinaman was employing maybe half a dozen people," Trevor said. "But then it tripled. The Nineties started running with us, and that raised our numbers. They were a PNP crew from over on Ninety-eighth Street in East New York, and some of the guys came from Rockfort in eastern Kingston. Lenox Williams was one of them;

he was Count Ossie's son. All these men grew up in the Gully, in Rockfort or in Wareika Hill. They'd been hanging together for a long time."

With fresh troops, Chinaman found it easier to manage his territory. After creating a base of operations for his people at Sterling Place and sending a few recruits down to Dallas to sell crack for the posse there, Chinaman himself stayed in Brooklyn and kept a low profile. He liked to stay indoors at the White House and watch videos; Trevor recalled that among the don's favorites were Al Pacino's *Scarface* and anything with Jimmy Cagney. He also loved to watch the videos of the Easter treats in McGregor Gully. They proved how powerful Chinaman was back home.

"I remember one night when we were all sitting around, looking at one of the treat videos," Trevor said. "Paul Burke was in some of the shots—the former chairman of the PNP's youth organization. But the JLP was in power then, and Chinaman was just laughing at how pathetic Burke looked, trailing around the Gully behind Chinaman's own people. He laughed and said that the tables were turned now."

Things got nasty very soon after that, when the Reid brothers made their play to take over the posse. Unable to maintain control over his own rebellious troops, Chinaman began fighting the war of attrition that ultimately brought the Gully down. The police got their biggest break when Chinaman had Fitzy Reid killed: Fitzy's brother Danny was terrified that he would be next, so he turned himself in to the cops and told them everything he knew.

I stayed with Trevor and Crystal in Miami for three days, hanging out at the Shalimar and cruising through the city at night.

My car had a tape deck, and I'd brought down some of Trevor's favorite music, ska from the late fifties and early reggae from the sixties. The tunes raised bittersweet memories.

"Baby, I only wish you could have seen the life in Kingston then," he said one night when we had gone out to get some vegetarian pizza. "There were no guns yet, and the Gully was the sweetest spot. I would wake up in the mornings and just lie in the green grass, listening to the hummingbirds buzzing through the air. They were so tame I used to catch them in my hand, hold them for a minute, and then let them go. You'll never see that kind of life come back to Jamaica again."

We were listening to an old Skatellite tape from the sixties. "That's Roland Alphonso playing saxophone," Trevor said. We both knew Roland from Crown Heights, where he lives now. Old and ailing, he sits on a little folding chair at the Apache Bakery, where Jamaicans come to buy patties at lunchtime, selling his tapes and chatting with anyone who cares to listen about the old days.

"Roland is lucky to be alive," Trevor said. "So many are gone now." He reeled off the names of musical stars who had died by the gun: Peter Tosh and Carly Barrett, who also played with Bob Marley; the popular deejay named Free-I, who was killed in a robbery; and the gifted young singer TenorSaw, whom Chinaman brought up from Kingston for Brooklyn shows. "He stayed with us at 1367," Trevor said. "He didn't want to go back to Jamaica. But then he started smoking crack because he got so down. He felt like he wasn't being treated right in the music business. So he got some coke and went to Texas to sell it. Someone killed him there."

On the night before I left, there was a concert in Fort Lauderdale with Judy Mowatt, the elegant singer who used to perform with Bob Marley's back-up chorus, the I-Three's. She still carries

Bob's torch, singing anthems to African womanhood and beaming her female self-respect into a Jamaican music scene that is dominated now by the dance hall men; they don't sing about much else besides pussy and guns. Trevor had known her "from morning," but he had not seen her in years. He knew that Robbie Shakespeare, his boyhood friend from McGregor Gully, would be playing bass for Mowatt, and Trevor loved the thought of surprising them at the show.

The club and the audience were small, and we sat right by the stage on a little rise of steps, watching the Rastafarian sisters in their Ethiopian robes skanking regally through song after song. Mowatt gave a generous show, singing for almost two hours without a break. She spotted Trevor from the stage right away and beamed him a huge smile. He had tears in his eyes by the end of her set, when she did a song called "Warrior Queen," her hymn to history's great women of color. She sang to Rosa Parks and Nanny of the Maroons, Harriet Tubman, and Ethiopia's Queen Makeda, and Trevor could not resist shouting with joy. "Teach them, Judy!" he cried, and Mowatt smiled down at him like a queen.

We went backstage to see her and Robbie Shakespeare. A tribe of women hovered around her, and the scene was light-years away from the usual backstage gathering at reggae shows, where bored girlfriends wait for their star-boys to get enough adulation. Mowatt sat enthroned, mopping her brow and autographing pictures. The men were on the sidelines, sipping their Red Stripes and rolling spliffs. Trevor was in a corner with Robbie.

"Bones," Robbie was saying as if he was seeing a ghost. "Bones. Mon, it's good to see you. It's good to see you're still alive."

We were both quiet at first on the drive back to Miami. I

could almost read Trevor's thoughts: that his days with Bob and Rita, Judy, and Robbie were gone like the hummingbirds in McGregor Gully. We began talking, in a nostalgic way, about the years before he came to Brooklyn, when he was still a hopeful activist for the PNP.

Some of his memories were laced with humor. He thought back to Manley's ill-fated friendship with Fidel Castro and the Brigadista work exchange with Cuba, and he told a story about the Rastafarians who had gone on the program and torn up their living quarters in a vegetarian rampage after their Cuban hosts tried to feed them pork. A year later, on his 1977 state visit to Jamaica, Fidel did everything he could to avoid shaking hands with Trevor and the Rastafarian contingent who went to meet him. Trevor also laughed at the memory of how hysterical the Americans were over Jamaica's brief flirtation with Cuba.

"You know, in spite of all the propaganda, Fidel took a very dim view of Jamaicans. Maybe it was the Rastafarian thing, I don't know. The Cubans really just considered us as troublemakers. They knew that we weren't revolutionary material. Fidel didn't want us on his hands."

Trevor said that even though the PNP's tribalists had high hopes of getting guns from Cuba, their dreams never came true. They tried to arrange some shipments in the year before the 1980 election, when Seaga's forces were arming themselves with help from the CIA, but Castro was not interested in turning Jamaica into another Angola.

"There were a couple of crates of M16s, but they were relics of the Vietnam days—dirty, broken-down guns that would have had to be seriously repaired before they'd even work. And meanwhile, Seaga's people were getting their guns from the United States. They had the necessary connections on the wharves."

The JLP had such superior firepower by then that gunmen

like Jim Brown tried to lure PNP warriors into the Labourite camp with the promise of weapons. "I knew from Bucky Marshall that the Tivolites were getting those guns," Trevor said. "And Rockers, the same Hot Stepper guy who later advised me to kill Chinaman up in Brooklyn, had gone into Tivoli a couple of times. They'd taken him into some underground hideout where they had stacks of guns still wrapped in plastic, all kinds of automatic weapons.

"And Rockers was impressed, believe you me. He said, 'Bones, we don't have nothin' compared to this.' They'd shown him their stash because they were trying to woo the Steppers over to the JLP side. But the only good guns the PNP seemed able to get their hands on were ones that renegade soldiers from the JDF [Jamaican Defense Force] stole and sold to us."

I was letting my tape recorder do the work of listening while I drove; we were back in Miami by then and I was trying not to miss the exit for Liberty City. But Trevor's offhand remark about the soldiers who stole guns brought me up short. I remembered David D'Costa's story of the soldier who'd died in Kingston after being accused of stealing army guns.

"Did you ever know anyone named Anthony Williams?" I asked.

Trevor looked over at me from the passenger's seat. The mercury-vapor lights from the highway threw their brutal glare across his face.

"Oh, God," he moaned. "How you know 'bout Willie?"

I told him David D'Costa's story.

"I've tried to forget about Willie after all these years," Trevor sighed. "Yeah, I knew him well. He was always desperate for money, and he didn't care who he sold those guns to. They were Sterlings, and we all wanted them.

"He came to me in the Gully the night before he died, with

five stolen guns from Up Park Camp. He'd tried to sell them to Balla Reid. But Balla was dry on account of the Ogilvie inquiry. I didn't have any money either, but I told Willie to check me on the following Monday. He couldn't wait that long. So he went over to Rema, and they murdered him for the guns.

"You know why it really cut me up when they told me he was dead? Because I had just talked to the man Friday night, and on Monday I heard he was dead. I don't like remembering Willie. Turn off the tape."

Anthony Williams was only a name to me, but somehow he became a symbolic, spectral presence after that night. Like so many other lost lives, his had briefly linked two people I had come to know, from either side of the underground's abyss. David D'Costa and Trevor Phillips would never meet, but both the journalist and the gang member would always remember a terrified young soldier whose path had collided once with theirs.

Trevor and I said good-bye in the Shalimar's parking lot as the sky was streaking into dawn.

"I don't know when I'll see you again," he said. "But thanks for everything. I'm coming back to New York one of these days, and you'll know when I do."

"Why come back?" I asked. "Things seem better for you here."

"No," he answered. "I miss the runnin's in New York."

He came back with Crystal a few months later, and their daughter was born in the winter of 1993. They were living in the Bronx, close to a Jamaican gatehouse where Trevor hung out. He still had a Glock like the one he'd carried in Miami, and one night he brandished it at Crystal during a quarrel. She called the police and Trevor was arrested. When they ran his name through their computer, they saw that he was on parole but had not been to see his officer in seven years.

Basil Wilson, the man who had brought me together with Trevor, wrote a letter in his behalf to the judge who presided at his hearing, as did I. He could have served a seven-year sentence—one year in jail for every year that he had violated his parole—but he was given only a year.

Trevor called me almost every day from jail and wrote many letters. He said that ever since he had decided to help me with the book, only Basil Wilson had supported the idea; all of his other friends had told him that I was an informer. "My hope was always that you were, in fact, someone who really wanted to write about this sordid turn of events," Trevor wrote, "and give as much of the human and inhumane factors to make the picture whole."

This letter was long and full. When he wrote it, near the end of his prison term, he was facing the prospect of being deported to Jamaica when he came out. And this released an eloquent flood of thoughts; the letter was his own farewell to the years in which we had worked together. Like Brambles on that night long ago when I was about to leave Kingston, Trevor wanted to make certain that I understood the lessons he had tried to teach me.

If you know as many people as I do who have died from the violence attendant to the Jamaican experience, with gang-related political rivalries and the drug-posse evolution of the gangs, as well as the assortment of posses now in vogue across the urban United States . . . and if you know that, due to the failure of society to overcome racism and make solid changes in the images being projected (to the youths most of all), most of these posses are now made up of Blacks, Hispanics, and Whites who are born citizens of this country and cannot be deported anywhere. Then maybe you will come to understand why "'mi haffi' cry fi de youths," as SuperCat puts it in one of his raps.

When a don dies or goes to prison for a long sentence, the hungry youths—hungry for the image and the power, if not just for food—always move into position (though they know the risks and the odds) to take their place as the band plays on.

Since the more fortunate members of society have ways and means to insulate themselves from the general violence, we daily have to live with it. I want to be sure that you really understand us. When you have to go to sleep and wake up to the body counts, you will have experienced our reality—when the count invariably includes a family member or friend. Someone who could have gone to college and earned a degree, instead of "Jungle" or "Tivoli" or "the crackhouse" or "the spot."

As I read these words, I remembered what Basil Wilson had said about Trevor: had he been born somewhere other than McGregor Gully, there was no telling what he might have become.

Trevor had written this valediction from the loneliness and isolation of his cell. He ended it in a spirit of wary affirmation: whether I was "author or agent," he said, he had nevertheless trusted me to tell his truth.

"Remember that, no matter how much you empathize with us or try to 'research' us—to us belong the sorrows of being trapped in this cruel experience. Only our hearts feel the pain."

EPILOGUE

On the first Sunday in February 1992, Jim Brown's twenty-four-year-old son, "Jah-T," was shot off his motorcycle in downtown Kingston by a gunman from the PNP. Jah-T had been running things in Tivoli Gardens since his father was in prison awaiting extradition to the United States. At the time he was killed, Jah-T was making arrangements for the annual Tivoli dance in memory of Claudie Massop, the community's beloved godfather who died almost fourteen years to the day before Jah-T himself was gunned down.

This killing sparked a downtown Kingston rampage in which close to twenty people died. The battle began in the emergency room at Kingston Public Hospital, where enraged Tivolites mobbed the doctors who had vainly tried to resuscitate Jah-T. The crowd was convinced that the hospital staff had not done all they could to save the don, so they kicked down the door of the emergency room and threatened to kill at least fifty doctors and nurses in retaliation for Jah-T's death.

After news of his demise flashed through West Kingston, gunmen from Tivoli Gardens vented their fury on sufferers from the nearby PNP garrison of Hannah Town. They kicked and shot their way into tenement yards in a frenzy of rape and murder that was a nightmare replay of 1980. This was simple justice. The JLP's don had been murdered, and as one Tivolite said, "Nuff PNP haffi' go dead now."

Three weeks later Jah-T was given the equivalent of a state funeral. His supporters wanted to bury him in Tivoli Gardens, next to Claudie Massop, but instead Jah-T was interred in May Pen Cemetery. Seaga himself led the throng of twenty thousand mourners, mostly young men and women whom the *Gleaner* described as "dressed in the most stunning black designs with gold accessories." The don's girlfriend, known to all as Foxy, walked beside Seaga in a tight black dress. Jah-T was laid out in a black casket with silver handles that cost forty thousand dollars in Jamaican currency, and he was dressed for the hereafter in a white satin shirt and a suit of black velvet. The Kingston press excoriated Seaga for attending the funeral of a well-known thug.

On the afternoon of the day Jah-T was buried, Jim Brown was burned to death in a conflagration in his prison cell. The British Privy Council had denied his extradition appeal, and agents from the Drug Enforcement Administration were waiting in Kingston to put him on a plane to Miami. Brown had vowed that if he went to trial in the United States, he would tell the world everything he knew about Seaga and the Shower posse. "Is not I-one goin' down alone," he had said to a fellow prisoner shortly before he died. No one ever found out who set the mysterious fire in his cell, but everyone knew that both Vivian Blake and Seaga wanted Brown dead.

Seaga attended the funeral, along with other prominent JLP politicians, like Babsy Grange, the councillor for Tivoli Gardens, and Ryan Peralto, the member of Parliament who once paid Delroy Edwards to shoot up Southside for the JLP. Seaga addressed a grieving crowd in Tivoli Gardens a few days before

Jim Brown was buried, and a reporter asked him whether the don had "enjoyed the sanction of a politician." Seaga's answer was angry. "As long as you and other people keep to think of the man with a background and to look at the background rather than where he stands in his community, you will always ask a question like that," Seaga said. "Ask the lawyer if he looks at that background. Ask the clergyman who takes a confession if he looks at that background. Ask him if the man who he is ministering to looks at that background. Look at the man in terms of how the community respects him and treats him as a protector."

The protector and his son were gone, but it would not be long before the JLP would find some other "community leader," as a gunman is politely called, to take their place in West Kingston. Vivian Blake, Jim Brown's partner in the Shower posse, filled this role for two more years, until he was arrested in January 1994 on an extradition warrant. As of this writing he is expected to stand trial in Florida for the Shower's crimes.

A month after Jim Brown was killed, Michael Manley relinquished the prime ministership of Jamaica. He had been fighting cancer for five years, and the time had come for him to step down. The leadership of his party and Jamaica passed to Percival James Patterson, affectionately known as "P.J." He is considered by Jamaicans to be their very first black prime minister; although the dark-skinned Hugh Shearer had held the position briefly in the 1960s, he was from the JLP and never enjoyed the widespread popularity accorded to P. J. Patterson.

I was in Jamaica when Manley stepped down, and I listened to his farewell speech to Parliament on my car radio as I drove through the lush hills in the parish of St. Elizabeth, where Manley had fought some of his first public battles as a labor organizer in the bauxite plants. I was on my way to interview the journalist Wilmot Perkins at the radio station in Mandeville where he hosts a call-in show.

Perkins is the undisputed elder statesman of Jamaican journalists: a tall, imposing man with piercing eyes and extraordinarily bushy eyebrows who speaks in the elegant cadences of an educated West Indian. He is the only media figure who has never stopped badgering Manley and Seaga about their links to gunmen, and Manley is still threatening him with a libel suit for remarks that Perkins made several years ago on his show. I have known him long enough to appreciate and fear the sharp-tongued wit that has reduced some of his guests to tears on the air.

As I drove to Mandeville, listening to Manley's sonorous voice ringing out in Parliament for the last time, I waited for him to say something about the political violence that had just spilled fresh blood in West Kingston. But he only spoke blithely about the admirable "consensus and agreement" between Jamaica's two parties, glossing over the viciousness that has turned his country into a battlefield for the past twenty-five years.

Perkins had just finished his program when I arrived. We talked for a while about the end of the Manley era, and then I asked him for his theory of Jim Brown's death. He would not say that Seaga was behind it, but his description of the death scene made it clear that he knew the fire had to have been ordered by a power higher than the prison guards.

"The fire brigade man said that when they were called, they weren't taken to [Brown's] cell. The army man who went in said that when he arrived, he saw a man's body on the ground, where it had been overturned out of the stretcher, and an argument raging between the police and the soldiers on one hand and the prison warders on the other as to whether the man ought to be taken to hospital. He was there for more than an hour before they moved him. Somebody wanted to make damned sure he was dead. I am told that he died of pulmonary edema, the result of inhaling flames. That seems to me to suggest that there was one bitch of a fire going in that cell."

Perkins shot me a look full of meaning. "There's a nasty underbelly to politics in this country," he said.

Perkins had a few political cartoons taped to the wall behind his desk. Next to them was an astonishing dub poem from a ghetto bard who had signed himself only as "Wayne." It had obviously been written by someone who spoke the language of the sufferers and also knew who Ogun, the Yoruba god of war, and Karl Marx were.

Nihilist?
Lumpen?
Uptown bullshit.
Respect I a' deal wid.
Respect me area, respect me brethren, respect me woman.
Diss me, an' you momma, poppa, granny, pickney a' go feel it.
Diss me, an' a one bullet fire.
It no matter. I 'ave a dog heart.
If me dead, a so man born fi' dead.
Accepting this offering, Papa Ogun sits on his hilltop,
Wondering when his own mortality will be tested.
And in history's dustbin, Marx bides his time.

"Where did you get this?" I asked Perkins.

He shrugged. "My secretary brought it from Kingston," he answered. He raised his bushy eyebrows in gleeful affirmation of the poem's excellence. "I don't know anything else about it. But it's quite something, isn't it?"

The poem resonated with ominous echoes after Kingston's recent bloodletting. Years later, when I was searching for a title for this book, I spent an evening in New York with Perry Henzell, the producer of *The Harder They Come*. We wanted to find a phrase to express the fearsome inevitability of the posses and the bitter resignation of their young soldiers to death.

I remembered the poem. I said, "A so man born fi' dead."

Brambles left New York for Miami just after I made the trip to Jamaica in the aftermath of Jim Brown's death.

He had been in the city for four years, and he was exhausted by the tribulations of being an illegal alien in the underground and squatting in the Crown Heights crack house with no job. This fourth and final winter had broken his spirit. He had lost most of his precious camera equipment after entrusting it to Shenda, who seemed to have a safer place with Mack than Brambles had at the crack house. But she'd left the cartons in her car trunk and it was broken into one night.

"I don't know where I goin' to cotch in Miami," Brambles said on the night before I went down to Kingston and he came to my place with a suitcase full of clothing and shoes for his children. But I knew that he was going to join his brother, the crack dealer.

"Why don't you go home?" I asked. "You know how much Natalie and Ricky miss you."

I knew the catch-22, the rule that says you don't go back to Jamaica from America poor and in disgrace. So I knew that Brambles might never go back and that Natalie and Ricky would go on now without their father, despite the promise he had made to himself, to them, and to me many years ago in Kingston: "Thru I grow without a mother and a father, I say me own pickney not goin' to grow without me." The children were living with their half-sister in Southside, and I promised Brambles that I would spend time with them and take many rolls of pictures.

He is in Miami now, working for his brother. But the man is a crackhead who also loves to bet at the track, so Brambles sees most of the profits go up in smoke. He lives in a motel without a telephone, so I can't reach him unless he calls me from the street, which he does from time to time. He has a secondhand camera now and vows to start taking pictures again. Sometimes he talks seriously about going home.

Shenda is still in Brooklyn, and we see each other often. She has a new boyfriend who treats her well, and she doesn't smoke much anymore. She went home to Jamaica for Christmas of 1993 and had a joyous reunion with her parents and her son and twin daughters. The boy is a man now, soon to graduate from his mother's alma mater, the University of the West Indies, and the twins are star students at a private school. They were raised by Shenda's parents and they have grown up well.

Her ticket had an open return, and I hoped that she might stay in Jamaica. But she called in early January to say that she was coming back. I knew enough not to argue, but I asked her why, and she explained that it was too painful to be there without any money; it had been more than wonderful to see her son and daughters, but it humiliated her when they asked her for things she couldn't give them. "You must know when something is finished," Shenda said. "You have to know when it's time to go."

Trevor is in an upstate New York penitentiary, serving his one-year sentence. In his absence, Crystal and I became friends. The birth of her daughter changed her life. She entered a job-training program for women on welfare and stayed with it until she graduated. A few months before Trevor was due to be released, she and the baby left New York. Trevor saw this as a desertion, but Crystal said that she would not let her child grow up in a ghetto in the Bronx.

Just before she left, she took Trevor's Glock to her local police precinct; New York had initiated a buy-back program to get weapons off the street, and Crystal got a seventy-five-dollar gift certificate at The Gap for the gun. She bought clothes for her child. Then she went home to be with her mother in the South and found work in her hometown.

Trevor will soon be out of prison. When I told Basil Wilson that Crystal had given away Trevor's gun, he was gladdened for only a moment. "As soon as he comes out, he will get another," Basil said. "You cannot be a ranking on the street without a gun."

Eric "Chinaman" Vassell, the fugitive leader of the McGregor Gully posse, was finally arrested in Kingston in September 1994. He is awaiting extradition to the United States.

Shortly after Vassell was arrested, Edward Seaga gave a list with the names of thirteen Tivoli gangsters to Trevor MacMillan, the new police commissioner. The list was partly a publicity stunt, but it also signalled Seaga's inability to control his own West Kingston constituency. The Tivoli gunmen were outdoing themselves with a recent spate of armed robbery and rape in Tivoli and in Rema, the ghetto nearby. Seaga said he had warned the criminals, but the dons had told him that since Seaga had not given them their guns, he could not tell them what to do. "The horse already gone through the gate," said one unapologetic Tivolite. Wilmot Perkins called Seaga's list "a cry from a drowning man. Do not mistake it for the herald of a better

future. But give him credit: at least he knows he's drowning."
The police commissioner declared that his men were not going
to round up suspects at Seaga's behest, without evidence or
charges against them. The names on the list were never made
public.

The Tivolite don behind the rampage against Rema was none
other than Christopher "Dudus" Coke, another of Jim Brown's
sons. Paradoxically, it was a peacemaker's overture that had ig-
nited Coke's rage: Ziggy Marley, Bob's son, was building a recording studio almost on the border of Trench Town and Rema,
trying to provide aspiring musicians there with a community
base. Ziggy didn't give the construction work to Dudus and his
posse, so the Tivoli don was taking his revenge. He was following in Jim Brown's footsteps, much as Ziggy was dancing in his
own father's light.